The
HUDSON

RIVERS OF AMERICA
edited by Carl Carmer

as planned and started by
Constance Lindsay Skinner
associate editor Jean Crawford

The
HUDSON

by CARL CARMER

illustrated by STOW WENGENROTH

HOLT, RINEHART AND WINSTON
New York   Chicago   San Francisco

TO THE MEMORY OF
CONSTANCE LINDSAY SKINNER
EDITOR OF RIVERS OF AMERICA

Contents

Preface to the 1974 Edition

THROUGH long centuries, the dark high land stood awaiting its discovery. White surf breaking on its walls heightened the effect of its loneliness when, at last, a ship captain heard the splashing and sought its meaning. Henry Hudson, Elizabethan explorer, called his son to his side and bade him listen. From the prow of the little vessel, the *Half Moon*, a property of the Dutch East India Company, the father and his son soon became aware that there was a break in the level shores before them that might lead their sturdy craft into lands that had never before been visited by white men or perhaps—just perhaps—it might serve to bring her into areas somehow recognizable as parts of China.

For this was a time wherein the dreams of all explorers were of a short passage to the Orient, a waterway that would shorten all journeys to a wildly prosperous future where, as always, trade would promise riches.

Whether or not other adventurers had found this country before (there had been whispers of it on the docks of many a sea-going nation and Hudson had even made other efforts to find it), the existence of a stream from the north which here entered the Atlantic was now a fact to be entered on the pages of all atlases. The English captain realized the importance of his discovery at once and set his sails for a northbound journey. Past the long narrow island to his starboard (now Manhattan) he skimmed. Now he would be able to find the truth about the strange myths and legends with which his confreres had teased his mind. But in a long stretch of fair weather he soon found himself frustrated by shallow unnavigable waters which he knew were far from the deeper reaches of China. Crestfallen he returned across the Atlantic to report to his Dutch employers that his effort had failed. He had, however, left to the river a name that it will bear "as long as its waters run."

In this, the latest edition of *The Hudson* which was first published in the Rivers of America series of which I am editor, I have added the results of my further researches in the history of the big stream. I have attempted to inform my readers of such recent incidents worthy of inclusion.

As for the relationship of Captain Henry Hudson, English employee of Dutch authorities, his Elizabethan contemporaries had not yet sufficiently recognized his importance.

As might have been expected, many American settlers found the Hudson's banks inviting for residences. Its little bays protected them and served as adequate shelters from the strong tides of the changeable river. Small towns sprang up and water intercourses between them were established. Public buildings, by that time the outstanding houses, had begun to reflect the architecture of the Dutch, the English, and other folk of heterogeneous backgrounds. The governments of these new communities found their tasks made easier by a joining of their duties, regardless of such difficulties as differing languages.

As a very late-comer indeed to the upriver banks, I went as far north on the Hudson as I thought safe, and during my first year of occupancy of its shores I looked out from the windows of my eight-sided century-old house and saw an inexplicable red carpet had been laid upon the green surface of my three acres of lawn. I rubbed my eyes and discovered that that did not alter the color. My yard had changed from its natural green to a brilliant red. Out on my circular veranda I dashed and became aware that I was looking upon a shining quilt of birds, and that they were engaged in eating a substance of which I had no knowledge. Their brilliant feathers had dyed the close-knit greensward with a flaming splendor.

I was standing transfixed by a sight that neither I nor my gathering neighbors had ever seen before. I looked into my "bird books" for an explanation, but none of the pages about tanagers (described by my reference library as "birds of the new world") gave me information as to their flocking habits.

Even as I sought such meagre knowledge as was available, I still watched. Already the commuting trains were filled with eager ornithologists seeking to witness the strange phenomenon. Our schools at Irvington had dismissed their classes. The whole Hudson Valley seemed alive with the shining scarlet creatures. My lawn had been blessed with a coat of red paint. The birds had neglected the upper stories, but soon we were to find that this visit had been limited only to the areas of our immediate neighborhood. Ornithologists had begun to arrive at our railroad station and scientists were asking throughout the valley how they could make their way to Octagon House. We made sandwiches to appease the hunger of our visitors.

When the noon train came in, it was crowded with earnest photographers who had filled their cameras with rolls of color films.

Suddenly we noted a decrease in the number of eager naturalists. One by one they seemed to be slipping away. I saw a group of five enthusiasts walking south along the aqueduct and I heard them exclaiming in disappointment. They had expected to see the birds forming a red pathway along the top of the old covered waterway that had been conveying its stream down into New York's Central Park for nearly a century, and one of my neighbors pointed out that on a hot day like this one the inmates of Sing Sing prison were accustomed to making use of the waters only a few miles away from the Croton River to augment their shallow shower baths.

Now the tanagers, as if at a given signal, joined in a magnificent flock and forsook my lawn, leaving my acres desolate. Next morning I looked for them. I walked down to the railroad station and my heart leaped. I beheld two tanagers clinging to the Irvington station sign, but as I looked they flew away. I had had my day of blessing and it had gone.

I sat in the reception room of Farrar and Rinehart, Publishers, awaiting a morning audience with John Farrar, when a woman, dressed in black tumbling lace, came into the reception room. She was a large handsome woman with very dark hair, heavily rouged cheeks, and it was obvious that she was elated.

"That Stanley Rinehart," she said, "is a perfect Blackfoot."

From the emphatic tone of her voice, I realized that she regarded her statement as the highest compliment that she could pay anyone. I also knew that I was looking upon a celebrated champion of all causes of the American Indian, Constance Lindsay Skinner. The Blackfoot tribe, moreover, was her favorite of all the Indian groups that inhabited the northwestern land near which she lived. The Blackfeet are tall and possessed of more than usual intelligence, and Miss Skinner regarded them as superior to all other western Indian nations.

"A series of books allowing our rivers, which were the nation's first roads, to tell the story of our early history," she said addressing me and the other occupants of the waiting room. "And we will want each volume to be written not by a formal historian but by a poet."

I did not realize that the following moment was one that would inevitably change my own life. I was later to discover, however, that it changed the direction of my writing efforts from the social investigation of limited areas of American states to a freer attitude toward wider expanses than those credited by man as political perimeters.

As a result of her conference, I was soon to find out that the firm had indeed accepted her project. With remarkable dispatch (for publishers), they had persuaded one of their treasured authors that he should begin to write a volume about a river. He was poet Robert P. Tristram Coffin, later a winner of a Pulitzer Prize, and he had chosen to write about the river he most loved—the Kennebec. This venture proved so successful both for the author and publisher that the series was well under way, and I was told that I had been chosen to write the volume to be entitled *The Hudson.*

During the next three years, I found myself wandering the banks of the great stream for a hundred and fifty miles. My plans led me to travel north along the east bank of the river in my automobile and whenever I saw any road allowing me access to the flowing stream to take it. Inevitably I would reach a house that overlooked the water and just as inevitably I would find a house occupied by people who loved their home.

And when I told them I intended to write a book about "their" river nothing would satisfy them but my sitting where I would get the "best view" while they told me the lore of the reaches on which they lived.

Most of the facts of the new country's early history are recorded in the book you are about to read. They have been up-dated from time to time as history has unfolded itself and American readers have given them changes of emphasis. When I searched behind the revolution of 1775, I found that for generations it was concealed from most readers that there was an unsuccessful earlier revolt in 1766 during which the first shots against British redcoats were fired by farmers who lived along the Hudson.

To obtain the details of this story, I went to the New York State capitol at Albany and sought the aid of a department of old and rare books. I told the ladies who were working there that I had been informed of their treasured manuscripts of the years of the late 1770's.

"Perhaps your informants were not aware of the fire of 1911 that destroyed those very papers," said one of my hearers, dryly. I had thought that this material would constitute a narrative particularly important to the history of our state and I was desolate. There seemed to be nothing I could do that might lead to my uncovering the story. I sat down disconsolate—and sat—and sat—until I realized that I must be embarrassing the whole personnel of the office.

I had risen to leave when one of the workers cried, "Wait," and she dashed into a part of the office that was filled with decaying yellow papers.

"These are old records that the firemen tried to save in 1911 but found they couldn't," she said. "Some of them might be what you want."

Together we set to work identifying the contents of her find.

"Look, look," she cried as she drew from the tumbled mess a bundle of flame-blackened pages tied together by a raveled brown string. Holding it aloft she read loudly and triumphantly:

"Minutes of the Secretary of the Committee for the City of New York, 1766," and she was instantly breaking the string.

"He was a good secretary," she said excitedly. "He kept extra wide margins and he packed his pages tight. That kept them from burning in the center. Every word he wrote is there."

I grabbed the pages she released and thumbed through them. There were the names I had been seeking—"William Prendergast and his wife, the former Mehitable Wing—Justice Horsmanden." She had found the narrative of the agricultural revolt of the Westchester County farmers against British authority—now

considered by many historians as the first militant action
of the War of the American Revolution.

I came to know a couple as enthusiastic about the
Hudson as even I had become—Mr. and Mrs. Benjamin
West Frazier who, sharing a lasting love of the Hudson,
were bent on its flowing as it did in the nation's early
days. The Fraziers had in the last few years busied themselves in opposing the invasion of various industries along
the stream's banks. They had especially fought the efforts of an industrial company named Consolidated
Edison to deface Storm King, the most cherished and
beautiful of the mountains in the Hudson Highlands.
The Fraziers found joy in allying themselves with
the members of the Scenic Hudson Preservation Conference (which had been organized at my residence, Octagon House, a short time before), and they have been of
invaluable assistance ever since.

When I began this essay to add to the contents of
this book such information as I felt was worthy of inclusion, I was somewhat astonished to find that I had
omitted any reference to two of its oldest but most important buildings, which stand close above Hudson
water. One of these is a small, pillared chapel which was
built during the Civil War years—the Chapel of Our
Lady at Cold Spring. Its walls still stand but the approach to it is steep and dangerous. The eldest of the
fishermen who live nearby told me that no religious
services had been held in it since 1906 because members
of the Roman Catholic faith had moved to another
church. The walls have fought off the slow ravages of
the years and still present their rounded brick columns

for the support of the graceful roof which unhappily
admits rain, snow, and whatever other handicaps the
weather may bring.

When the beautiful white residence, Boscobel, was
moved to the north some fifteen miles to an eminence
that points its lovely facade downriver, an exquisite
formal sanctuary built close by for followers of the
Christian God could not fail to call attention to itself
and the Fraziers seized upon the opportunity to recommend its being restored to its original uses. A meeting of
those lovers of its beauty in the area was announced and
it was attended not only by prominent members of the
Roman Catholic Church, but by all who recognized the
quality and distinction of the chapel's presence at the
very summit of the river's banks. Here, with complete
unanimity, all present joined the ecumenical agreement
that the little church be restored and dedicated to all
causes of righteousness and humanity. It is expected even
as I write that on the next Sabbath-in-the-sun the sharp-
prowed dories of the Hudson fishermen will be setting
out in the down-and-up tides and from both the east
and west banks to join the vast fleet moored below the
chapel, now renewed beneath the cross that gives it
sacred meaning.

From the high steps, when they come from their
meditations and prayers, the worshipers may catch
glimpses of a vast and spreading gray building that has,
ever since its opening in the year 1825, been also devoted
to the redemption of men. Its walls support dark armed
citadels that allow no freedom to those whom they confine, and the irony of the propinquity of the Chapel of
Our Lady at Cold Spring and the New York State Cor-

rectional Facility (once known as Sing Sing) now gives philosophers sad contemplation.

CARL CARMER

Irvington-on-Hudson, New York
September, 1973

Preface

IN this book I have tried to tell the story of the people who have lived in the Hudson valley. I have tried to be objective and unprejudiced, but my friends who are historians say that a pure objectivity cannot be obtained, and I believe them. I confess, therefore, that whatever prejudices I may have favor my subject. There is more in this volume about large groups and the leaders that represent them than there is about individuals who became uniquely distinguished—more about tenants than landlords, more about privates than generals, more about workers than employers.

Since a work of this sort might go on indefinitely and into many volumes, I have sought other limitations. I have tried to keep as near to the stream as I could and to avoid, where I thought it possible, things that happened out of sight of Hudson water.

The Hudson is rich in material and there will be people who will accept the boundaries I have set for myself and still object to my sins of omission. To them I can only answer that what I have chosen to tell here in this book seemed to me to be the best to tell.

Carl Carmer

The
HUDSON

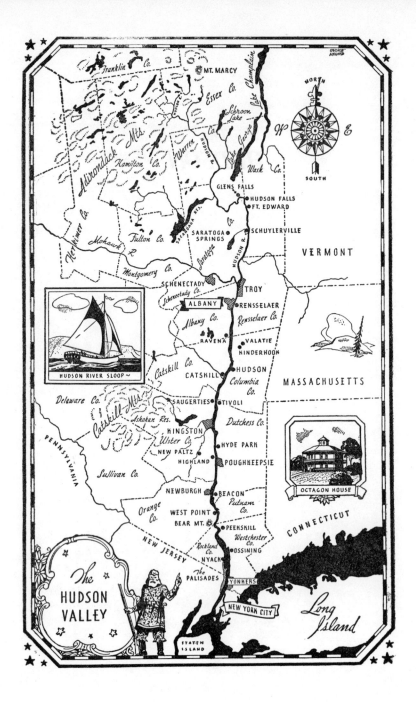

GEORGE ANNAND

MT. MARCY

Franklin Co.

Essex Co.

Lake Champlain

Schroon Lake

Adirondack Mts.

Hamilton Co.

Warren Co.

Lake George

Herkimer Co.

Fulton Co.

Sacandaga Res.

Mohawk R.

Wash. Co.

GLENS FALLS

HUDSON FALLS
FT. EDWARD

SCHUYLERVILLE

SARATOGA SPRINGS

Saratoga Co.

VERMONT

Montgomery Co.

Schenectady Co.

SCHENECTADY

ALBANY

Albany Co.

RAVENA

TROY

RENSSELAER

Rensselaer Co.

VALATIE

KINDERHOOK

HUDSON

CATSKILL

Columbia Co.

MASSACHUSETTS

HUDSON RIVER SLOOP~

Delaware Co.

Catskill Co.

Catskill Mts.

SAUGERTIES

TIVOLI

Ashokan Res.

KINGSTON

Ulster Co.

Dutchess Co.

PENNSYLVANIA

NEW PALTZ

HIGHLAND

HYDE PARK

POUGHKEEPSIE

Sullivan Co.

NEWBURGH

BEACON

WEST POINT

Putnam Co.

OCTAGON HOUSE

Orange Co.

BEAR MT.

PEEKSKILL

Westchester Co.

Rockland Co.

OSSINING

NEW JERSEY

NYACK

The PALISADES

CONNECTICUT

YONKERS

The HUDSON VALLEY

NEW YORK CITY

Long Island

STATEN ISLAND

NORTH

W E

SOUTH

I

To Make a River

FROM rocks as old as any in the world fresh
waters rise into a little lake beside the highest Adirondack peak, Mount Marcy. Before the mountains, fold-
ing, raised island heads above the Grenville Sea these
rocks were there. Once they were higher, when molten
masses burst their crust to force tongues upward, lifting
steeper summits to the sky. But the old rocks sank again
and, in the years that followed, tilting and warping
the surfaces of earth, tropic oceans washed them
smooth and streams of ice, miles deep, made scars upon
their sides.

The little lake is younger than the rocks and
younger than the glaciers, but older than man. In the
whole state of New York it is the highest body of water
to feed an ever-flowing outlet. When the naturalist
Verplanck Colvin, in 1872, climbed through woods of
spruce and balsam and white cedar to its bank it had a
lovely name. He was so overcome with the emotion
proper to his period and the occasion, however, that he
wrote, in a sentimental report to the New York State
legislature: "Far above the chilly waters of Lake Avalanche, at an elevation of 4,293 feet, is *Summit Water,*
a minute, unpretending tear of the clouds, as it were—
a lovely pool shivering in the breeze of the mountains. . . ." The lawmakers were so overcome by this

3

coincidental flowering in their midst of literary effort and the "pathetic fallacy" that lovely Summit Water soon officially became *Lake Tear of the Clouds*.

The rocky peak of Marcy, once called Tahawus—the cloud splitter—by the Indians, looks down into the mirror of Lake Tear. East of the peak, beyond Panther Gorge, stands the dome called Haystack, to the north stands Table Top, to the south Skylight, and westward rises Mount MacIntyre.

The clear water of the ancient rocks spills from the lake to shallow Feldspar Brook. Through its ripples shine the stones of its bed. Green, gold, blue, they glitter with iridescent labradorite. Down the crystalline slope the water plunges to join with other brooks, the Up Hill and the Upper Twin. Another fork descending in the shadow of Calamity Mountain from Flowed Lands and the Falls of Hanging Spear meets it to form the swift Opalescent River. And the Opalescent, running south and then west, at the hill town of Newcomb becomes the Hudson.

Flowing south then to Indian River Junction and between Bad Luck and Kettle mountains, keeping east of the steep sides of Ruby and Balm of Gilead, the thin stream meets the splashing Schroon. There the Hudson widens into a strong river running south between gentler shores broken by the mouths of streams: Stony Creek, Wolf Creek, the Sacandaga River. Below the last of these it flows east in level meanders, dropping after a few miles into an old and broad north-south channel. To this, for more than the first hundred miles of its course the Hudson has been in actuality a tributary.

The channel runs almost straight south, deepening

as it goes. The last towering ice sheet that slid down from the north over most of New York State, blocking the St. Lawrence outlet and making the Mohawk River and the Great Lakes drain through the Hudson, was split by the Adirondack heights; its southern portion was forced into seaward progress between the high folded hills. It deepened the course of the great river as it moved.

From the point of its southward turn into the old glacial channel the Hudson flows through a gorge within an older valley. The floor of the gorge from almost as far north as Albany to its mouth lies below the level of the sea, creating a fiord or estuary where the fresh waters are ever subject to the invasion of salty ocean tides. Through a land of ice-built terraces the Hudson runs south to the northern gate of its highland canyon. On the west behind the terraces the Catskills lift the folded floors of ancient tropic seas, sediments bearing corals, starfishes, sea lilies which once had life beneath warm waters. East of the river and its eastern terraces lie the Taconics, which moved up into the sky before the Catskills were born.

There was a time, some of the scientists say, when the Hudson, before it reached the highland barrier, wandered off to the southwest through Pennsylvania where it joined the Susquehanna and emptied its waters into Chesapeake Bay. Another stream, whose source was far to the south, gradually by headward erosion moved its beginnings northward until it captured and incorporated the runaway and straightened its course oceanward. That course led through a barrier of ancient mica-laden rocks upreared into the high ridges of the Appalachians. The Hudson worked its way through those ridges, aided by the glaciers that forced their masses southward through its valley, smoothing the northern slopes, carrying boulders away from the southern, leaving behind high-frowning cliffs, digging a channel so deep that its floor is in places nearly a thousand feet below sea level.

Through the gateway peaks, Storm King and Breakneck, the river flows southward past Mount Taurus on the east, Bear Mountain on the west, and emerges from the gap between the mountains known as Dunderberg and Anthony's Nose. A few miles farther along, after passing between High Tor Mountain and Prickly Pear Hill, the gorge widens and the river spreads to its greatest width, more than three and a half miles at Haverstraw Bay. For the next dozen miles the stream narrows gradually and the west side becomes a sheer columned wall of hard basalt rising 350 feet in its lower segments, 550 feet at its full height. This rock poured from the earth's interior as molten liquid and inserted itself in a thick hard sill between layers of sandstone, forming a giant sandwich. The sandstone cover has been worn off near the river, leaving the hard brown wall towering above the water in an awesome vertical precipice, the Palisades.

The river runs past the narrow island called Manhattan into New York Bay, thence between Staten Island on the west and Long Island on the east to the Atlantic. But the end of its channel is not yet. Cut into the floor of the ocean, it extends far out to the southeast. A generally accepted theory is that at some date before the existence of man the water level of the Atlantic dropped ten to fifteen thousand feet. When the last of the four great ice sheets was on the land, a mighty river gushed from the end of the glacier that had covered the Hudson valley and roared downward, cutting deep into the soft sediment of the former ocean floor, to a new shore line nearly 150 miles farther out than the old one. For thousands of years the great stream ran, constantly lowering its level and digging one of the deepest canyons the world has ever known. From a shallow beginning, as scientists have discovered by soundings, the floor of the gorge dropped steeply until in some places it reached a depth of 3,600 feet, a thousand feet deeper than the Royal Gorge of the Colorado. Had there been human life then, a traveler in a boat on the Hudson might have looked up to the blue sky between walls more than two miles high. But no man has yet seen, or probably ever will see, this stupendous natural phenomenon. After the river had created it, the salt sea returned and buried the canyon thousands of feet below the tossing waves.

The most recent surveys of the United States Coast and Geodetic Survey do not completely confirm or contradict this theory. They point out that the Hudson Submarine Channel begins about three miles southeast of Ambrose Lightship where it is a flat-bottomed valley a mile and a half wide and twenty to thirty feet below the ocean floor. It runs in a sweeping curve, continually broadening and deepening until, ninety miles from its beginning, it is obscured by a delta formation.

Three miles southeast of this delta lies the beginning of the great canyon. The government survey soundings have shown that it slopes downward at the average rate of 150 feet a mile and that when it has reached its amazing 3,600-foot depth below the ocean floor its width from rim to rim is about five and a half miles.

In that canyon where once apparently the Hudson ran in sunlight and shadow between walls almost inconceivably high there is now only the twilight of the great sea depths. The naturalist-explorer William Beebe has sent his nets far down into that water-dusk and has written that in the Hudson gorge there swims a blind fish, whose eye-pockets are glowing headlights to attract smaller fish close enough to be caught and swallowed, and "a tiny white thread of a fish," with eyes "far out on the ends of impossibly slender stalks." Another dweller of these submarine depths is a round fish of glowing silver that keeps "all its batteries of green and violet lights turned downward while it stares unmovably and piously upward." Here are pale-violet humpbacked shrimp, and shrimp exuding clouds of scarlet flame, "active opals, gleaming and scintillating as they twist and turn," and a long bronze and black "scimitar-fanged sea-dragon."

Near the edge of the continental shelf—the elevation a hundred miles wide above the ocean floor, which geologists believe was once dry land—the Hudson channel makes one last plunge downward. The grade is so steep that the 1,200-foot drop has been called the "undersea falls." Actually, in the days when the river dashed through the gorge there must have been furious rapids here. At the seaward limit of the most recent surveys 135 miles southeast of Ambrose Lightship, the bottom of the canyon is 7,500 feet below the water's surface and 1,500 feet below the ocean's floor. Somewhere beyond that point the Hudson channel finally ends in the immensity of the Atlantic.

2

Old Moon Into Stars

WANDERERS from the Eastern Hemisphere crossed the Bering Straits into the north land and became the first Americans. Increasing with the generations, they spread southward along the west coast, then eastward. No one knows how long it took them to cross the mountains, deserts, plains, rivers, of the continent, but the story of the journey was remembered and often told among a people called the Algonkins. For a reason long forgotten they had set out from their homes beside the blue Pacific to travel toward the sunrise until they would come to the water-that-flows-two-ways.

Long years of wandering and of wars followed, but at last the Algonkins came to the banks of a wide river and saw with excitement the down current stopped, then overcome, by the rush of upstreaming tides. They had found the water-that-flows-two-ways. Eagerly they spread out along the shores, organizing small tribes, painting and engraving rocks and trees with tribal insignia as a manner of staking out exclusive hunting rights in certain areas. On the western banks settled the large association of tribes called the Lenape. Across from the big island at the river's mouth was the land of the Raritans, and north of them lay the wooded shores that belonged to the Hackensacks, the Tappans, the Haverstraws. All these were joined in the Lenape alliance of the Unami, the Turtle. Above them was another such Lenape union, the Minsi, or Wolf, brotherhood among whose river tribes were the Waranawankongs, the Catskills, the Wawarsings.

Across the Hudson from the Lenape were the homes of other Algonkin peoples—the Manhattans, the Wappingers. And to the north of these, from the site of Albany to the two big lakes now called Lake George and Lake Champlain, lived the strongest of all the Algonkin tribes, the Mohicans, who had taken their very name from the old prophecy—people-of-the-water-that-flows-two-ways.

The Hudson River Algonkins were a simple people and they were good to look at. Possibly their journey from the west coast had killed off the weak, leaving the strong to mate and produce a fine race. Their dusky bodies were muscular and tall and symmetrical. White settlers found them more pleasing to the eye than to the nose, however, for they rubbed themselves with the odorous greases of slain wild animals and went about naked to the waist in warm weather. During the summer months the clothing of a man was a breech clout, hip-length leggings of tanned hide, and soft-soled moccasins. He never wore a long feather war bonnet like the headdresses that decorated his western cousins. The River Indian often burned off with hot stones most of the hair on his head, leaving a strip of stiff short hair running from the forehead to the back of the neck and, hanging from the crown, one long lock—the scalp lock coveted by his enemies.

The women's leggings were knee-high and their square leather aprons, tied about the waist, did not reach to the knees. Aside from moccasins, their only other articles of apparel were square beaded caps which covered the long black braids caught up on their heads. In cold weather both men and women wore, carelessly slung to windward, handsome robes of wildcat, wolf, bear, deerskin or mantles of gorgeous turkey feathers.

The River Indians pleased themselves aesthetically with much colorful decoration. They painted their faces and the exposed parts of their bodies with dyes made from the colored clay of the riverbank or from the juices of berries. The men wore necklaces of opalescent shells and sometimes hung pendants of colored stones on their chests. The women covered their clothes with shell beads, not only to be more beautiful but to show how rich and socially important they were.

The Indians lived well beside the big river which some called the Mannahatta, others the Shatemuc. The woods were so full of birds that the noise of their twittering overwhelmed the sound of the hunter's approach. There was red meat among the valley trees, too, to be brought down with arrows from hickory bows—deer, bear, and raccoon. In the water swam countless fish— the heavy leaping sturgeon, the striped bass, the slim herring, the lavender-scaled shad running in millions upriver every spring. And all a lazy man who was also hungry need do to satisfy his appetite was walk into the river shallows and pick up a meal of oysters.

Well fed by the water, the Indians sported in it and upon it. They swam as well as the river otters and they built boats from single big trees, making the trunks hollow by burning and scraping. Few, if any, took the pains to build a birchbark canoe such as the Indians of the north woods used. A craft of lightness and delicacy fashioned for the swift attacks and swifter flights of human conflict seemed unnecessary to them. Most of the causes of aggressive war, economic causes at least, had been removed by the generous stream. Now that they lived by the water-that-flows-two-ways portages to other waters were not to be contemplated.

The Indian villages along the Hudson looked like clusters of very large wooden bowls turned upside down, little replicas of the rounded hills behind them. Hickory poles set into the ground and bent over, to be tied together at their meeting, formed the framework on which the bark walls rested. A hole in the center of the roof allowed the smoke from the fireplace, built deep in the ground just below it, to escape. Long poles, hung horizontally from the roof on strong withes, held drying corn, food baskets, household utensils, clothes. Around the inside wall ran a curving bench on which the Indians sat and also slept.

In their clearings beside the broad, sun-flecked river the women of the tribes hoed the maize fields, tended the yellow pumpkins that lay between the tall green plants, hoed the beans, watched over the playing children while their husbands fished and hunted. When night had come and the roasted meats and the loaves of maize bread had been eaten, the Indians sat outside their houses and watched the stars as their fathers before them had done—until those pinpoints of light in the deep blue arc above them could make no movement they did not anticipate. They measured the time of their plantings by the alternation of the constellations, their harvestings by the autumn moons.

The Hudson River Indians wished they could fight better whenever the Mohawks left the rich valley that bears their name and came down the river in well-

organized war parties to demand tribute. Only the
Mohicans sometimes dared to resist them. The southern
Algonkin tribes usually submitted meekly. Though their
warriors were big and strong, the sight of a single Mohawk in war dress would scare the wits out of a half
dozen of them—so well had the Iroquois spread the
reputation of their fiercest tribes. The strongly governed
Iroquois federation, made up of Mohawks, Cayugas,
Onondagas, Oneidas, and Senecas, was usually content
to rest upon its fertile lands along the Mohawk and the
Genesee, but its rulers knew that in an emergency they
could always rob the Hudson valley tribes.

The River tribes were too loosely organized, too
fond of the ways of peace to be victorious in their wars.
It would seem from their history that the ebbing and
flowing water which the Algonkins so long sought had
in the end betrayed them for, by making them happy
and contented, it had caused them to think too much on
peace.

The highest officer in the government of the Mohicans, the sachem, devoted himself only to the problems of peaceful living. An ancient account says that
the sachem was looked upon as a great tree under whose
shade all the tribe might rest. "His business is to con-
template the welfare of his people day and night—how
to promote their peace and happiness . . . whatever he
does for his nation must be done out of friendship and
good will." Only in time of actual war was the authority
of this counselor superseded by that of "the Hero," the
battle leader. It is not surprising that the first white
man known to have visited a tribe of the River Indians,
Henry Hudson, spoke of his hosts as "loving people."

The wide tidal stream beside them inspired the

Indians' belief in supernatural beings. They cowered beside the fires in the bowl-like houses wondering how they had offended as Minewawa, goddess of the valley, hurled lightnings down upon them and growled at them in thunder. But they were soon dancing to thank her as the soft rains followed, making the gardens fertile, and the burning of their votive tobacco sent clouds of pungent smoke toward her dwelling beyond the Catskill peaks where in Onteora, "land of the sky," lived many gods. It was Minewawa, the River Indians said, who hung the new moon above those peaks and it was she who took it down when it had grown old and cut it up into little stars which she cast about her in the western sky.

Like children in ecstatic fear of the dark, the Indians listened to the ghost spirit Jeebi speaking through the wailing monotony of the whippoorwill; they looked for dark monsters among the river rushes which the Wahwahtaysee—the fireflies—tried to reveal with their flashing lanterns; they told tales of the pukwidjinnies— the little men who seemed to materialize in the valley dusk as soon as the sun was behind the hills but who often disappeared before one's very eyes.

The squaws putting their papooses to sleep ("squaw" and "papoose" were Algonkin words which the Iroquois claimed to despise) told the little Indians of the naked bear who lived in a valley shut off by circling high hills, great Mishemokwa, who was very hard to kill and who sometimes ate bad children. The old men spoke of the Wendegoes, big men of the woods who tore down oak trees and clubbed the storm spirits with them. The elders said, too, that in the thunder-storms that sweep across the Hudson valley on many summer days they could hear the groans and shrieks of rebel spirits captured by the powerful spirit, Manitou, who imprisoned them behind the river hills he had built up to hide himself and his victims from mortal eyes. And when the old men had related these tales, the young Indian girls sitting together told each other of sunny hours in the afternoon when they had heard the sound of splashing in the shallow river bays and had tried to catch the Neebanawbaigs, water spirits, at their play.

One hot, hazy day these simple, fanciful savages living beside their broad river saw a strange giant moving smoothly over the water. Some of them thought it a fish sent by a distant devil to bring them evil; others, seeing the sun's rays on its big white wings, thought it a bird sent by the god of light and prepared to worship it.

3

"A Pleasant Land to See"

ON a July day of the year 1524 in the little French seaport of Dieppe, Giovanni da Verrazano, Florentine explorer, penned a letter to his employer, "his most serene and Christian Majesty" Francis I of France.

"We found a pleasant place below steep little hills," he wrote. "And from among those hills a mighty deep-mouthed river ran into the sea. . . . We rode at anchor in a spot well guarded from the wind, and we passed into the river with the *Dauphin's* one small boat."

The next few sentences told the rest of the simple incident. These men who had left Captain da Verrazano's vessel, the *Dauphin,* had sailed half a league into the land—where the river made a pleasant lake about three leagues in compass—and there had heard a friendly shouting and had seen, rushing down the wooded banks, many people "clad in the feathers of fouls of divers hues." Some of the crowd had launched small craft, mottling the sunny surface with bright colors as feather-mantled oarsmen rowed frantically toward the arriving boat. Then on a sudden ("as is wont to fall out in sailing") the foreigners felt upon their faces a contrary flaw of wind and to their great discontent they were forced to put about and retrace their course. Once aboard the *Dauphin* they had weighed anchor, spread sail, and dipping steadily eastward had vanished from the sight of the disappointed natives. Da Verrazano had come to the mouth of a river that would one day bear the name of an explorer yet unborn—and had sailed away.

Eighty-five years and a few days after da Verrazano had written his letter to King Francis a little 80-ton Dutch yacht was beating northward along the low sandy seacoast of what is now New Jersey. Manned by a tough, quarrelsome English and Dutch crew, the shallow-bottomed, high-pooped little *Half Moon* was commanded by an experienced and distinguished English sea captain, Henry Hudson. He had been employed by the Dutch East India Company to try to find the Northwest Passage to China. There had been trouble between the Dutch and English members of his crew in northern waters and he had made peace by sailing southward as far as Virginia. Now, after a short stop at the mouth of the Delaware, Henry Hudson was following the coast line northward with curiosity.

On the heavy morning of September 2, 1609, the men on the *Half Moon* saw a great fire that seemed to hang in the sky, for no land showed beneath it. Later the sun burned away the mists and they saw land "all like broken Ilands," and they sailed into a bay into which flowed a big stream.

The light of the sunny afternoon was mellowing and the evening calm had come as they dropped anchor in the quiet harbor. When the stars began to show through the clear air they saw to the north of them high hills, bluer than the deepening blue of the sky. "This is a very good land to fall with and a pleasant land to see," wrote English Robert Juet, an officer of the boat, at the end of that day.

The next morning, when the wind had cleared away the dawn murk, they weighed anchor and stood to the northward, finding the land "very pleasant and high and bold." They spent many hours in sounding and found anchorage near the mouth of the river. On September fourth they sent out a boat to fish and her men caught ten mullets and a ray so big that it took four sailors to haul it in. Some of the natives of the country came aboard clad in loose deerskins and feather mantles and carrying big green leaves of tobacco, yellow ears of maize, brown loaves of corn bread. About their necks hung ornaments of reddish copper and their tobacco pipes were of the same gleaming metal. When Captain Hudson returned their visit by going ashore soon thereafter "the swarthy natives all stood and sang in their fashion." He was delighted with their country. "It is as pleasant a land as one can tread upon," he wrote, and Robert Juet entered in his journal that the country was full of great and tall oaks. An expedition of five men sent out to explore the river to the north reported that the lands in that direction "were as pleasant with grass and flowers and goodly trees as ever they had seen, and very sweet smells came from them." But on the way back to the ship these men, commanded by John Coleman, an Englishman, were interrupted in their aesthetic reveries by the swift attack of two boatloads of natives. Slowly John Coleman bled to death with an arrow deep in his throat. Two of his men were in agony, struck by the flying shafts. Darkness came and with it a driving rain. All night the four rowed aimlessly about on the black river with the dead body of their

leader. It was ten o'clock in the morning before they
were back on the safe high decks of the *Half Moon.*

After that they were careful. When, on the ninth
of the month, two long canoes approached, their occupants badly disguising hostile intent with a pretense at
barter, the sailors took two of them prisoner, dressed
them in red coats to make them look ridiculous, and
drove the rest away. The heat of early September, moist
and breathless, had settled upon the river and the ship
slowly sailed northward. Day after day dawned into
hot sunlight. On the fourteenth they glided past the
pillared twelve-mile wall of the Palisades and through
the lake that would someday be known as Haverstraw
Bay. The shadows of the Hill of Thunder lengthened
over their white sails as they turned into the channel
of the highlands and saw, beyond the swirling waters
of the narrow race, the Mountain Bear crouching in the
blue heavens. "The land grew high," wrote Robert Juet.
"The river is full of fish."

They lay at anchor among the mountains that
night, and the next morning before they were under
way their two captives squirmed out of a port and swam
ashore. They waited until the wind had filled the *Half
Moon's* sails and she was moving indifferently upriver
out of their sight before they shouted derisively at her.

Still the fair hot weather continued. High above
the ship lay the blue ramparts of *Onteora,* Land of the
Sky, guarded by the night-squalling wildcats that were
to give them their Dutch name. In sight of these high
blue mountains Henry Hudson crossed in a native canoe
to the eastern shore of the river with the old chief of a
small tribe of forty men and seventeen women. The
Indians were gathered to greet the white captain "in

THE MOON ROLLED A SALTY T

NST MOUNTAIN WATERS

a house well constructed of oak bark and circular in shape . . . with an arched roof." There the Englishman saw great stores of corn and beans and outside, drying in the hot sun, "enough to load three ships besides what was growing in the fields." And there, sitting on a mat spread for him, he partook of a feast of pigeons, which had just been shot, and fat dog, hastily killed and skinned with shells from the riverbank.

The river was getting shallower now. Any hope that Hudson may have had that he was discovering a passage to China had vanished. But each day was sunny and golden and the autumn colors were dimmed only by the valley mists that turned bold contrasts into pastel harmonies. The friendly, simple people of the river were happy to see the strangers and brought them grapes and corn, pumpkins and tobacco, and the precious skins of beaver and otter, to be traded for beads and knives and hatchets. Great crowds of the natives came to see the white-winged ship and Henry Hudson, a little distrustful, invited some of the chiefs to his cabin where he plied them with wine and *aqua vitae* until "they were all merrie." But even much alcohol brought out no treachery in the group. At least one of them was too drunk to go ashore that night and his companions were obviously worried over his strange condition. When they returned to the *Half Moon* late the next morning, however, they were so pleased to see him safe and sound that they gave Henry Hudson presents of tobacco and shell beads, making a great ceremony of it. One of them delivered a florid oration and they "shewed him all the country round about" and there was a feast of venison, brought on board on an enormous platter.

That night, after fifteen days of sunny weather, a typical upriver shower swept upon them. In the midst of it at ten o'clock came the hail of the *Half Moon's* small boat that had gone north in the morning to take soundings. Weary and wet, the crew reported that they had rowed eight or nine leagues to the end of navigable water and had returned.

At noon of the next day, September twenty-third, in air cleaned and cooled by the night's rain, the explorers started on their return journey. Again each day was filled with sun but the autumn winds were brisker. Out of the south, on the twenty-fifth, came a gale so strong that there was no combating it; the *Half Moon* rode at anchor while her men went for a walk on the west side of the river "and found good ground for Corne and other Garden herbs with great store of goodly Oakes, and Walnut trees, and Chestnut trees, Ewe trees and trees of sweet wood in great abundance, and great store of Slate for houses, and other good stones." All the rest of the month, while the reds and golds of the valley trees flamed in the air and made the water a kaleidoscopic mirror, they dropped steadily downstream, stopping here and there for pleasant converse and trade with the simple people of the shore. On the last day they were close to the gentle slopes that now hold Newburgh—"a very pleasant place to build a Town on"—and there in the afternoon they anchored, for the southeast wind was blowing a stiff gale between the mountains. The gaunt rocks cropping out from the high barren crests, the blasted trees that had found no sustenance on stony slopes, filled the wanderers with hopeful surmise that there might be valuable minerals in this region.

Their last three days on the river—the first three of October—saw an unhappy ending to their explorations. For hours a native in a canoe had kept hanging under the stern of the *Half Moon*. When he saw the opportunity he climbed up the rudder and into an open window in the stern. There he stole Robert Juet's pillow, two of his shirts and two bandoleers and began the steep return to his craft. The first mate saw him and shot him dead. At once all the natives who had come aboard to trade leaped over the sides. Some struck out for shore, leaving their canoes behind. The white men put out a small boat to pick up the stolen articles and a swimmer tried with one hand to roll it over in the water. The crew's cook grabbed a sword and cut the hand off.

The next day was spent in a running fight with natives bent on revenge. Two war canoes followed the *Half Moon* as it moved south, their occupants discharging volleys of arrows. Two of the attackers were killed by musket fire. Two more were shot when about a hundred of them waited at a point of land for the ship to pass. Another canoe lost five or six men before it withdrew and left the white men to sail down to peaceful anchorage beside the big island of Mannahatta at the river's mouth. There, in a lowering twilight, they saw a cliff "of the colour of a white greene as though it were either Copper or Silver Myne." A northeaster blew fiercely that night, hurtling great gusts of rain against the sides of the ship. The men had a hard time holding anchorage the next day against strong shifting winds and more rain.

"The fourth, was faire weather, and the wind at North North-west, we weighed and came out of the

River into which we had run so faire. . . . And by twelve of the clocke we were cleere of all the Inlet. Then we took in our Boat, and set our mayne-sayle and sprit-sayle and our top-sayles, and steered away East South-east, and South-east by East off into the mayne sea."

4

The Hard Blond Traders

MOST of the first white settlers of the high-walled valley which Henry Hudson had claimed for the Dutch spoke French as their natural language. Fifteen years after the explorer's voyage on the stream he called "Great River of the Mountains" these people came to build their homes on its banks. Meanwhile a few Dutch ships had visited the river and returned to Holland loaded with skins of beaver, mink, otter, and wildcat. The New Netherland Company, organized in 1614, obtained a monopoly on the river trade and sent out fur expeditions so successful that two years later its sponsors asked for continuance of its charter. But the Dutch government decided to leave the river open to competition for a few years while it planned a powerful monopolistic stock company to handle the American trade—the West India Company.

That organization was founded in 1621, and in April of 1624 thirty families of Walloons embarked on the ship *New Netherland,* under Captain Cornelis Jacobsen May, bound for the Hudson's mouth. They were mostly Protestant refugees, farmers from the South Netherlands where they had felt the pressure of Roman Catholic Spain. On the deck of the *New Netherland,* as she rocked in the harbor of Amsterdam on March thirtieth, they listened politely as two magistrates publicly read to them the "Provisional Order" of the West India Company. They must obey orders, be loyal Reformed Calvinists, convert the heathen wild men. They must live where they are told for at least six years, lending a hand in all communal enterprises, selling all materials for export to the company, recognizing the company's rights to all mining properties and pearl fisheries. They must not sell for profit the products of their handicraft (this to protect Holland industry). They must plant only what they are ordered to sow. They must be careful not to trade with outsiders or tell them about the business or profits of the company, and they must be honest and respectful in their dealings with the natives.

Through the English Channel and the Bay of Biscay was the route, and then the Canary Isles rose in fresh bright colors from the sea. The Savage Islands lay beyond, and white sand shores beneath Virginia's tufted pines. Soft breezes and the moon of May performed their spell upon the pioneer Walloons, for Caterina Trico long years later said she saw four weddings on the deck below the wind-filled sails.

The "River of the Mountains" was now officially the "River of the Prince Mauritius," named to honor that remarkable Dutch soldier and strategist, Maurice of Orange. At its mouth the *New Netherland* paused to disembark her passengers. Some of them set out for the big river to the south, the Delaware. Others sought the "Fresh River," the Connecticut. Eight men stayed where they were to begin the permanent settlement of Manhattan Island. Then Captain May, with about eighteen families of Walloons, sailed up the river to the foot of the long hill on which Albany now stands. There on the west bank, about opposite where a Dutch fort and trading center, Fort Nassau, had been built and abandoned, he and the men of the new community set up a quadrangular stockade of logs new cut from the near-by woods, and called it Fort Orange.

Now the two towns, one at the mouth of the river and one a hundred and fifty miles north, began to grow and develop. While the Fort Orange Walloons were trying to learn enough Dutch words and Indian words to carry on the business of an upriver trading post, the Manhattan group, having built small hutlike dwellings of sod and bark, were asking the West India Company to send them a preacher—at least someone with the proper authority to baptize babies. At once the bearer of the message, Bastiaen Jansen Crol, a layman who had qualified for the position of Comforter of the Sick on ships going to and from the new colony, was authorized to perform not only baptisms but marriages as well.

Crol arrived at Manhattan on the River of the Prince Mauritius at about the same time as Willem Verhulst, who took over governorship of the colony from Captain May. They had not more than begun their work when their responsibilities were increased by the arrival of three ships—*Horse, Cow,* and *Sheep*—each containing the cargo indicated by the name, and a swift yacht, the *Mackerel,* which held few fish but brought forty-five new colonists. The cattle were soon peacefully grazing in meadows upriver from the little settlement at the foot of Manhattan, and farming on the Hudson had begun.

But agriculture did not thrive along the big river. Though the West India Company was committed to efforts at colonizing, it had found the profits of fur cargoes absorbing most of its interest. It found, too, that, while it was easy to encourage "petty traders who swarm hither with great industry, reap immense profit and exhaust the country without adding anything to its population or security," it was difficult to get worthy farmers and craftsmen to leave a prosperous, safe, free Holland for the wild and precarious shores of a little-known river.

In order to allay criticism of its failure in this respect and to satisfy the desires of major stockholders who wanted to participate as individuals in the benefits of the rich new land, the directors of the company established in 1629, by a "Charter of Freedoms and Exemptions," the Patroon System. The charter permitted grants of great river estates to members of the company who would, within four years after accepting the terms of a contract, establish on the lands proffered them settlements of at least fifty persons. The patroonships might extend sixteen miles along one shore of the river or eight miles along both shores, "and as far inland as the situation of the occupants will permit." The patroon had to purchase the title to his lands from the Indians but, once having obtained it, he might hold the land as a "perpetual fief of inheritance." He need not pay duties for eight years and his tenants did not have to pay the taxes of the province for a decade.

Six patroonships were immediately signed for by eager investors—two on the Delaware River, two on the Connecticut, two on the Hudson. Six years later only one remained.

A prosperous jeweler of Amsterdam, Kiliaen Van Rensselaer, registered himself for a patroonship on the

Hudson in the late autumn of 1629. By the beginning of the new year he had obtained the services as agent of Comforter of the Sick Crol, who had risen to high office in the community at Fort Orange. Completely disregarding the limitations set by the charter to which he had agreed two months before, Van Rensselaer ordered Crol to secure for him on both sides of the river near Fort Orange as much land as possible even if the claim extended north and south of the fort for twenty miles or more. Crol made three purchases of land so vaguely defined that for many years the Van Rensselaers felt justified in claiming all lands on both sides of the river from Barren Island, eleven miles below Fort Orange, to the mouth of the Mohawk, nine miles above it. The inland limit on either side was left indefinite.

The story of the greed of the Van Rensselaer patroons is not a pretty one. They made use of the West India Company whenever it could serve them, and they fought the company relentlessly whenever this was to their advantage. The first patroon never set foot on the great Hudson River estate which he named Rensselaerswyck, but he gave much of his time to figuring out unethical ways by which his pocketbook might be made fat by traffic on his distant acres. He even ordered a fortified castle to be built on Barren Island at the southern end of his claimed dominion and attempted to enforce by arms a monopolistic edict prohibiting any trader not under contract to him from sailing into the waters of his patroonship. As for his tenants, he treated them with hostile suspicion as stupid peasants and, claiming as excuse that they deceived him, bulldozed and cheated them. In the spring of 1639 he wrote to William Kieft, director of New Netherland: "I would not like to have my people get too wise and figure out their master's profit, especially in matters in which they themselves are somewhat interested . . . these I would rather keep a secret between the company and myself. . . . I shall then be better able to trade with my people and to satisfy them." He set up a commissary at which he sold supplies to his tenants at outrageous profit to himself.

Most evil of all his machinations, if Maria, wife of his son Jeremias, is to be believed, he conceived the idea that he had founded Rensselaerswyck "in order that his children, with God's mercy, might live off it and that they should not alienate it." Whether or not she told the truth, Maria affirmed this policy after the death of her husband (who dissented) and, though she and her progeny owned a property so vast they could hardly compute its extent, they thereafter refused to sell any of it. Thus was established a feudal sort of tenant system which was to torment the farmers of the Hudson valley into sporadic armed warfare over a period of two hundred years.

The perpetual leasehold by which a farmer might live in a house and till fields for his lifetime, provided that he agreed to give each year a share of his crops and his increase of livestock to the owner of the land, became the greatest single instrument of injustice in the whole history of the Hudson valley. Scornfully in 1650 Cornelis Van Tienhoven, secretary to the director general (then Pieter Stuyvesant), wrote to the High and Mighty Lords of the Dutch States-General that in Rensselaerswyck "no one down to the present time can possess a foot of land of his own but is obliged to take upon rent all the land which he cultivates."

Winning the war against the rents was to be more important to the tenants of the river farms during the two centuries of oppression that followed than winning the War of the Revolution, because unfair rents were an immediate local disaster that touched their daily lives. Many a rent-distressed countryman fought against the British in the earliest of America's wars for democracy believing that, once the Revolution was won, the feudal system initiated by the first Van Rensselaer patroon would be abolished by a new republican government and the Tory-owned estates would be confiscated and divided up into small farms for independent and democratic farmers. At the end of the long war, however, such idealists were to find that while the new government abolished the right of entail, by which the eldest son inherited the estate in its entirety on the death of his father, the rich river families who had supported General Washington were united in preserving their vast acres to their own uses and even adding to their holdings by absorbing the confiscated lands of the Tories. The tenant farmers were then forced to submit to the perpetuation of the unfair practices of the landlords, who made aristocratic pretensions in the democratic state, or fight. Again and again they chose to fight, but it was not until the middle of the nineteenth century that the special privileges of the holders of the Hudson estates were abolished.

The antirent struggle was a long war fought by successive generations and throughout two centuries it vitally affected the life of a large portion of the people who lived along the Hudson. It was a war between two ways of life, and the fundamental ideas of both had been brought to the river shores from the Old World. One was the way of the aristocrat, based on belief in the superiority of the few. It was Europe's old way, destined to periodic revival. The other was the way of democracy, based on belief in the dignity and deserving of honest persons. The people, dreaming of a new land where men might have equal rights, fought for their river, claiming it as their own. The landholders, assuming aristocratic privilege, denied them.

As the three units of organized living—Fort Amsterdam, Fort Orange, and Rensselaerswyck—began to grow, life on the Hudson River took on a character that has not been understood by the American people generally for a hundred years. Washington Irving's charmingly written and immensely popular caricature, the *Knickerbocker History of New York*, has done more to create widespread misconception of the Dutch period than any other one agency. Despite its author's insistence that it was an effort at comic distortion of truth for the purpose of entertainment, American readers have found it so delightfully compelling that they have accepted its characterizations seriously. As a matter of fact, it is doubtful if Irving's work, however pleasing, is a real caricature since by definition of that term it should present exaggerations of actual characteristics.

The Dutch were not the fatheaded, fat-bottomed, sleepy, sillily pompous folk of the *Knickerbocker History*. Nor were the two colonies at the foot and the head of the navigable Hudson so prevailingly Dutch as to be permeated by the characteristics of the people of the Netherland States. Van Rensselaer's advertising of the joys of life on his patroonship brought few of his countrymen to Rensselaerswyck. But the prospect of quick profits in various ways, including the counterfeiting of Indian Wampum, the accepted medium of exchange, brought to that colony and to the Walloon settlement at Fort Orange as opportunistic a lot of roistering adventurers as ever swarmed about a newly discovered gold field, a rough, tough, quarrelsome crew of Irishmen, Swedes, Germans, Danes, Englishmen, all with but one idea of conduct—every man for himself. Most of them were illiterate. Few were unintelligent. They were hard, shrewd, lawless, brave, and cruel.

On Manhattan an equally polyglot society was developing. Father Isaac Jogues, a Jesuit missionary rescued by the Dutch from slavery among the Mohawk Indians, recorded that in 1643 Director General Kieft told him "there were persons there of eighteen different languages." They were a hard-drinking and profane lot, exercising their creative imaginations by inventing oaths so fanciful as to approach poetry and by applying such picturesque names to their drinks as Kill Devil (well-earned title of Barbados rum), Little Mill, Ship's Sails, Hans in the Cellar, The Abbot and His Monks, Great and Small Fisheries, Bride's Tears.

The drunken and profane frontiersmen who made up the heterogeneous groups at New Amsterdam and Fort Orange were rough in their play and in their ideas of entertainment. In a favorite game, Clubbing the Cat, puss was imprisoned in a cask hung in the middle of a tightly stretched rope. Players stood a given distance away and hurled clubs at the cask. The winner was he who broke the cask and let the animal escape. Another game, Pulling the Goose, consisted of riding a horse full gallop under a goose that hung with greased head down from a rope stretched across the road. The rider who yanked the bird free won the game. Variations of this pastime were played with a rabbit or an eel for the booty. Dutchmen have always loved to skate and their enjoyment of the smooth frozen surface of the Hudson during the long winter months, when a barrier of impenetrable forests and ice floes separated Fort Orange from New Amsterdam, soon brought most of their comrades to the river to try their skill.

As for humor along the Hudson in the early Dutch days, it consisted mostly of practical joking. The Dutch loved to serenade newlyweds with raucous horning and often planted at night a strangely decorated pole outside the door of the happy couple's home to embarrass them when morning light had come. They loved to gallop their horses through town at top speed in the daytime and to disturb the night by firing their guns and shouting. A frightened Indian seemed always a funny sight until they discovered how dangerous he could be. Trader David DeVries sailed his sloop stealthily in past Sandy Hook one evening and came quietly to anchor under Fort Amsterdam at about two o'clock in the morning without being observed. He waited until dawn began to break and then suddenly fired three guns that made a terrific clamor echoing against the walls of the fort and "caused the people to spring out of their beds all at once."

At a tent party inside the fort two months later, Trumpeter Anthony Van Corlaer got himself into a fist fight with two of his associates by unexpectedly blowing his loud trumpet in their ears. When the British took over the government of the Hudson valley they were frequently unable to see anything funny in such antics and were much less tolerant of them than the Dutch had been. There was, for instance, the time Jan

Conell and Dirck Bradt brought a common soldier into Willem Gysbertse's tavern near Fort Orange and gravely introduced him as Captain Mosely, a commander of three hundred men who had come up the Hudson to drive away the River Indians. This so impressed the credulous landlord that he served free drinks to the three conspirators all that evening just as they had planned. But the next morning after their host had very importantly told the mission of his distinguished soldier guest the Indians began taking to the deep woods. Jan Conell and Dirck Bradt soon thereafter found themselves seated in uncomfortable positions in the stocks and condemned to pay Willem Gysbertse a tavern bill which they regarded as exorbitant.

The tendency to regard a charge against them as exorbitant and all their own prices as reasonable was thoroughly typical of the majority of early Hudson River settlers. Indeed, they were loyal to nothing save profits. They did not care who ruled over them so long as they were acquiring wealth. They complained of the West India Company's monopoly of the fur trade and frequently smuggled beaver pelts into New England where they got more money for them. They were very jealous of their opportunities for trade. In the spring of 1655 the New Amsterdam preacher Megapolensis complained bitterly to the authorities in Holland of the influx of Jewish immigrants. In a violent denunciation that foreshadowed more recent vilification of unoffending Hebrews, he declared: "These people have no other God than the Mammon of unrighteousness, and no other aim than to get possession of Christian property, and to overcome all other merchants by drawing all trade to themselves. Therefore, we request . . . that the godless rascals, who are of no benefit to the country, but look at everything for their own profit, may be sent away from here."

The traders of the Hudson shore even mistrusted each other and made rules to govern the general conduct that would make cheating difficult. At Fort Orange it was forbidden to run up the hill to meet Indians coming in to trade, to entertain Indians overnight in a white man's house, to send children to play (and incidentally to trade) with Indians. When the English invaders arrived at the mouth of the Hudson, the traders gladly disregarded all questions of loyalty to the Dutch lords overseas and submitted to the new rule because they thought the English governors would ask a smaller share of their earnings than the Dutch had demanded.

Most unfortunate of all the characteristics of the queerly mixed collection of early settlers on the Hudson was their quarrelsome bumptiousness. They squabbled with the Swedes to the south of them on the Delaware, with the English in the Yankee settlements to the north, with the neighboring savages. They complained against their directors and the patroons, and they fought against each other.

These men and women were actually quick to anger, peppery, captious, nervously active. Though they have often been praised for maintaining friendly relations with the Indians, they treated them very badly. They kept peace only with the powerful Iroquois who lived to the northwest along the Mohawk and Genesee rivers and whom they heartily feared. The first war of the Dutch with the Hudson River Indians was begun by fussy, incompetent Director Kieft who "to break their mouths" ordered the midnight massacre of a tribe of pitiful fugitives who were fleeing a war party of Iroquoian Mohawks and had sought Dutch protection. Another was caused by the murder of an Indian girl by a farmer who saw her stealing his apples. An upriver conflict started when a band of settlers fired a volley into a group of Indians who had been hired by whites to husk corn and had got drunk on their pay. A more serious uprising occurred when the natives discovered that the Dutch had been sending Indian captives into slavery in Curaçao.

The Dutch were also constantly quarreling among themselves and their spats were not confined to ordinary citizens but involved distinguished burghers as well, including the many directors general, most of whom held office for a short time only. Wordy warfare between representatives of the church and government officials were far from unusual. The colony preacher and its director were frequently thrown together and almost as frequently at odds. The first fully ordained minister at New Amsterdam found his habitual avoidance of profanity no bar to forceful expression when he wrote to his patron in Holland that Director Pieter Minuit was "a slippery fellow, who under the painted mask of honesty, is a compound of all iniquity and wickedness. For he is accustomed to the telling of lies, in which he abounds, and to the use of horrible oaths and execrations."

Dominie Bogardus, in particular, was the terror of successive leaders. He opened up on the fourth director, Van Twiller, by calling him a "child of Satan" and promising to preach a sermon against him on the next Sunday that would make him shake in his shoes. Yet a short while after, lured by a case of excellent claret that had been brought to the west bank of the Hudson by Cornelis Van Voorst, he joined Van Twiller in an evening row across the river to try a bottle or two. After disposing of several samples he became quarrelsome and argued hotly with his host and the director over the circumstances of a recent murder. Later all the group became merry and friendly and Van Voorst, to celebrate the reconciliation and salute his guests as they put out on the river, fired an old cannon which stood on the palisade before his home. This proved a more spectacular gesture than he had intended, for the blast set fire to the house and burned it to the ground, making his friends' progress across the river as light as day.

A few years later, in 1646, Dominie Bogardus seized the opportunity at a gay wedding to attack Director Kieft and his associates: "In Africa which has a climate of intense heat different species of animals come together by which various monsters are generated. But I know not from whence, in such a temperate climate as this, such monsters of men are produced." Hotheaded Kieft answered with a formal written protest, pointing out the differences between certain rites which the dominie had conducted when "dead drunk" as contrasted with ceremonies he had performed when only "pretty drunk." Then, knowing what thunders against him would issue from the house of God on the following Sunday, he ordered the Fort Amsterdam drum corps to beat a loud tattoo just outside the church door during the morning services. He made doubly sure that the good man's shouts would not be heard, by having the fort cannon fired frequently in the course of the sermon "as if he had ordered it out a-Maying."

Another wedding, that of the dominie's daughter, found this same director and preacher reconciled and plotting against the guests. The two conspirators had agreed that a new church was necessary to the colony and planned to do something about it. By the time the usual drinking had reached the fourth or fifth round of Bride's Tears the scheming officials brought forth a subscription sheet and in no time at all had the merry guests competing with each other as to who should pledge most to so worthy a cause. Many a burgher groaned the next morning as he remembered signing away more guilders than he could afford in a moment of alcoholic and religious exaltation. Their bitter complaining got all the way to the authorities in Holland before they were satisfied.

Most illuminating example of the way in which Washington Irving divested the touchy, rough-and-ready characters of the Hudson River settlements of their natural vehemence and drive is in his relation of the exciting brush between Govert Loockermans, captain of the sloop *Good Hope,* and Nicolas Coorn, in command of Van Rensselaer's fortifications at the foot of Barren Island. According to court records, Loockermans, who was generally considered a bold fellow by his associates, a smuggler of powder and ball to the Indians yet not above killing one if occasion seemed to demand it, was sailing downriver past Barren with a crew of nine, seven of whom were under twenty-eight years of age, when Coorn demanded that he lower his colors in salute with the single word:

"Strike!"

"For whom?" said Captain Loockermans.

"For the right of Rensselaerswyck," shouted Coorn.

"I'll strike for no one," answered Loockermans, "except the Prince of Orange and the man I work for."

At that Nicolas Coorn fired a cannon and the ball whistled through the mainsail of the *Good Hope* and cut one of the shrouds, a halyard, and a gasket.

Govert Loockermans held the staff of the flag of the Prince of Orange in his hand as he shouted his answer to this insult:

"Fire, you dogs; and the devil take you."

Coorn fired again but the ball went wild. Thereupon an Indian standing beside him, and quite possibly out of patience with his marksmanship, let fly with his gun and the charge went through the colors of the Prince of Orange just about a foot above Govert Loockermans's head. Before more damage could be done the sloop was out of range down the river.

Irving tells this story very amusingly. The changes he makes in it to give it his typical flavor, however, are interesting. He says that Govert Loockermans "of few words but great bottom, was seated on the high poop, quietly smoking his pipe," when he was called upon to lower his colors, that he took his pipe out of his mouth only when he answered Coorn, that he never left his chair or stopped puffing, "maintained a smothered, though swelling silence" until the sloop had got down-river among the Highlands where he swore so mightily that the echoes of his oaths still "give particular effect to the thunderstorms in that neighborhood." Thus for purposes of caricature Irving changes the overcholeric Govert Loockermans from a bold, active, shrewd smuggler and Indian fighter, the captain of a crew of hot-blooded young sailors, into one of his typical wide-

rear, slow-wit Dutch fatheads. A reader of the actual
contemporary records would know that, the Dutch
being what they were, the air immediately below Barren
Island was suddenly charged with a series of profound,
fanciful, and defiant oaths as the *Good Hope* dropped
downriver, and that the leader of the chorus, striding
about in his rage and waving the tattered ensign of the
Prince of Orange, was her very articulate captain.

Years after that ludicrous incident, the patroon and
the West India Company were still carrying on fierce
quarrels. Brant Van Slichtenhorst, director of Rensselaerswyck and the "old gray thief" to most of the dwellers at Fort Orange, built a number of houses beneath
the guns of the fort during the years between 1648 and
1651. They would be in the line of fire in case of an Indian raid. The soldier inhabitants complained to Director Pieter Stuyvesant in New Amsterdam. That
honest official ordered the building stopped. Van
Slichtenhorst answered by putting up a house within
pistol shot of the fort. The quarrel dragged on for
months, was dormant through the winter of 1651.

As soon as the river was free of ice in the spring
Stuyvesant, realizing that the "gray thief" was scheming
to claim the land on which the fort stood for his employers, took passage upriver. In a towering rage he strode
up the hill at Fort Orange on his famous silver-studded
wooden leg, and ordered the soldiers to march to Van
Slichtenhorst's house and take down the patroon's flag.
The soldiers fired a volley and took down the colors.
Then Old Silver Peg laid out the boundaries of the land
he claimed for the West India Company and announced
that the land which they enclosed would henceforth

be known as Beverwyck. He set up a court with three magistrates to hear all criminal and civil cases in Fort Orange and Beverwyck. Law and order were about to descend on the fur traders.

The Regeneration of Jochem Wessels

I<small>T</small> is possible that the honorable judges of the West India Company's new court would not have accepted their appointments so complacently had they known what difficulties were in store for them. The citizens in Beverwyck were slow to accustom themselves to disciplined living. One family in particular was often to be haled before them—from their second meeting on through many years. And since nearly the whole of the social history of the Beverwyck settlement is to be found in the story the court records tell of the life of Jochem Wessels and his wife, it deserves relating.

When old Captain Willem Juriaens stopped baking in his cracked oven on the bank of the Hudson in the spring of 1652 his next-door neighbors, baker Jochem Wessels and his wife Gertrude, were relieved. Two bakeries next door to each other in a town of a hundred houses like Beverwyck might easily be confused, especially by Indians.

Jan Van Hoesen and his family took over the captain's house and lot. They agreed to pay the old fellow for the use of it by letting him live there and eat as much of their food as he would need in the few years of life left him. Both Van Hoesen and his neighbor Wessels had been born in North German territory, and all might have gone well between the dwellers on the plot that is now the park in front of the Delaware and Hudson Building in Albany, if there had not been another clause in the agreement already mentioned. It read that Willem Juriaens would give Jan Van Hoesen the use of his bakeshop and tools and would teach him the baker's trade. Van Hoesen at forty-seven was only ten years older than Jochem Wessels and Jochem knew he was not the type of man to sit and wait for Indians to become confused between two houses. He would go out and get customers. Competition was not dead as the Wessels family had supposed. It would be heavier than ever.

Gertrude Wessels' reaction to her discovery of this situation was a simple one. She had had two broods of children, one by her first husband, Hoffmeyer, in a Dutch colony in Brazil and one by Jochem, and she sallied out on an April day to defend them both. When she saw Jan Van Hoesen's wife, Volckgen, she walked up to her and said, "You're a low woman and I can prove it." Then she doubled up her fist and struck Volckgen with all the power in her strong right arm.

Gertrude was probably surprised when a deputy came for her the next Tuesday and took her to the two-story frame building with the pavilion roof standing close to Fort Orange. Agreeably, however, she climbed the steep stair and entered, through the trap door at the top, the one big room of the second floor. There she saw a half dozen of the burghers of Beverwyck sitting about in dignity. One of them informed her that she had been haled into the second regular session of the Inferior Court of Justice of the town of Beverwyck on the complaint of Volckgen Van Hoesen who charged her with abusive language and assault.

The newly made magistrates must have been embarrassed by what happened. Gertrude had not been accustomed to dealing with an unco-operative neighbor by other method than the one she had used and she resented the innovation. She repeated what she had said about Volckgen with colorful embroidery. Then she told the court what would happen to each of them personally if they tried any nonsense with her. The written record of her trial ends with these words: "The defendant is for her abusive language and assault and threats made here against the court condemned to pay a fine of six guilders, with order to leave the plaintiff henceforth in peace."

The last admonition seems not to have been too well obeyed. Within the next two weeks the court saw fit to assign the old captain's lot to the Van Hoesens permanently. In a rage Jochem Wessels built a pigsty in front of the Van Hoesen door. The court commented on this bold action a few days later: "It is decided that whereas the said baker . . . had constructed an obstruction and nuisance to the house of the aforesaid Jan Van Hoesen it is ordered that he must within the time of three days tear down the said pigsty." When Jochem heard the decision he went home and buckled on his sword, ran back to the courthouse and up the stairs. Waving his blade about in the air he appeared suddenly through the trap door and interrupted proceedings by calling Magistrate Volckert Jans bad names and demanding that he come outdoors and fight like a man.

Two mornings later the court met in extraordinary session to hear Volckert Jans's charges. They decided that this last crime of Jochem's was serious enough to be referred to the authorities at Manhattan for action.

And they were the more exasperated when they had to meet again in the afternoon to consider a further offense. Jochem had been telling everybody who would listen that the magistrates had rushed from the morning session to advise Jan Van Hoesen what they had just done to his archenemy. The court decided he would have to prove this accusation of undignified conduct or suffer an "arbitrary sentence."

In the meantime Volckgen Van Hoesen had entered another charge against Gertrude Wessels claiming she had been slandered. Upon being asked whether she had anything to declare against her neighbor's wife, Gertrude was compelled by lack of proof to say a reluctant "No," and was fined fifty guilders. The setback proved not to have weakened her spirit in the least, however, and now for the first time she began to fight back with the new weapon that had surprised and wounded her. By August she had trapped her own especial enemy neatly. Haled into court for having started a fight, Volckgen Van Hoesen and her good friend Styntgen Laurens pleaded that they had attacked Gertrude only after she had provoked them to it by calling them dirty names. No witness had been near enough to hear Gertrude (probably she had been waiting for just the right conditions) and the two defendants were fined twelve guilders apiece. The suspicious court added to the sentence the despairing admonition: "Parties on both sides are furthermore ordered to hold their tongues and to leave each other in peace, as otherwise the court will take such measures as shall be found necessary."

Watchfully the Wesselses now bided their time. By the beginning of the year Jochem had thought up a new onslaught. He charged Jan Van Hoesen with illegally occupying the house and lot which really belonged to poor old Captain Juriaens. When the court asked him to give security or bind himself in the old man's favor, however, he backed down and withdrew suit, not without whispering about that the chief magistrate had offered Jan Van Hoesen ownership of the old captain's property in return for a bribe of three beavers. The Van Hoesens answered the attack by throwing hot ashes and glowing embers against the clapboards of Jochem's house and the court had to send a messenger to make them stop.

Meanwhile Old Silver Peg in Manhattan had been hearing things about the quality and weight of the bread Jochem and his associates were baking. Complaints sent downriver stated that the bakers were making sugar buns, cookies, and pretzels from good flour and selling them to the Indians, who so loved sweets that they would pay almost any price for them. The remnants of the ground meal were being made into bread for the citizenry and conditions were getting so bad that the heathen were eating flour while the Christians were eating bran.

Immediately the honorable director general sent a letter prohibiting the sale to Indians of all white breads and cakes. The Beverwyck bakers made a fearful to-do over that. In desperation they presented a petition to the court asking "permission to sell some white bread to the Indians, especially cake." The petition was taken to New Amsterdam by the president of the court and other magistrates who were making the trip to confer with Stuyvesant. Upon receiving it that dignitary sent his own especial representative, Cornelis Van Tienhoeven, up to Beverwyck with the returning magistrates to see to the enforcement of his regulations with regard to both brewing and baking.

Now the embarrassment to which Jochem Wessels had subjected the court reached a dizzy height. During the absence of the chief magistrate Jochem had baked a fine batch of sweet cookies and then, standing before his bakeshop, had blown upon his big horn to advertise to the Indians that his wares were done to a nice brown and ready for sale. To add to this brazen defiance of law and order, as Jan Van Hoesen was plaintively pointing out, Jochem had not torn down the pigpen he had been given three days to destroy eleven months before.

Patience was at an end. The magistrates condemned Jochem to pay a fine of fifty guilders within twenty-four hours, commenting in their decision on the evil consequences which might arise . . . especially at this juncture of time—that is, with Old Silver Peg's own representative looking on—in the matter of "disregarding the well meant ordinances of the Honorable Director General."

But the officer from New Amsterdam was not satisfied. He presented a written complaint and the court had to go further. In a long decision in which all Jochem's crimes were enumerated—slander, attacking a magistrate, false accusations, refusal "to move the pigpen which he had erected in front of his neighbor's door to his annoyance and detriment," charging the chief magistrate with soliciting a bribe—"all of which are matters of very serious consequences," the court unanimously decided "to condemn him, on promise and in hopes of better behaviour" to pay an additional fine of a hundred guilders. Begun with sounding dignity and emphasis, .the decision moves on to state with judicial sternness that the fine must be paid within twenty-four hours "or the double amount within forty-eight hours and so on in succession." It ends hopefully: "Also that he shall immediately tear down and remove the pigpen or that it shall be immediately torn down by order of the court."

To complete their work of establishing order during the visit of Van Tienhoven the court continued by disciplining the old captain whom Jochem had been encouraging to revolt against the provisions of his contract. "Furthermore, to prevent all further disputes and differences," said the judge, "it is ordered that Willem Juriaens shall have to comport himself as a decent old man should and at noon and in the evening come to meals at regular hours as is proper and shall also have to be satisfied with the ordinary food which Jan Van Hoesen daily supplies for himself and his family." This pleased Jan and his family so much that they began triumphantly throwing their slops on Jochem's lot until the court enjoined them against the practice. It put Jochem in a bad temper. He took it out on Mariken Ten Haer by getting into an argument with her at a rival baker's house and giving her a good beating.

Then, when all must have seemed darkest to Jochem Wessels, victory suddenly sat upon his banners. From the most unexpected source of all, the camp of his relentless enemy, came news of almost incredible joy. The captain had proved too hot for his apprentice to handle and Jan Van Hoesen was refusing to feed him. Jan said the old man had broken his word in failing "to teach him to bake and by hiding the baking utensils and making it impossible for him to do so."

The captain complained, but the court decided that

Jan was right and the agreement was void. The old man
should be allowed to live in his bakehouse, however, until he died. They added that, in view of his extreme poverty, Jan should pay him 125 guilders for improvements
he had made in the garden. Apparently they, too, had
found the old man difficult, for the record ends with an
admonition in which, incidentally, the magistrates list
themselves in distinguished company: "And in case it
should hereafter be found that the plaintiff Willem
Juriaens, according to his custom, should continue to
blaspheme and abuse the name of God or His Service, or
any of the magistrates of the court, whether in general
or particular, he shall without exception be corrected
by the court, either by the infliction of banishment or
corporal punishment, as the case may require."

Now Jochem rejoiced. There was but one bakery
in the neighborhood and that was his own. Moreover,
since the whole happy situation had been achieved by
the court, he began to alter his attitude toward authority. It would be unfair to intimate that he who had
been the plague of the law became its champion overnight, but he was trying to make amends. The law had
done away with a threat of competition that had caused
him embarrassment. He would support the law.

Accordingly, on February 3, 1654, the contented
baker presented himself as a voluntary witness before
the court and answered questions about the crimes of a
drunken Dutchman named Jacob Stoll, generally known
as Hap. From his testimony the court learned that Hap
had come to the guardhouse of Fort Orange one day of
the previous summer just after guardmount, when
Jochem was corporal of the guard. Incensed by something or other Hap had gone home to get his sword, and

came back brandishing it with the avowed intent of clearing out the guardhouse. Finding the village school-master, Mr. Adrian, standing inside by the fire, Hap had called him a burgher's dog and given him a handker-chief with which to defend himself while he attacked him with a sword. Then he had turned on Corporal Jochem and, holding his naked blade close to that offi-cer's nose, had said, "I dare you to draw your colonel's rapier," and had tried to fight with him "life for life." Finally he had gone outside and called out to all by-standers that if they wanted a fight he was their man, emphasizing this remark by firing his gun.

After having given such valuable aid to the court, Jochem backslid a month later by getting into a fight over old man Juriaens's chickens. Jacob Willemsz testi-fied that he had seen Jochem chase some setting hens off their nests and had remonstrated saying, "What do you mean? They are the old captain's hens." At this Jochem had immediately invited him to come outside and fight and, not accepting a refusal, had grabbed him by the throat and given him a sound beating, calling him an old dog. To which Jochem answered only that Jacob had returned the blows, pulled his hair, and called him a dog. Jochem had to pay thirty guilders for that ex-hibition of temper and behaved himself for another month.

Then Hendrick Andriessen haled him into court for shooting his dog in the public street. Jochem got out of that by agreeably offering "to have a young dog trained with others and when trained to deliver it to the plaintiff." The court decided that this was a fair agree-ment but added that, "as the deed was done in the pub-lic street and the plaintiff's dog was killed," Jochem must pay a fine of one beaver. That made Gertrude Wessels so angry that she shouted "abusive and slanderous words" against the court and was summoned to answer for it at a future session.

The next period of model behavior on the part of Jochem was much longer. Old Silver Peg sent up to Beverwyck an urgent appeal for a loan of money to help in the fortifying of Manhattan and the court called upon the "most prosperous and loyal citizens" to subscribe. Possibly flattered to be included in such a category, Jochem offered five beavers and forty florins— just one beaver and eight florins more than Jan Van Hoesen. A week later he strengthened his support of good government by appearing as a witness to aid the prosecution of Elmerhuysen Kleyn and Gerrit Van Slichtenhorst for selling brandy to Indians. Jochem said that he had seen the defendants fill a glass with brandy which the Indian took in his hand and drank down. The Indian had then come out of the defendants' house drunk, picked up a maul lying near the Van Hoesen house, and used it to beat down the door of the Wessels homestead. Thereupon he had "greatly molested" Gertrude, the children, and himself.

Continuing to exert a restraining and dignifying influence upon the community, Jochem began the new year of 1655 by appearing as a witness against scandalmonger Cornelis Vos, who had apparently applied nicknames so appropriate to the houses of various respected burghers that the whole town was bandying them about and getting many a mean laugh out of it. He had called one house *The Cuckoo's Nest* and another *The House of Bad Manners*. One he had named *Birdsong* after a famous disorderly street in the town of Gouda in Holland, and another *The Savingsbank* because of its miserly inhabitants. Mr. Van Rensselaer's house he called *Early Spoiled* and Mother Bogardus's *The Vulture's World,* and he had entitled the town eating house *The Seldom Satisfied.* These names, said Jochem, he had learned at the harvest feast of farmer Oom Dirrick and he was informed they had been invented by Cornelis Vos. Though his testimony did not convict Cornelis, it showed Jochem Wessels on the side of decency and order and prepared the magistrates somewhat for the almost incredible next step.

As soon as he had finished his testimony about the nicknames Jochem said that he and a neighbor of his had a request to make of the court. The neighbor turned out to be Jan Van Hoesen, no longer planning to be a baker, and the two men in friendly agreement requested that the court order the old captain's house be put in repair because it might, in its present condition, cause a serious fire in Beverwyck. A month later they brought the matter up again and got the court to order the old man not to bake in the house until it had been repaired. Then for more than a year the two former enemies kept after the magistrates to take some action, a year that must have witnessed many a friendly conference. Finally they persuaded the court to appoint a committee to solicit loans toward repairing the house and authorize repayment from a mortgage on it. Jochem furnished thirteen boards and the roof timbers, and Jan twenty-five boards.

Meanwhile the now pleasantly co-operative and charitably minded baker was finding that the rewards of virtue are not always immediate. Some of his neighbors who apparently did not believe in his change of heart intimated that the good beer which the night watch on his rounds had found a group of Indians guzzling was in a pail they had seen in the Wessels house.

And Gerrit Van Slichtenhorst, against whose illegal sale of brandy Jochem had testified so glibly, picked a fight with him one July day when they were piling firewood. Gerrit went after Jochem with an ax and Jochem ran home and got his sword and chased Gerrit up the street and into the house of Thomas Paul. Peaceloving Mr. Paul had no sooner succeeded in getting Jochem to surrender his sword than Gerrit returned to the fray and jumped on his disarmed enemy. The struggling men fell to the floor and Jochem, having twisted himself to a position above Gerrit, was "trying to mutilate and ruin him" when onlookers intervened. Possibly realizing at that moment that the whole affair was somewhat undignified for him in his new role, Jochem got up and hurried home. Then Gerrit rushed to his own house and emerged waving a cutlass with which he chased Jochem about the town and struck a mighty blow which was intercepted by the transom bar over the door of Thomas Paul's house, "committing private injury and violence against the person and the house of the aforesaid Thomas Paul."

Both Gerrit and Jochem were fined for this indulgence of their tempers but Jochem had to pay more than Gerrit, a hundred guilders and costs. Moreover, at the session during which he was fined he was obliged to undergo the humiliation of hearing Jacob Willemsz, with whom he had fought about the old captain's hens, and Thomas Paul, whose privacy he had invaded, testify that on the previous Saturday they had seen an Indian stroll out of the Wessels bakeshop munching an oblong sugar bun. So strong in good deeds had Jochem become by this time, however, that his offer to swear that he had not committed the crime of selling the tidbit to the savage was sufficient and the case was dismissed.

Now that he had passed the age of forty the joys and woes of family life began to settle upon Jochem Wessels. His good-for-nothing stepson, Willem Hoffmeyer, got into trouble by selling beer to the Indians. He had twice sailed his canoe up the Hudson and peddled a cargo of half-barrels of beer. In fact, he had even employed one Indian as his agent to sell the beverage to Indian customers. Willem was banished for three years and fined 500 guilders, which Jochem gave bond for and eventually had to pay. He must have been somewhat consoled, however, when his own daughter Catryna married one of the richest and most distinguished men in Beverwyck, Abraham Staats, surgeon, trader, and magistrate, who as a member of the court had had ample opportunity of knowing his parents-in-law.

The tone of the judges in their dealings with Jochem now underwent a change. This was probably not so much because there was a new chief magistrate, the first one having gone crazy, as because of Jochem's continued good behavior. When, as a citizen deserving of consideration, he asked for a grant of land for a garden he was informed that "The court will take the request under advisement and after inspection of the place requested accommodate the said Jochem in all fairness."

By 1657 the Wesselses and the Van Hoesens were such close friends that one of the Van Hoesen girls was working as a maid at the house next door. But the old unhappy status was temporarily revived when Jan sued Gertrude Wessels for having kicked his daughter in the chest. Gertrude said that the girl had been impudent and that she had kicked her, but in a place considerably removed from the chest. Jan replied that wherever it had landed the kick had been administered from behind while his daughter was bending over and that it had caused her much pain. The court fined Gertrude thirty guilders and costs "for the pain."

From then on Jochem and Gertrude Wessels led a prosperous and comparatively uneventful life. At the age of fifty-five Jochem flared up and became the old hothead for a while when Captain Baker intimated that Gertrude (whose son was now over thirty-five) was a loose woman. Demanding reparation of his honor, the baker brought the English captain into court which was then presided over by Abraham Staats—the insulted old lady's son-in-law. When the captain produced an affidavit from a doddering alcoholic named Claes Wip in support of his accusation Jochem produced one from the same old drunk declaring that to the best of his knowledge Gertrude was a good woman. "Therefore," declared the honorable court, "the honor of both parties remains intact and they are to live together in peace."

So full of the love of humankind did Jochem become that he once paid a fine for having harbored overnight two elderly Indians whom his kind heart would not allow him to turn out into the autumn darkness. He must have done well in the baking business, for one burgher "being located in a street where there is no business" asked the court for the privilege of living next to him in the busy section on the steep bank of the

Hudson. Later two others aspired to live in lots bordering Jochem's.

Gradually he became a devout and influential leader in the Lutheran church. Then in 1672, at the behest of Mr. Philip Schuyler, the members of the court personally investigated the work of the Lutherans in extending the gate to their churchyard and warned the builders not to go beyond the limits allotted them. Hearing this, Jochem returned to his old pastime by telling the magistrates they had weak minds and that the one who had been a tailor had better go back to his job. Sergeant Parker gave evidence of this indecorum to the magistrates assembled in court and Jochem promptly called him a liar. For this he was fined twenty-five florins, the Lutherans were again reminded of the limitations placed on their gate, and the court ended its decision with an injunction: "Above all, a perpetual silence and obligation to keep still is hereupon imposed upon Jochem, the baker."

Three years later, in December, 1675, Willem Hoffmeyer, now a man of family nearing forty, sued the Lutheran congregation for the sum of 174 guilders which he said was due him for reading service in the church. Jochem Wessels, respected senior elder and the plaintiff's stepfather, replied in court that Willem had earned no such amount, having failed to read the service on many occasions when he was supposed to. The court was regarding this as a dignified and acceptable answer from a responsible elderly citizen until Willem explained he had not always been able to read services when he was supposed to because stepfather Jochem had several times stolen the key of the church from him.

In February, 1680, death imposed on Jochem Wessels "a perpetual silence and obligation to keep still." So far as is known, this is the only admonition of the sort he ever obeyed.

6

By the Grace of God—The English

STRANGE omens filled the Hudson valley with an atmosphere of dread in the early spring of 1663. The ground shook, the river overflowed, a plague of small-pox was visited upon the people. The next year when a British fleet of five vessels suddenly appeared and appropriated for James, Duke of York and brother of Charles II of England, the Dutch colony of New Netherland, many thought the disaster so presaged was at hand.

Not so the English. No sooner had Colonel Richard Nicolls and his troops taken control of New Amsterdam from Old Silver Peg than they and their countrymen went busily about explaining that England had a just claim to the colony based on the discoveries of Cabot and Smith and that the bloodlessness of the conquest proved beyond question that God willed the English to rule the shores of Hudson's River.

Whoever had ruled it, the settlers were satisfied. There was little change in their lives. Under the English duke's government they kept their lands and other properties, and they were pleased that the duties and taxes levied upon them by the greedy West India Company were abolished. They began to prosper.

New Amsterdam was New York, Rondout was Kingston, Beverwyck was Albany, the River of the

Prince Mauritius was the Hudson, but the complexion of the valley was the same. The reports of English visitors to the Hudson's shores were lyric and fulsome. Daniel Denton offered the highest praise an Englishman can give: "The climate hath such an affinity with that of England that it breeds ordinarily no alteration to those which remove thither." Once having assured his countrymen that they would keep their British identities in the exotic faraway river land, he abandoned native restraint to say that "the Country itself sends forth such a fragrant smell that it may be perceived at Sea," that the new settler would find there prodigal quantities of deer, turkeys, geese, pigeons, ducks and that, if weary of the hunt, he might catch a plentiful supply of fish in the river before fishing became a bore. "If there be any terrestrial Canaan," sang the pen of Daniel Denton, " 'tis surely here, where the land floweth with milk and honey."

"It's a Climate of a Sweet and wholesome breath," wrote the Reverend Charles Wolley. ". . . Nature kindly drains and purgeth it with Fontanels . . . and shelters it with the umbrellas of all sorts of trees."

John Miller wrote: "The air of this province is very good . . . generally very clear and thin . . . nor does there want in the summer the Southern breezes which daily, almost, rise about 9 or 10 in the morning & continue till sunset. . . . A sober Englishman may go into it live there & come out of it again without any seasoning or other sickness caused meerly by the Country."

A little book from Holland, *In Praise of New Netherland,* came to the Dutch along the river. Between

its covers lay a long poem written by Jacob Steendam
in lyric reminiscence of his eight years on Manhattan:

> This is the land, with milk and honey flowing
> With healing herbs like thistles freely growing
> The place where buds of Aaron's rod are blowing
> O, this is Eden!

Such psalms had their effect. Eagerly land investors
sought grants along the river shores. British confirmation
of the rights of the Van Rensselaers in their patroonship
as a manor gave others ideas of grandeur, particularly
Robert Livingston, whose father, a poor Presbyterian
minister, had been exiled from Scotland into Holland and
had there brought up his shrewd, redheaded opportunistic son. Robert came to the upper Hudson in 1674 and
had soon become town clerk of Albany. A few years
later, according to folk legend, he was called aboard a
yacht on the Hudson to make the will of Nicolaes Van
Rensselaer, considered queer by his relatives ever since
his oracular announcement, that Charles Stuart would
one day sit upon the throne of his father, had proved
true. "Nicolaes the Prophet," as he sometimes called
himself, was breathing his last on the boat, but at sight of
Livingston he had strength enough to order him away.
"Anyone but you," folks say he cried, "for you will
marry my widow." Fourteen months after Nicolaes died
Robert Livingston obligingly made that prediction also
come true.

Mistress Van Rensselaer had been born Alida
Schuyler, and the marriage connected the young Scot
with two of the richest and most powerful upriver
families. He at once set out to gain control of as much

of the Van Rensselaer property as he could and at the same time to obtain other lands along the river.

Despite his religious upbringing and the fact that in the generations behind him the Livingstons claimed distinction as a family, Robert Livingston had soon acquired a reputation for acquisitiveness and greed in a group characterized by both those qualities. Two English governors testified to this: Benjamin Fletcher, with the statement that Livingston's "whole thirst" was "at any rate and by any ways" for riches; Richard Bellomont, with the charge that as a purveyor of supplies to the military of the province he had "pinched an estate out of the poor soldiers' bellies." Indeed, Governor Fletcher became so violently prejudiced as to state that the Scottish clerk never spent sixpence without expecting twelve in return and that "his beginning being a little Bookkeeper he has screwed himself into one of the most considerable estates in the province."

That estate, twelve miles long on the east bank of the Hudson south of Rensselaerswyck and spread fanwise to a thirty-mile boundary along the Massachusetts line, comprised more than 160,000 acres and was but one of several extravagant grants which the British government was soon to regret having made. The next decade saw vast domains along the lower Hudson go to Frederick Philipse, to Stephen Van Cortlandt, and on the west bank, to Captain John Evans. The medieval feudal system of permanent leases, on whose rents the Van Rensselaers were living comfortably, was at once adopted in all such holdings and the manor lords of the Hudson had been established in a power that only generations of rebelling farmers would finally destroy.

The English governors soon discovered that such

large grants to single families were resulting in a slowing of development. Settlers preferred to live where they could own their own land. Arguing against the extravagant grants, a governor wrote: "Mr. Livingston has on his great grant . . . but 4 or 5 cottages as I am told men that live in vassalage under him and work for him are too poor to be farmers." But just as this sort of antagonism was developing a danger of confiscation of his property, Robert Livingston found opportunity to destroy it. The Atlantic's winds were blowing that opportunity to him.

7

The Tarmakers

IN the sunny spring of 1707 a French army under Marshal Villars marched into the valley of the Rhine, confiscating the old wines and the new vegetables of the farmers, trampling and laying waste their fertile lands. The soldiers overran most of Germany before their return in September, when once more the Rhineland planters were despoiled.

Desperately the people of Alsace and Baden and their neighbor districts tried to remedy the damage war had done. All through the spring and summer of 1708 they worked their land and nursed their crops. Then, as October began, a north wind blew.

When the month had ended the valley was so cold, the farmers said afterward, that they could not coax a flame out of firewood in the open air. By January their precious wines had turned into solid blocks of ice inside the casks. Then flying birds were stopped in flight, and fell stiff and frozen to the earth. A man could not spit without the water of his mouth becoming a shiny pellet before it rattled on the frost-hardened ground. Until April the cold continued. By that time the fruit trees and the vines had died. Once more there could be no happy harvest.

Taxes were rising throughout the German Empire. The princes of the states along the Rhine, dazzled by the glories of Louis XIV, the "Sun Monarch," sought to emulate his extravagances. When their subjects had paid the state its demands they had nothing left. Starvation stalked the country.

Into the valley that desolate and despairing spring came a book which showed at its beginning a picture of smiling, kindly Anne, queen of the English, and title pages printed in letters of gold. It told of a faraway fragrant Canaan, a land of river valleys, warm and peaceful, where food was to be had for the taking. The people called it the "Golden Book" and pored over its lyric pages night after night. English agents began to appear among them, speaking the praises of Queen Anne and of her rich lands in Carolina and Pennsylvania.

A preacher, Joshua Kocherthal, was visiting the farms around the town of Landau in the Rhenish Palatinate. He was ready of tongue and enthusiastic. In a few weeks he had persuaded a band to join him in a journey to England whence, he promised, they would be sent to fertile homes in America. There were forty-one in the group when they set out down the Rhine—ten men, ten women, and twenty-one children ranging from six months to fifteen years of age.

They made a happy trip down the river. People came to meet them along the shores and gave them food and clothing. The city council of Rotterdam sent a boat to meet them and convey them to a large island just off the Dutch coast. After that an English boat embarked them free of cost and took them to Harwich in England. There they were well taken care of by Queen Anne as she had promised. By the end of April Preacher Kocherthal was able to report to the London

Board of Trade that his fifteen Lutherans and twenty-six Calvinists were ready to help in settling a British colony. "One is a joyner," he said, "another a smith, the others all versed in gardening, husbandry, planting, and tillage."

Soon the queen had approved an order that Kocherthal's band "should be settled upon the Hudson River in the province of New York." She and her advisers had feared the effect of the hot weather of southern lands on people accustomed to cooler climate and she had also by this time been convinced that the manufacture of tar and other maritime necessities could be successfully established on the Hudson, thereby destroying the effect of the Swedish monopoly on such products. The Palatines, she felt, "might be useful to this kingdom in the production of naval stores and as a frontier against the French and their Indians."

In the middle of October the group, somewhat augmented by other German recruits, sailed for New York. The new governor of the province, Lord John Lovelace, was also aboard their ship, the *Globe*. After nine weeks on the water their first glimpse of the fragrant spring land promised by the Golden Book showed them snowy barren cliffs and frozen rivers. They disembarked in December and were cared for in New York until spring. When the valley of the great river was turning to fresh green, they sailed fifty-five miles up the Hudson and came ashore on the west bank to lands granted them by Governor Lovelace. There beside the clear waters of Quassaic Creek they built their homes and, remembering the old days of privation, called their settlement Newburgh.

Meanwhile, back in the valley of the Rhine, the

dream of the new and fruitful land was in the minds
of thousands. After nearly a quarter century of living
in little Hilgert Dorf kindly Gerhart Schaeffer went to
his mayor to ask for a certificate of character that he
might use where he was not known. "He has lived in
Hilgert Dorf with his wife for twenty-four years,"
wrote the mayor, "and has behaved himself well and
honestly, so that all those who lived near him regarded
him as a faithful neighbor and were entirely satisfied
with him and they would have been greatly pleased if
it should have been God's will that he should stay here
longer."

From the meadows of Alsace and Lorraine, from
as far south as the Swiss border town of Basle and as
far east as Bayreuth on the river Main, from the districts of Trèves and Spires and Hanau the refugees
from the war-despoiled, frozen land were sailing, drifting, plodding down the Rhine. By June a thousand a
week were pouring into Rotterdam. At the city's edge
in camp shacks covered with reeds they miserably
awaited the boats that would take them to England.
Vainly the English tried to stop the human tide that
was rolling in on them, but Rotterdam kept it moving.
By the middle of October more than eleven thousand
refugees were in and around London. They were encamped in tents along the Thames, in barns along
Nightingale Lane, in Deptford's big rope houses. One
large warehouse sheltered fourteen hundred of them.
They were a source of great curiosity and of great annoyance to Londoners. Walking abroad to see the Palatines was a popular Sunday amusement. One German,
sixty-four years old, made London athletic history by
wagering £100 he could walk three hundred miles in

Hyde Park in six days and won his money with a generous mile added. Like most refugees, however, the Germans were charged with taking employment away from
native citizens and frequently found themselves obliged
to defend their lives against violent attacks of English
mobs.

Winter had come again before the Palatines bound
for the banks of the Hudson were once more embarked.
Lord John Lovelace had died and handsome, literary
Robert Hunter, friend of Joseph Addison and Richard
Steele, had been made governor of New York. He was
to accompany the Palatine expedition to the province,
determined to make it pay for itself in naval stores for
the British fleet. Ten ships—the Germans called them
the "Wonder Fleet"—lay in the Thames late in December waiting for twenty-eight hundred passengers, the
largest single emigration to America in all the colonial
period.

The six months' voyage that followed held more
suffering than can easily be told. Packed into quarters
too limited for cattle, forced into darkness below deck
to breathe foul air and lie among vermin, these people
used to the outdoor life of a river valley could not live.
For four months the ten boats cruised along the southern coast of England awaiting the spring. On one of
them eighty had died before the end of April. On another a hundred were sick. Typhus broke out. The
younger children, weakened by lack of sunlight and
healthful food, died in scores. The disease caused such
ravages among them that for years thereafter it was
known as "Palatine fever." When the two months' sail
across the Atlantic was over, more than four hundred
had lost the Canaan of their dreams, though there were

thirty new babies who would begin their lives among its woods and streams.

In mid-June of 1710 the *Lyon,* first of the Wonder Fleet, sailed into New York harbor. The last came in on August second. Only nine reached port, for the *Herbert* was wrecked—without loss of life—on Long Island. The arrival of almost twenty-five hundred Germans increased the population at the mouth of the Hudson by about one-half. At once the New York City Council complained that the disease-ridden foreigners might cause a plague, not only threatening lives within the town but discouraging country people from coming in to trade. And so the whole lot were landed on Nutten (now Governor's) Island where they camped during the summer. Their first months in the new land were not the happy rich days they had seen in visions. Only Peter Romers, coffinmaker, was prospering. He sold two hundred and fifty of his boxes that summer.

The Palatines sailed to their new home through an aisle of autumn land brilliant with the glowing red of maples, the yellow of river oaks, the deep green of the pines on which they were to depend for their living. Robert Hunter had bought them more than 60,000 acres of crown lands, once a part of Governor Benjamin Fletcher's west-bank grant to Captain John Evans, "The Manor of Fletcherdon." He had also acquired for them eight hundred acres bordering these on the north from one Thomas Fullerton, and 6,000 more across the river from Robert Livingston, who was happily waiting for these German flies to be entangled in his web. By selling a few of his less desirable acres and the rights to make tar from trees on some of his own property, he had obtained from the government a good price for the land, a number of fat contracts to supply the newcomers, and several hundred prospective customers for his real estate.

More than eighteen hundred Germans were landed from the river sloops after their hundred-mile sail on the Hudson. Livingston had food and tent poles waiting for them. Tents were soon replaced by laid-up log cabins, which suddenly stood complete, clay stuffed in the chinks, on lots of 40 by 50 feet. There was a continuous sound of axes as in the next few months seven little German towns sprang up on the steep slopes of the Hudson. Three of them, Elizabeth Town, George Town, New Town, looked across the broad stream toward the other four on Livingston's east side and at the Taghanick ridges above them down which light spilled upon the river when a morning had come. Hunterstown, Queensbury, Annsburg, Haysbury looked back at the three lying far below the crooked crests of the Catskills that turned a deep and misty purple when the sun was at last behind them and a day was done.

The autumn colors on the mountains had faded and their peaks were powdered with snow when the Germans turned to the business expected of them. If they were to be freed from obligation to the British crown and become independent landholders they must make and ship enough tar to meet the expenses of their transportation and settlement. When their debts had been paid, Queen Anne had promised that she would give every family a plot of forty acres for each of its members. All that winter the immigrants planned the coming season. Richard Sackett, a neighboring farmer who claimed some experience, had been appointed instructor in tarmaking and his eager pupils walked back and forth between the east camp and the west on the frozen surface of the river discussing his theories.

Meanwhile, the food which the government had promised them until they were self-supporting became steadily worse. Jean Cast, a Frenchman, whose sloop carried supplies to the east camp, found it necessary to complain to Governor Hunter that Livingston was cheating the settlers in selling them flour by weight in barrels that weighed three and four pounds more than he claimed. At the same time Cast said to the governor, "I never saw salted meat so poor nor packed with so much salt as this pork was. In truth one eighth of it was salt."

When the river was open once more and days were warmer, the sound of the axes began again. The tar-makers were at work under Sackett's direction, barking the north quarter of each pine's circumference about two feet. In the autumn the instructor said they would bark the south quarter a little more than that. In the second spring they would bark the east quarter something over two and a half feet and in the second autumn the west quarter would lose about three feet. Finally, in the second winter the trees were to be felled, and the barked portions cut out and carried to a kiln where slow roasting would sweat the tar into a trench which would conduct it to their casks. The eager Germans barked a hundred thousand trees that first spring.

The two years of waiting before results could be measured seemed very long to the ill-fed tarmakers unaccustomed to working in thick forests. By this time they had discovered that the Golden Book and the agents of the crown had deceived them about the land to which they had come so trustingly. There was talk of a smaller, fairer, more fertile valley to the northwest, the valley of Schoharie, where a man might be free to till his own soil and need not eat bad food or work at an outlandish occupation. Whispers went around. Governor Hunter, on a visit of inspection, suddenly found himself in the midst of an organized secret society of more than three hundred men who had sworn that they would desert the settlement and march to the Schoharie. They cried out to him that they would rather lose their lives at once than remain where they were. They would not stay on these Hudson River lands and work for Queen Anne's fleet all their lives. Hunter realized that he was in danger of capture, perhaps of being killed, and managed to escape the malcontents until he could lead a detachment of seventy soldiers from Albany into their towns. Helpless then, the rebellious ones were forced to give up their guns and submit themselves to the governor's mercy. By that time Robert Hunter was almost as disillusioned over his protégés as they were over the navy stores project. He never quite forgave these people for the humiliation to which they had subjected him. He had worked hard for them and had frequently spent money from his own pockets for their support.

The first barking season got off to a good start. By the beginning of summer Hunter was reporting: "Our Tar work goes on as we could wish God continue it." While their fathers wielded the axes the German boys and girls ran about the woods along the river and back of it toward the mountains, picking up pine knots, and by the end of the first week in June they had delivered so many to the smoking kilns that Mr. Sackett had been able to run off sixty barrels of tar from them and still have left a pile big enough to sweat out sixty more. Indeed, so plentiful were the knots that he was renting wagons and teams from Mr. Livingston, ever obliging for a profit, to bring them in. Soon tar casks were not to be had, and Sackett was using the barrels in which the detested salt pork had been shipped.

Then in the middle of the summer of 1711 discouragements fell upon the seven towns in an increasing shower. Queen Anne decided to send colonial troops on a second expedition against the French and their Indian allies in Canada and three hundred of the bravest and strongest German tarmakers were marched north to join her army. This accomplished nothing save the slowing of the tar manufacture. Work was further handicapped by the failure of Sackett's methods. In some cases the pitch pines had not been barked sufficiently when the sap was descending; in others, as Hunter pointed out, "the trees being barked by an unskilful and unruly multitude were for the most part pierced in the inward rind contrary to strict directions."

Accustomed to the solitary labor of the farmer or the vine grower, the tarmakers found themselves wholly unsuited to working in gangs like lumberjacks and they were disgusted with the barrenness of the lands on which they lived. They longed to plant and to harvest and they grumbled, saying to each other that they had come to America to secure lands on which their descendants could support themselves "and that we cannot do here."

Lastly, through no fault of his own, Governor Hunter's support of the venture was failing. Unsympathetic Tories had succeeded the favorably inclined

Whigs to power in England. The House of Commons had passed two resolutions: "That the inviting and bringing over into this kingdom of the Palatines . . . was an extravagant and unreasonable charge . . . and a scandalous misapplication of the public money" and "That whoever advised the bringing over the poor Palatines into this kingdom was an enemy to the Queen and kingdom."

As a result, Governor Hunter found it harder and harder to obtain funds for the maintenance of his charges. Hope of collecting from the government the large sums he had spent on them grew dim. Somehow he managed to keep them fed during the next winter and to continue them at work through the summer of 1712. At last he could do no more. In despair he told the Germans that after the first weeks in September they must support themselves. With only about two thousand barrels of tar to its credit, the business of making naval stores had failed.

Desperate, the poor people awaited the winter. Some of them scattered up and down the Hudson's banks looking for work. Others seemed too stunned by the bad news to do anything for themselves. Once more they underwent an ordeal of suffering, a torture worse even than the six months' Atlantic voyage, for then they had had hope and faith in a new rich land. Now that land had failed them and the early snows were falling.

Spring finally came and summer and their minister, the Reverend John Frederick Haeger, was writing back to London to his employers, the Society for the Propagation of the Gospel: "they boil grass and the children eat the leaves of the trees. I have seen old men and women cry that it should almost have moved a stone."

Gradually, as the months went by, some of the inhabitants of the east camp's three towns, now all included in the village which is, in memory of them, called Germantown, and the people who lived in the west bank's four towns, still called inclusively West Camp, spread out along the Hudson. Some of them went back to New York City. Others settled in Hackensack. Some went a few miles south of the east camp to settle a little town. Remembering the other river from whose banks they had come with high hopes, they called it Rhinebeck. One group, crushed by disaster, stayed on the lands of Livingston Manor and suffered the fate of all manor tenants—a gradual accumulation of debts to the landlord that eventually resulted in rebellion. Five hundred marched northwest into the hill-circled valley through whose bottom lands winds the shining little Schoharie.

More than a thousand Germans now left along the Hudson invaded the life about them and made strong impressions on it. A boy who had been but thirteen when the Wonder Fleet brought him to New York, John Peter Zenger, became a printer's apprentice, then the publisher of a paper. Twenty-two years later, when Governor William Cosby tried to ride in roughshod tyranny over the representatives of the people, Zenger went to jail rather than suppress the stinging truths his New York *Weekly Journal* spread abroad in black ink. His acquittal of the charge of libel proved a victory for freedom of the press whose echoes still sound along the Hudson's shores.

German ways and Dutch ways intermingled along

the Hudson. Observers a century later assumed that all upriver life that was not obviously English must be Dutch. When Washington Irving came to visit in Kindernook and wandered the country round about, the Rhineland influences had been at work for a century. There are those who say—and Dominie Delber W. Clark of Coxsackie, a great scholar of the early days, is among them—that the little fellows whom Rip Van Winkle found bowling among the Catskills are very like the gnomes, the kobolds, the Nibelungs that folks have always known may sometimes be seen at work and play in the valley of the Rhine. The Winkels were a family who came to the Hudson with the tarmakers. And the folklore of the Rhine contains more than one long nap like Rip's—Friedrich Barbarossa's slumber in the cave of the Kyffhäuser, for example. Perhaps in his great classic of early life on the Hudson Washington Irving was unwittingly writing out of a poetic folk background that did not lie on the Netherland banks of the Rhine as it nears the sea, but beyond them on those high green shores haunted by water-maidens.

8

"Both Your Houses"

THE Hudson valley developed rapidly during the first half of the eighteenth century. The poor Palatines were only a part of the trend of immigration to the new land. Englishmen came in great numbers and settled beside the river. Wide fields of flax bordered the water north of New York, and other river acres were given over to maize and wheat. Hundreds of sloops were bringing trade to the river ports. New York City prospered and its rich merchants bought country seats on the Hudson at Hoboken and farther upriver at Greenwich. The manor lords had increased their holdings enormously. In Westchester County by mid-century nearly five-sixths of the inhabitants were manor tenants. Servants of the well-to-do included a few indentured white people, both free and slave Indians, and many Negro slaves. The city was gay, irreligious, extravagant. The popular Earl of Bellomont, governor at the turn of the century, had been severely criticized because of his personal friendship with the notorious Captain William Kidd who, though possibly more sinned against than sinning, was executed for piracy. Nevertheless, Bellomont had made serious efforts at reforming current abuses.

Queen Anne appointed her nephew Edward Hyde, Lord Cornbury, to succeed Bellomont in 1702. Cornbury and his wife scandalized the town. Lady Cornbury had an unfortunate habit of asking people whom she visited to give her expensive articles which she saw about the house and happened to admire. Cornbury made an elaborate event out of his first trip up the Hudson to Albany. He had his sloop decorated in gaudy colors and the crew dressed in fancy new uniforms almost as brilliant as his own peacock apparel. On later occasions he indulged a fancy for parading the streets of New York fashionably dressed in women's clothes. He was arrogant, spendthrift, dishonest.

After Cornbury had been ordered home in disgrace, Governors Lovelace and Hunter struggled through their problems with the Palatines.

Serious differences now began to spring up among the people as prosperity settled upon the river. There was jealousy between regions. In 1749 Peter Kalm, Swedish visitor, was noting that "The avarice and selfishness of the people of Albany are well known throughout all North America, by the English, by the French, and even by the Dutch in the lower part of New York province. If a Jew, who understands the art of getting forward pretty well, should settle amongst them, they would not fail to ruin him."

Lewis Morris, resident of the Hudson valley, wrote into his will a few years later:

"It is my desire that my son Gouverneur Morris may have the best education that is to be had in Europe or America, but my express will and directions are that he be never sent for that purpose to the Colony of Connecticut lest he should imbibe in his youth that low craft and cunning so incident to the people of that country, which is so interwoven in their constitutions that all their art cannot disguise it from the world, though many of them under the sanctified garb of religion have endeavored to impose themselves on the world as honest men."

Governor William Cosby assumed office some months after the death of John Montgomerie in 1731. He brought to the colony an order from the king requiring that the salary of the governor's office during the period between governors be shared equally by him and Rip Van Dam, president of the City Council, who had been acting as governor. Van Dam had collected the full amount and refused to share it. Cosby referred the matter to the judges of the Supreme Court and Chief Justice Lewis Morris (he who hated Connecticut) disclaimed jurisdiction. Cosby thereupon removed Morris as chief justice.

The great landholders immediately split into bitter factions. De Lancey and Philipse aligned themselves against Livingston and Morris. It was the beginning of a rift that would end only when the downriver De Lancey group had been driven from the country by the Continental patriots in the War of the Revolution. The Livingston and Morris group gained the immediate advantage as they were to gain the later one. Andrew Hamilton, elderly Philadelphia lawyer, won the first skirmish by an inspired speech in defense of John Peter Zenger who had been sued for libel for his attacks on Cosby in the New York *Weekly Journal*. Zenger's acquittal was a victory for democratic idealism, but the quarreling manor lords were not greatly concerned with idealism at the moment. There was arising a situation which would cause them to forget their differences and unite against foes they feared more than each other.

9

"Without Indecorum of Behaviour"

QUAKER HILL was hard to climb in 1754. The families of the Friends who had settled on its crest in the hope of being left alone had chosen well. Few strangers dared the steep narrow trail that led from Pawling over five miles of tangled, rock-strewn woods to the high tableland jutting into the Harlem's green valley. One came often through, urging his tired horse as far as the hill's airiest acre where the tall house of Jedediah Wing looked out over treetops far below to the fabric of the Catskills that seemed to hang in folds from the blue ceiling of the Hudson. The ways of Quakers are grave and simple and Kilkenny Irishman William Prendergast must have found it hard to look properly solemn while sixteen-year-old Mehitabel Wing demurely cared for her ten little brothers and sisters. He must have had trouble, too, in catching a moment alone with her to tell her what was on his mind, for the Wings were orthodox Friends and could not favor the wedding of a daughter to a man outside the sect. But William Prendergast was a strategist and he had a way with him. It was not many weeks before he and Mehitabel took the downtrail together to his farm on rolling acres at the tall hill's foot. And though William Prendergast was not a Quaker, the Wings loved him and were happy in their girl's happiness. In about a year young Matthew

81

Prendergast arrived, to the delight of both families, and the Wings came down the hill more often than the Prendergasts went up.

Mehitabel was twenty-six before James was born. Hard times had come to William Prendergast by then. His crops had been poor and he was behind in his rent to fat Frederick Philipse who owned not only the Prendergast farm but thousands of acres near by, tens of thousands in Westchester County, and a great manor house overlooking the Hudson at Yonkers. Prendergast had taken his acres in perpetual lease from the manor lord before he had married Mehitabel. Now that he was the father of two sons the terms of that lease were irksome. He might not will his land to his wife or his sons without the consent of Frederick Philipse. If, after William's death, that consent was granted, Mehitabel or the boys must pay the manor lord a third of the value of the farm in order to keep it. Whoever held the lease, moreover, must each year pay to the manor lord for the privilege a portion of his crops, his poultry, his labor.

To an eighteenth-century Kilkenny Protestant the idea of protesting rents paid to absentee landlords could not have been a new one. It is doubtful, nevertheless, that William Prendergast would have lost his Irish temper if it had not been for one sudden realization. On a trip to Yonkers he found out that Frederick Philipse, sitting in gross dignity over his manorial court while he sentenced recalcitrant tenants to corporal punishment and imprisonment, himself paid the British crown for his vast holdings an annual quitrent of four pounds, twelve shillings. That amount was exactly what William Prendergast was obliged to pay yearly for his few acres. The irony of it galled his soul. Mehitabel was soon to bear a third baby. He needed all the money he could get to help her and his growing family. Yet the fat man in his big house in Yonkers would not even let him own the land he lived on.

Mehitabel was lonely while her child was coming. William was seldom at home. All the current of his magnetic person was turned toward one goal—the righting of an injustice. His neighbors believed in him and they were, like him, desperate. A deep muttering rose when imperious Elizabeth Philipse, fat Frederick's wife, drove out in her careening coach, her four black horses galloping along the river road so close to the Hudson that they seemed to be racing with their images in the clear water.

The waiting woman in the farmhouse at the foot of Quaker Hill did not approve of violence. The gentle Friends in whose meetinghouse she had been taught were strict in their pacific doctrines. But she could spend little time in argument with a husband who would not stay to be argued with. She must have known an outbreak was near. Yet it came with shattering suddenness. On a day when the hill beside the house had turned a fresh green news came that the sheriffs had pounced upon two farmers for not paying their rent and jailed them in New York where they would be safe from rescue. The next morning William Prendergast rode out from Pawling and Mehitabel knew that he would not be back by sundown. Somehow or other she got her two children and herself up the steep trail to her father's house. On the high hilltop she waited for news of her husband, and the coming of the baby.

In the next few days William Prendergast called for an army, and amazingly an army answered. Hun-

dreds of farmers rallied round him. With sword drawn,
he addressed them in the fields of Dutchess and Westchester, saying that the manor lords had made him a
desperate man.

"If any officer attempts to take me till this dispute
with the landlords is settled," he shouted, "I'll make
daylight shine through him!"

Again and again he drilled the farmers, marching
them up and down their meadows. "Pay your honest
debts," he said to them, "as honest men should—but not
a shilling for rent." Then with a company of his men
he made a sudden raid on Justice Peters, whose decisions
had thrown many a manor tenant into jail, gave that
magistrate a ducking, dragged him through the mud,
beat him with a whip. And when Peters objected, crying out that he was a representative of his Majesty the
king, William Prendergast shouted in a rage: "If the
king were here I would serve him the same way. Mobs
have brought kings to before now and will again." With
that he told his men it was time to march on New
York, and they would meet together on the following
Monday, each man to bring six days' provisions, arms
and ammunition. They would have their comrades out
of the New York jail, he said, or die in the attempt.

A thousand farmers joined Prendergast on that
Monday, April fifteenth. They marched into the manors
of the Hudson Highlands and declared manor rents
abolished. They dispossessed tenants who had taken
over the acres of farmers ejected for debt and put the
former owners back on the land. In vain the manor
lords denounced them as "Levelers," old-time communists whom even radical Cromwell had rebuked for
"trying to make the tenant as liberal a fortune as the

landlord." They accepted the appellation and marched on. Throughout the lower Hudson valley the farmers left their spring plowing, took down their guns, rode out to join their neighbors. William Prendergast was riding at the head of a growing army of vengeance that steadily moved southward on New York.

Few New Yorkers slept well the following nights. Every sloop and every courier from the north brought bad news. Near midnight of the twentieth a horseman dashed through the little city into Fort George at the foot of Manhattan Island. A few moments later General Thomas Gage ordered all officers and men of his New York City command into the fort. Frightened citizens, watching orderlies round up the soldiers and hurry them from the taverns and pleasure parks toward the Battery, knew what had happened. The terrible Prendergast and his Westchester men were on their way downriver. They might enter the city at any time.

The long night passed and they had not come. Four days of anguished waiting went by. Then a courier brought word that the farmer army was on Cortlandt Manor and had pronounced all Westchester manor rents invalid. Another four days and Ben Randolph, loyal tenant, galloped into town to report that three hundred farmers of Cortlandt Manor had met at North Castle and were riding to join Prendergast. A letter arrived from the marchers saying that if Cortlandt refused their demands they would tear his town house down about his ears. General Gage ordered the militia to be ready, and the tacit admission that his regulars might not be able to beat back the invaders scared New Yorkers into a panic not moderated by the City Council's readily accepted suggestion that Governor Sir

Henry Moore, Baronet, Captain General, issue a proc-lamation "offering a Reward of One Hundred Pounds for apprehending William Pendergrass, the head and leader of said Rioters."

The last day of April passed slowly. The City Council, sitting in almost continuous session, heard the news that the Levelers had reached King's Bridge. New Yorkers were on the verge of hysteria. On May Day, they said, the march of the terrible Prendergast would surely reach its goal. He might even decide on a surprise attack in the darkness of the night before. The farmers were rough, desperate fellows and their leader was a madman. No one knew what might happen before the invaders were driven back. Many a burgher waited through the long night, gun in hand, beside his barred door. But at dawn the hoofs of the farmers' cavalry were not yet clumping through the streets.

Early in the morning the sentinels outside Fort George were suddenly on the alert as six horsemen rode boldly down upon them. The soldiers were relieved when, on being challenged, the riders explained that they came as a committee from Prendergast and his men to explain their opinions and actions to the gov-ernor and city officers. Sir Henry Moore received them, listened to their statement that they considered their quarrel to be only with the landlords, and then escorted them about the fort. He told them that General Gage was resolved to defend the jail with his entire command and he showed them a detachment of his Britannic Majesty's Grenadiers assembled in a sturdy red square. The six excused themselves and rode hastily back to their leader. Hours passed. There was no attack. Night came and went. In the morning the waiting was over.

The news ran with magic speed ahead of the galloping messengers. Prendergast and his farmers had turned about and were headed upriver. New York was saved.

Then suddenly the city was noisy with swaggering fellows full of bravado. Fired by the enthusiastic rejoicing and eager for the £100 reward, Alderman Brewington boasted that he, singlehanded, would capture the cowardly outlaw leader who was now running away. To prove that he meant it, Mr. Brewington set out along the river road. He had ridden but a few hours when he met a genial fellow who gladly conversed with him on the events of the past few days. His new companion was so pleasant that Alderman Brewington finally, under pledge of secrecy, revealed his identity and the plan by which he expected to capture the Leveler leader. Hardly had the two bade each other hearty farewells at the parting of their ways when a friendly countryman revealed to the city officer that he had been riding with William Prendergast. The whole city appreciated that joke, though the laughter held a strained note.

No word of her husband had reached the Quaker girl waiting in her father's house, but he was on his way back to her and, though he had not taken New York, he led a victorious army. Everywhere he marched the farmers of the Hudson valley welcomed him as their deliverer. Hundreds of Livingston Manor tenants had risen in arms at his arrival, denouncing the rents. Just as he reached Dutchess County, Sheriff James Livingston had jailed John Way in Poughkeepsie for not paying rent to Petrus Ten Broeck. Pistol and sword in hand, Prendergast marched on Poughkeepsie and emptied the jail. He caught Petrus Ten Broeck in the town and made him withdraw the charge. Now daily couriers raced for New York from the Livingstons, the Philipses, the Ten Broecks, begging Sir Henry Moore to do something. They told anxious officials that Prendergast had sworn to restore to each of his followers the lands from which the manor lords had driven them and that he was keeping his oath. They said that almost a thousand of his force were still with him and that he was moving about the river country forcing law-abiding citizens out of their homes and installing the communist Levelers in their places. The authorities of the region sent word that they were helpless since the invaders were connected by family ties throughout the countryside and the militia could not be depended upon to fire on their relatives and neighbors.

The rebel leader was riding more proudly now and with more serious purpose than ever, for he was the father of a third son, Jedediah, named after the Quaker grandfather whose house had been his birthplace. A part of Mehitabel's waiting was over and she and her parents rejoiced in the little boy. The period of happiness was short. Before Jedediah was a month old his father was suddenly to face the complete demolition of his dreams.

Urged by the City Council, Governor Moore applied to General Gage for three hundred troops to restore law and order to the entire British province, and the general acted briskly. The 28th Regiment of Grenadiers was on sloops bound from Albany to New York and he ordered them disembarked at Poughkeepsie. When William Prendergast heard that the redcoats had landed, he knew he was in deep trouble and, like many another distressed husband, decided that he would resist it with his wife at his side. Hastily he marched for home.

The Levelers' army had shrunk to a straggling remnant when they wearily clambered up the last few slanting yards to the old meetinghouse on Quaker Hill. They knew that the jig was up but they refused to leave the man who had risked so much for them. And so they barricaded the doors of the House of Peace and trained their guns out its windows on the path their pursuers would soon be taking. Meanwhile in the big white house at the crest of the hill, William Prendergast told his young wife the story of his first success and his present fearful danger.

Desperately Prendergast's allies on the upriver Van Rensselaer Manor tried to create a diversion. Captain Robert Noble, who had been fighting the manor lords for fifteen years, gathered some sixty of the valley farmers in a house on the manor. Immediately Sheriff Harmanus Schuyler advanced with a hundred and fifty militiamen. The first shot from the besieged set the sheriff's hat and his white wig to describing graceful separate parabolas. At the end of the first attack Militiaman Cornelius Ten Broeck was dead, stretched out beside seven wounded comrades and, though they had three dead and many injured, the farmers were still fighting. When with incredible courage they made a successful sortie to reach Captain Noble's house, which had been fortified with breastworks for just such an emergency, Sheriff Schuyler, wig and hat retrieved, galloped off to Poughkeepsie to demand that the redcoats return north at once.

But Major Browne, commander of the 28th, was too shrewd a soldier to be tricked. His job was to hunt down Prendergast, and he set out for Quaker Hill as soon as his troops were landed. Mehitabel and William, looking down on the umbrella tops of distant elms that hid the little town of Fredericksburg (now Patterson), heard the sullen thudding of musketry and knew that there was little hope left. Beneath the green foliage at a little wooden bridge across the Swamp River, Browne's Grenadiers had suddenly come face to face with thirty Levelers riding to join their commander in the meeting-house. In a trice the farmers were off their horses and into a field of tall corn. Nine years before the "shot heard 'round the world" was fired at a bridge in Massachusetts these New York countrymen dared defend themselves with arms against the British Grenadiers. Two of Browne's men were killed at the first volley from the corn. The soldiers charged in among the tall stalks but the field was still and empty. Their enemies had withdrawn.

Next morning the redcoats reached the cleared ground about the meetinghouse. Whether Prendergast had spent the night encouraging his men or had been prevailed upon to leave earlier no one knows. Whatever the time of his departure, the effect on Major Browne was the same when he realized that no one of the half a hundred farmers who marched that morning under a white flag from the meetinghouse doorway into his custody was the outlaw leader. The soldiery had taken fifty prisoners, but William Prendergast at large among the hills would be as great a menace as ever. The expedition had failed of its main purpose so long as the bitter, eloquent Irishman was free. It must have been small comfort to the major, not knowing the lady, to be informed that Mehitabel Prendergast, on hearing that her husband was not one of the prisoners, had gone to look for him—to persuade him to surrender himself to the mercy of the governor. It would have been an interesting experience to hear what Mehitabel told William when she found him, more interesting to see the face of Major Browne when the two of them—the twenty-eight-year-old girl in her Quaker dress and bonnet and the desperate rebel chief he and his Grenadiers could not catch—rode confidently side by side into his camp.

The surrender must have seemed a humiliating anticlimax, but he was not fool enough to waste time considering it or expressing his thanks. He put Prendergast in the middle of his Grenadiers and set them marching for Poughkeepsie as fast as their tired legs would swing them along. Hundreds of farmers followed just out of musket range. More Levelers joined the pursuit with every mile traversed. There was talk of rescue. The jail at Poughkeepsie had been emptied once. The farmers swore they would tear it stone from stone this time.

The major took no chances. He marched Prendergast right through Poughkeepsie to the river wharf. Before the pursuers were aware of the strategy, Prendergast and a heavy guard were aboard a Hudson River sloop and sailing for New York. There, on the morning of July tenth, a curious crowd watched an armed detachment march ashore, guarding the lonely figure of a man who had caused the whole city a week of sleepless anxiety less than three months before.

During the month of Prendergast's imprisonment in New York, affairs upriver did not improve. A farmer avenged his leader's capture by shooting in the right knee Private George Henry, of Captain Skene's com··

pany of the 28th, and Private Henry, though sent downriver to a New York hospital, died. Robert Noble and his farmers on the Van Rensselaer Manor were raising the devil again, and on July nineteenth General Gage sent a company of the 46th Regiment with three field pieces north on a sloop bound for Claverack to help Harmanus Schuyler. At about the same date a Poughkeepsie grand jury indicted William Prendergast for high treason.

In the following week a special trial commission was appointed in New York, and great dignitaries embarked for Poughkeepsie: the Honorable David Horsmanden, chief justice of the Supreme Court of the province; Judge Robert R. Livingston, of the same court; members of his Majesty's Council; the attorney general, with his assistant, plump, cockeyed James Duane—whose wife was a Livingston—and others. Two days after they had sailed William Prendergast, under strong guard, was taken aboard a sloop bound upriver. His wife was waiting at the wharf at Poughkeepsie when the soldiers marched him off the boat.

And when William Prendergast was brought into the crowded courtroom on August sixth, Mehitabel Prendergast walked beside him. A jury consisting of some of the most respectable freeholders was soon selected. Then, as the first of the twenty-four hours of the dramatic trial began, the Quaker wife suddenly showed the power with which she had brought her rebellious husband in from the hills. The curious crowds in the courtroom, the thousands in New York and the settlements along the Hudson eagerly awaiting news, were at first bewildered, then delighted as the center of attention moved directly from the strong character of the prisoner to that of his stronger wife. For as the attorney general brought out the damning evidence against William Prendergast, leader of riots, thief of property, captain of rebels, speaker of treason against his Royal Majesty, Mehitabel Prendergast thwarted his every move. Obviously enchanted by her, the Poughkeepsie correspondent of the New York *Gazette or Weekly Post Boy* informed his downriver readers that "solicitously attentive to every particular and without the least Impertinence or Indecorum of Behaviour, sedately anxious for her husband she never failed to make every Remark that might tend to extenuate the Offence and put his Conduct in the most favourable point of view not suffering one Circumstance that could be collected from the evidence or thought in his Favour to escape the Notice of the Court and the Jury."

"And when he came to make his Defence," continued the admiring reporter, "she stood behind him, reminded him of and suggested to him everything that could be mentioned to his advantage."

When the attorney general thundered out the charge that William Prendergast was the archconspirator and ringleader of all the rent rebels, she softly suggested that the real chief was "one Samuel Munro," who had stirred up her unfortunately weak husband to act as he did. (She knew that Munro was safe across the Massachusetts border and out of the court's jurisdiction.)

When the prosecutor condemned William with fiery rhetoric as a dangerous criminal, she gently interposed evidence that before the recent disturbances he had been "esteemed a sober, honest and industrious farmer, much beloved by his neighbors."

Tried beyond the limits of his temper by this, the attorney general suddenly rose and addressed Justice Horsmanden:

"Your Lordship, I move you that this woman be removed from the court, lest she too much influence the jury."

"She does not disturb the court," replied the chief justice, "nor does she speak unseasonably."

"Your Lordship, I do not think that she should speak at all, and I fear her very looks may too much influence the jury."

"For the same reason you might as well move the Prisoner himself be covered with a veil," snapped Justice Horsmanden.

Drearily the trial wound to its end before a court and audience exhausted by lack of sleep. Nevertheless, Mehitabel Prendergast's "affectionate assiduity fill'd every observer with a Tender Concern." With compelling personal magic she held the whole courtroom in her spell. But she could not change the history of the past weeks and she knew it. While the jury deliberated she clung to her husband, awaiting a verdict which they both knew must come.

"Guilty," said the jury foreman.

"Your verdict does not accord with the evidence in the opinion of the court," said the chief justice. "I must ask you to return to your deliberations."

New hope added to their torture. The wait until the jury was again ready must have seemed very long.

"Guilty," said the foreman, and hope was gone. There could only be one sentence.

"High treason against his Majesty—Friday the

twenty-sixth day of September—to be hanged by the neck until you are dead."

"God have mercy upon my soul," said William Prendergast, and the New York *Gazette* reporter wrote that he said it "with such earnestness and looked so distressed that the whole audience, even those least susceptible to compassion, were melted into tears."

As the solemn procession of the condemned man and his guards moved through crowds of sullen, muttering farmers toward the Poughkeepsie jail, Mehitabel Prendergast was mounting her horse. She had a last recourse to save her husband—Governor Sir Henry Moore. She had known in her heart what the verdict would be and she had prepared for it, even to the un-Quakerlike vanity of borrowing her sister Abigail's best dress—the white one with the blue stripe—and hoping that the worldly British executive would like her in it. Fort George was eighty miles away and every moment was precious for the carrying out of her plan.

She galloped down the King's Road, past Fish Kill and the waters of Oscawanna Creek, past Peek's Kill, between the steep green slopes of the Manitou Mountains on her left and the broad gleam of the Hudson on her right, past wide Tappan Bay, past King's Ferry and Tarrytown, past the great Philipse Manor House where fat Frederick and imperious Elizabeth lived richly off the rents of poor men like her husband and sometimes caused their deaths, and finally there was the ribbon of the Harlem below her and the slow little ferry. She dashed down the full length of Manhattan Island and into Fort George, begging even as she dismounted that she might see the governor.

Though there is no official record of the interview

between British Sir Henry and the provincial Quaker housewife, the story of it is a legend in the Wing family to this day. She strode up and down, so the Wing archives say, in her pretty blue-striped linen, and her arguments were so convincing and her looks so utterly appealing that the reserved British governor was moved to tears and, wiping his eyes, exclaimed:

"Your husband shall not suffer."

The governor immediately wrote out a reprieve for William Prendergast "respiting his execution until his Majesty's pleasure should be known," and then allowed Mehitabel to draw up in her own words the petition for a royal pardon. As soon as she was satisfied with that, she set out for Poughkeepsie. She knew too well what all the muttering and sullen looks had meant when her William had been marched from the court. His followers would storm the jail and have him out, undoing all her efforts unless she could get back in time to prevent them.

And so the ride back was more desperate even than that of the day before. Landmarks seemed farther apart. The waters of Fish Kill were a long, long ride to the north from Peek's Kill—and the last miles seemed interminable. Her fatigue when she reached the sheriff's door at Poughkeepsie must have been incredible. In less than three days she had ridden a horse a hundred and sixty miles, won the governor's favor, written the petition, obtained the reprieve—all these after the trial ordeal of twenty-four sleepless hours.

Even then her work was not finished. The day after she had left, Sheriff Livingston, anticipating difficulty in finding a hangman who would execute Prendergast, had advertised for one, offering "a good reward to any person inclined to assist" and promising to protect him and to disguise him so well that he would not be known. The publication of the advertisement had not had quite the result intended. As soon as it appeared there had been a casual drifting of men with sunburned faces and rough hands to join their comrades who had dared attend the trial in Poughkeepsie. Mehitabel had just delivered the reprieve to the disappointed sheriff and rushed to the jail to tell her husband of it when these men "without the least Tumult, Noise or previous Notice suddenly assembled at the Gaol." They told Prendergast they had come to release him and take him to a place of safety. But William knew better than to interfere with Mehitabel's plans. "Having received a reprieve he chose to remain where he was and await results." Moreover, he said, and it is safe to say that he was very earnest and tender about this, "if he should escape without any other Inconvenience, it would certainly be attended with the loss of his Property in this Government, which would reduce his Family to Poverty and Want." The *Gazette* reporter adds, "Upon this Answer which he persisted in the Company withdrew as suddenly and as quietly as they met, without doing the least Mischief of any Kind."

Six months later the "results" which William Prendergast chose to await became known. Obviously Sir Henry Moore had kept his word to Mehitabel, for a letter written to him by the Earl of Shelburne and dated at Whitehall, December 11, 1766, ends with these words: "I have laid before the King your letter of the 11th Oct. recommending W. Prendergast who was sentenced to death for treasonous Practices and Riots committed in Dutchess County, to the Royal mercy, and his Majesty has been gratiously pleased to grant him his pardon, relying that this instance of his Royal clemency will have a better effect in recalling these mistaken People to their duty than the most rigorous punishment."

So Mehitabel Prendergast brought her husband back to his acres on Philipse Manor and all up and down the river, except in the big houses, there was great rejoicing. The farmers had not won their battle and they were not to win it for nearly a hundred years but they were happy because William Prendergast was back on his farm with his wife and children.

If this were not a true tale it would end here. Life goes beyond the story endings, however, and there are always people who ask "What happened to them afterward?" The answer is—a great deal. Mehitabel bore William four more sons and six daughters, making a grand total of thirteen, all but one of whom lived to maturity. Not feeling comfortable on the Philipse Patent, the Prendergasts moved to Pittstown over in Rensselaer County for a while. Not feeling comfortable there either, they decided to move southwest where there was plenty of land a man might own by himself with no strings attached. So in the spring of 1805, when William was seventy-eight and Mehitabel was sixty-seven, they set out with four sons, five daughters, several sons-in-law, some grandchildren, and a Negro slave, twenty-nine of them in all, for Tennessee. Four covered wagons—the first two drawn by four-horse teams, the second two drawn by three-horse teams—and a barouche made up their caravan. William and his four sons cracked their whips over the straining horses as they made their way through the Pennsylvania hills, but Mehitabel sat in the barouche in the rear and kept her eye on things. When they reached Wheeling they bought a flatboat, drove their wagons and livestock aboard, and floated all the way to Louisville, Kentucky. Then they started cross-country again and ended up at Duck Creek, near Nashville, Tennessee. By that time they had decided they did not like southern country after all, and so they turned north. After hard going they struck General Paine's Lake Road in Ohio and before long they had reached the head of Chautauqua Lake in their old home state of New York. There, at the northwest corner of the lake, William and Mehitabel began farming again. One of their daughters who was a widow and one who was an old maid lived with them. Their son James brought his wife for a long visit with them in the autumn of 1810 just a year before he founded Jamestown, New York.

William was eighty-four that winter and the snows of February proved too much for him. Mehitabel lived a year and a half after he left her. In the early autumn of 1812, just forty-six years from the day of her long ride, she once more went to her husband.

"Never to Become Slaves"

THE third quarter of the eighteenth century saw the full flowering of cultured living among the manor lords. It saw, too, increasing dissatisfaction with the rule of England whose government looked on the riches of its colonial possessions as an easy source of revenue. Already in antagonistic groups, the landed river families found this a further cause for quarrel. The rich downriver families of De Lancey and Philipse loyally approved the British policy while the upriver Livingstons, Van Rensselaers, and Schuylers denounced it.

Sir Henry Moore brought his wife and daughter to Philip Schuyler's Albany house. "Sir Harry," wrote young Scottish Miss McVickar, who was also a visitor, "had never thought of business in his life . . . spent more than he had . . . was gay, good natured, and well-bred, affable and courteous, in a very high degree." He and his lady, continued the young observer, "were too fashionable and too much hurried, to find time for particular friendships, and too good natured and well-bred to make invidious distinctions." These charming people found the Schuylers most congenial hosts. So did many another Britisher, despite increasing differences of opinion. There was something graceful and appealing about life on the big Schuyler farm on the flats above

Albany, a life that was very like plantation life in the South. There were many black slaves, each with his pet raccoon, squirrel, crow. The fabulous, mammoth barn held fine saddle horses, and there was beautiful river country to ride through. There were distinguished guests and good food and intelligent conversation. And there were hundreds of interesting events to enjoy.

With the coming of every spring there was the awesome spectacle of the ice breaking up on the river. "Conceive a solid mass, from six to eight feet thick, bursting for many miles in one continued rupture . . . Thunder is no adequate image of this awful explosion." At the first cracking sound the whole populace of Albany ran for the river, not pausing to take off nightcaps or to put on overcoats. "People never dreamed of being obeyed by their slaves until after the ice was past . . . Every child and every Negro was sure to say 'Is not this like the day of Judgment?' and what they said everyone else thought."

There were spring days, too, when the sky was black with the drumming wings of millions of pigeons, and Indians and Negroes and whites stopped what they were doing to shoot down delicious food. There were others when the sturgeon began to run upriver and everybody was hard at work spearing the great bodies of the fish all day, and at night by the flares of hundreds of torches.

Lumber rafts were on the river as soon as the released waters were at their height. The settlers had put up sawmills on every stream north of Albany. After the logs had been cut the planks were drawn to the side of the Hudson where the "whole neighborhood assembled and made their joint stock into a large raft which was floated down the river with a man or two on it, who, with long poles, were always ready to steer it clear of those islands or shallows which might impede its course. . . . Sometimes one sees a whole family transported on this single conveyance; the mother calmly spinning, the children sporting about her, and the father fishing on one end."

In the summer the Schuylers and their guests might attend the Iroquois festival of the Green Corn and see their Indian neighbors dancing, hear their songs of thanksgiving, the beat of their drums, the jingle of their belled ankles. And on dull winter days the red-coated young officers of his Majesty's Grenadiers broke the monotony by producing high comedies like Farquhar's *The Beaux' Stratagem* and caused great scandal by casting healthy males in the female parts.

Life at the other manors was not very different from that described by the Scottish guest of the Schuylers. South along the river the Livingstons were prospering. A descendant, Helen Evertson Smith, writes of "great treasures of tapestries, pictures, inlaid cabinets, jewels, satins, velvets and laces, as well as old wines, delicate porcelains and expensive plate" imported by the family. "For miles along the eastern bank of the Hudson," she says, "above and below what is now Rhinebeck, almost every sightly eminence was capped with the fine residence of one of the grandchildren of the first Lord and Lady of Livingston Manor."

These people rode and hunted, patterning their leisurely lives after the customs of aristocratic rural England. They sent their sons abroad for education and travel. And every rent day the roads to the manor house were choked with wagons as the tenant farmers brought in the toll they had to pay for the privilege of working manor lands. From sunrise to sunset they patiently paraded to bring the manor lord a portion of their harvests—a tribute he had earned by inheritance from an ancestor who had been lucky enough to be first on the river land.

But by the late 1760's manor lords, tenants, and freeholders alike were beginning to feel the strained relationship between Hudson River people and British rulers. Some substantial farmers along the stream were satisfied with their homes and crops and decried the complaints of their less successful neighbors against the government's arbitrary taxes, but they were in the minority. Sir Henry Moore, who had been able to pour oil on the troubled waters, died. Stern, loyal Cadwallader Colden, who had been the power behind the governor, became more and more unpopular.

In 1765, during the Stamp Act Riots, a mob destroyed the fine Hudson River estate of Major James of the Royal Regiment of Artillery, who had expressed himself too freely about people who opposed the tax. On Golden Hill (the corner of Pearl and John streets) in New York City, in the middle of January, 1770, a party of British soldiers were provoked by members of the "Sons of Liberty," an anti-British organization, into attacking them with cutlasses. There the first blood of the long struggle for liberty was spilled.

Four years later on an April afternoon, after the tax on tea had been imposed, the ship *London* arrived at the mouth of the Hudson. Captain Chambers loudly protested to a committee of suspicious patriots that he had none of the detested commodity in the hold. They knew he was lying and in the early evening a band of active men rushed aboard and dumped the tea into the water. In Kinderhook at about the same time a committee of Dutch housewives stormed the shop of a tea dealer, tied him up, and sold his tea for him at their own prices. Thus Boston's famous "massacre" and "tea party" had their counterparts along the Hudson.

A few lean years added to the bitter discontent of the tradesmen and farmers of the valley. They assumed that the government was responsible for hard times. On April 20, 1775, a rider brought the news of Lexington into Albany. Up and down the river flashed the word. It was all the hotheaded English-haters needed to hear. They wasted no time in conciliatory preliminaries. If there was to be war, there would be no pretenses about it or about the purposes for which it was to be fought. It took them just a month to gather at Coxsackie on the river—the Dutchmen, the Swedes, the French Huguenots, the Palatine Germans of the Hudson valley—and there to express themselves. Two months before the famous Mecklenburg pronouncement of their comrades in North Carolina, more than a year before the Philadelphia Declaration of Independence, two hundred and twenty-five Hudson River men signed their names to a sheepskin parchment on which it had been written that they were resolved "never to become slaves." Led off by the signature of preacher John Schuneman, the names told the story of the valley: John Van Loon, Peter Janson, Cornelius DuBois, Abraham Carmer, William Wells. The Coxsackie Declaration of Independence was the first to say to the world that the settlers of America would not consent to be ruled save by themselves.

11

The Long Fight

THE people of the Hudson had been expecting the British. The broad streak of water between high banks was too obvious a division of the New England colonies from those of the south to be overlooked by strategists. Once the forces of the king had occupied it, the rebellion would be cut in two. Eagerly, in 1776, many of the conservative, prosperous farmers of the valley looked forward to the comforting sight of red-coats on the march to restore law and order. Even more ardently the downriver manor lords yearned for a sight of white sails of his Majesty's frigates beating upstream. British occupation of New York would, they were sure, moderate the radical ideas of the Livingstons and Van Rensselaers—traitors to their class who had espoused the cause of the discontented and rebellious lower classes along the river. The Livingstons, it was true, had less to gain by maintenance of the old order since the huge old manor had been prudently divided up by the family itself. They had discovered that the eldest son, who would by law of entail come into possession of the estate, had imprudently entered into business negotiations with the Spanish allies of the French during the French and Indian Wars, and had been bamboozled into a bankruptcy which would eventually sacrifice a great portion of his inheritance. James Duane, that same shrewd,

plump, cockeyed lawyer who had assisted in the prosecution of William Prendergast for offenses against the
manor lords in 1766, had arranged the division, not
without self-interest since his wife was a Livingston.
As for the Van Rensselaers, both political alliances and
political idealism—which did not extend far enough to
include abolishment of aristocratic manorial abuses—
led them to oppose the British. But the spearpoint of
the upriver resistance was not to be a representative of
the great landholders. He was a six-foot-four country
lawyer, George Clinton, son of a farmer in Ulster
County, where men plowed their own fields and milled
their own flour with millstones that ranked higher in
quality than the wheat they ground. He had married
a Hudson River Dutch girl, a Tappen of Kingston, and
he lived with his wife and two little daughters on a
hill farm in a house whose southern windows opened on
the great sweep of the Highlands. When George Clinton led, the traders of the unaristocratic west bank
knew that he could be trusted. He was fighting for
what they were fighting for.

When two river sloops scudded up to New Windsor to inform Clinton that on July eleventh the British
had come to the mouth of the river and the next day
had landed troops, he went out and told all the men
who lived near him. He had forty of them with him
when he reached weakly constructed Fort Montgomery
just north of the point where the Popolopen Kill flows
into the Hudson. From there he sent out a call for his
friends and neighbors—the militia—but he was bitterly
disappointed in the result. A thrifty farmer himself, he
had encouraged the militia to harvest their crops while
the enemy was still distant. But the summer had seen

one long march of thundershowers and now that the farmer-soldiers were desperately needed they were staying at home, regardless of orders, to finish the haying.

The provincial convention obligingly tried to help Clinton summon his soldiers from Ulster and Orange and Dutchess counties to the defense of the river by promising them a bounty of twenty dollars plus their regular pay. On the same day that it made the offer, the sixteenth of July, the *Rose* and the *Phoenix* and other boats of his Majesty's fleet appeared in the Tappan Zee and fired a few shots toward the shore. With even more arrogance, in the following few days, they sailed further up the river and sent out small landing parties. One fast sloop even stuck its curious nose within gunshot of Fort Montgomery.

Word of this raced through the valley. Farmers left their horses standing among the haycocks and made for the river. Their wives rushed to the fields, drove the horses to the house doors, loaded the wagons with their most precious belongings, and rolled away to visit relatives and friends not so close to danger. The back-river roads were full of creaking wheels and straining horses. At points where Clinton thought landings might be attempted he placed units of the increasing militia to do their best to kill invaders who dared step ashore.

In the meantime the nearness of the enemy made Clinton realize that by some stupidity Fort Montgomery had been built on a spot which would be untenable if the enemy occupied a hill south of the Popolopen. He wrote General Washington for permission to improve the fort and, without waiting for a reply, sent his militiamen up the hill with orders that read: "It is expected . . . that the Detachment of Militia now here, honorably employed in the Defence of their Country, will as Early each Morning as if working for themselves, which is truely the Case, turn out on Fatigue to forward and compleat these Works in Season." Washington not only concurred in Clinton's decision but sent him experienced Lieutenant Machin to supervise the building of the fortifications. An iron chain was hurriedly forged by the valley blacksmiths and stretched across the river from the foot of Anthony's Nose to a point just below the new breastworks, which had already been christened Fort Clinton.

The hated warships had been moored above the Tappan Zee more than two weeks when five small American boats—the *Lady Washington*, the *Shark*, the *Whiting*, the *Crown*, the *Spitfire*—sailed up the river after them. There was great shouting from the shore as the guns roared, and long echoes sounded in the hills. For an hour and a half the first and last naval battle on the Hudson continued. By that time the Americans had lost many men and knew that they could not drive the enemy craft away. They turned about and made for Spuyten Duyvil as fast as their sails would take them.

Another two weeks went by and the big boats still idled contemptuously about. In frenzied rage the rivermen at Poughkeepsie were building fire rafts and mooring them just above Fort Montgomery to await an opportune moment. Below the fort the militia had piled great pyramids of brush that on application of a torch would turn the river into an arena of light if the enemy vessels should dare to sail north under cover of darkness. And Captain Silas Talbot, whose fireship had been chased by the British warships from moorings just below the city, had anchored in a near-by cove and was plotting revenge.

Captain Talbot lay naked in the cabin of his ship. A full ebb tide and a warm wind fair from the north were driving the craft swiftly down the dark river. Seaman Priestly, as unclothed as his commanding officer, had weighed anchor at exactly two hours after midnight. As soon as the boat was under way he had helped the captain spread fresh priming on all trains leading to the fire barrels. Then they had baptized the whole craft with spirits of turpentine. Now Priestly lay just outside the forecastle, a lighted fuse in his hand, waiting for the bump of the prow against the Britisher. At that precise moment he would set the tiny spark to the powder train beside him and roll into the river. A boat would be near, with friends to row it, and he was one of the best swimmers on the Hudson. Just in case something went wrong, Silas Talbot held a second lighted fuse. He, too, would set it to a fire train, then jump for the sally port and escape to the boat. The British of the fleet had been the first to dare move up the Hudson. Let them be first to take the consequences.

The mid-August night was very dark and for a time Talbot could not see the hulk that lay somewhere ahead. Then it was towering above him—the *Asia*, with sixty-four guns that would blast his little tinderbox into eternal impotence if he could not drift into her. From high in the rigging came a piercing shriek—a boy's voice calling terror to the men on deck. Hoarse shouts answered. A cannon roared. A shot splashed into the water, then another. There was a splintering crash and the two men on the fireship wondered if this was the end of their careful planning. Their boat had a hole through the side but she was still drifting down on the *Asia*. She had not caught fire. Priestly was close enough to throw hooks across the gap now. Suddenly there was a shock and a groaning, rubbing noise. Two fuses dipped into gunpowder. A blinding flash!

When Talbot came to he was lying on the deck and flames were licking at his body. He was blind. He stood up and with hands outstretched tried to feel his way to the sally port. Everything he touched was afire. Frantically he rushed about—then he felt the rail and a moment later the coolness of the water. As he floundered about aimlessly the voice of Priestly was above him and he was lifted into the rowboat. Three big ships were firing on them, the men said, as they raced desperately for the west bank. The fireship was a pyramid of flame, making the whole river as light as day for the British gunners. Twice grapeshot skittered across the surface into their wooden hull but no one was hurt and the boat moved on. The *Asia* was not yet afire and the other ships had launched small craft to help her escape the flames. She had moved away. The fireship was burning alone on the water.

Blistered from head to foot, blind, naked, Talbot climbed out on land. Quickly his men dragged him into near-by woods. They led him, stumbling and only half conscious, for a mile or so through thick trees. Then he heard them asking where they were. "English Settlement," said a man's voice with a Dutch accent. No, they couldn't take in anybody—not a scarecrow like that—he would frighten the children. He was led away. Then a knock and a woman's voice in which fright and compassion mingled. She was an aged widow, all alone.

Yes, she would care for the poor man. The men laid him on the floor, covered him with a blanket, and went away. They must make a report; they could not help him more.

For days and nights Talbot lay there sightless, tortured by the burns. Then his sight began to come back. In a week he could recognize the fat bulk of General Knox filling up the doorway of the old woman's cabin. And behind the general came Dr. Eustis with bandages and healing ointments. Some days later Talbot was in Hackensack under friendly care. Comrades told him that on the night of his own vain attempt Ensign Thomas, of his regiment, with a 100-ton fire sloop had set fire to the 14-gun tender *Charlotta* in the Tappan Zee and burned her to the water, though he himself had been destroyed in the flames.

The British had had enough—the *Asia*, the *Phoenix*, the *Rose*, the *Tryal*, the *Shuldham* had all dropped downriver. They knew now that the farther up the Hudson they went the more trouble they could expect. They knew, too, that in the valley were men who hated them so wholeheartedly that they would gladly give up their lives in searing flame to drive them away.

General Washington had been having a hard time trying to repel the invaders at the river's mouth. He needed more troops and sent Clinton orders to march his command to Manhattan. Ten years after William Prendergast had led his farmer band down the king's highway in defiance of the New York redcoats, the giant lawyer-soldier rode at the head of eighteen hundred militia, some of whom must have ridden with

Prendergast, down the same road, against the same enemy. At Kingsbridge they halted.

A month later they dashed down Manhattan Island to Harlem Heights and helped hurl the British back in the first American victory of the Hudson valley warfare. Two weeks later they were encamped at White Plains. The men of Ulster and Orange and Dutchess were learning that war is a nervous, desperate, hard business. General Clinton described their experience in a letter:

"We had reason to apprehend an attack last night or by daybreak this morning. . . . Our lines were manned all night . . . and a most horrid night it was to lie in cold trenches. Uncovered as we are, drawn on fatigue, making redoubts, flashes, abatis and lines and retreating from them and the little temporary huts made for our comfort before they are well finished I fear will ultimately destroy our army without fighting."

After the disastrous defeat at White Plains in October, Clinton went back up the river, taking most of his men with him; Washington and his army crossed and fled south into New Jersey. The British stormed and captured Fort Washington, last Manhattan stronghold of the Continentals, though Margaret Corbin took her slain husband's place at the parapet and fired at the advancing red line until she was herself wounded three times. While Washington evaded pursuit there was a conference of American generals at Peekskill. Clinton suggested that he and his men begin the further defense of the Hudson by fortifying Polopel's Island and Constitution Island. The plan was approved.

At once most of the able-bodied revolutionists of

the valley went to work. Major General Philip Schuyler
came downriver from Albany with five hundred men
from the north counties to help with the Constitution
Island project. At his home in New Windsor, Clinton
directed the work on Polopel. Sunlight caught the
blades of three hundred new axes as the valley patriots
swung them high. They might be inexperienced soldiers
but these were weapons they knew how to use. Teams
and wagons choked the river roads. Spars and timber
and iron were on their way from Gilbert Livingston.
Boats and scows crowded about the islands. The weather
was stormy. The building of the foundations required
work in the icy water of December. There was a great
grumbling and a call for more rum to warm the men's
bellies. Work was interrupted to give help to Washington by a swift raid on New Jersey.

Then followed months of strained inactivity. The
Hudson was no longer the theater of war, but everyone
knew that the time would come when it would be
again. All winter and through the spring and summer
of 1777 the valley militia waited for the British. General Israel Putnam was now George Clinton's superior.
To keep up the morale of his volunteers he allowed
them to go back home to harvest their crops. Late in
September news came to Putnam that three thousand
men had arrived in New York as reinforcements to Sir
Henry Clinton's garrison of four thousand. From the
north came word that Burgoyne and his army were
marching on Albany from Montreal. There could be
but one conclusion. Sir Henry would soon be setting
out to meet him at Albany. In a week the entire length
of the Hudson would be swarming with redcoats unless
something could be done.

A Negro slave ran panic-stricken across the level pasture of the Becker farm that lay north of Saratoga. He had seen Indians in war paint down by the river. Breathless, he gasped out his news. The family knew how to interpret it. The painted heathen were Burgoyne's advance scouts. They were part and parcel of the damnable savages who had murdered and scalped pretty Jenny McCrea when she set out to visit her British fiancé, an officer under Burgoyne. Sight of them meant that the British Army was only a few miles away.

Farmer Becker ran to his brother's house a quarter of a mile off, while his wife packed as much of the family clothing as she could into a cask. Young John and a black boy went into the pasture to bridle the horses and hitch them to the wagons. They turned the squealing pigs loose in the woods. They dug holes in the earth and buried the hoes and rakes. By that time Mrs. Becker was ready to have the wagons loaded, and her husband had come back. At the farm dock where the light bateau was moored they emptied the wagons and carried their cargo of household treasures aboard. Then the wagons were sent back for another loading and flight downriver. Young John and the black boy took the canoe and paddled. That night the whole family was reunited at Vanderbergs' little settlement below Stillwater. Other families had come there too; so many that all beds were full and most of the men slept in the cattle sheds.

Early the next morning Farmer Becker rode back to his farm, because in the panic of the day before he had not tried to save his cows. He found them and drove them down to Vandenbergs'. By that time the road along the river was jammed. John Becker looked on all this with the wide-eyed interest of a nine-year-old and in later years he described it: "A long cavalcade of wagons filled with all kinds of furniture not often selected by the owners with reference to their use or value on occasions of alarm . . . stretched along the road." Many of the refugees were on horseback—sometimes two on a horse. Others not so fortunate were fleeing on foot, hurrying frantically to keep up with the wagons as they thought of the Indians and soldiers behind them.

Meanwhile, a strange army was marching downriver. The painted Indians were no novelty to the Americans, nor were the redcoats—but the Hessians, with their heavy, befeathered hats, ornamented with brass, their long-skirted coats, long swords, canteens the size of small barrels, their big queues of powdered hair, were foreign enough to infuriate the American provincials. Terrified by the rattlesnakes of the rocky north country, clumsy and helpless in their efforts to penetrate the wilderness of felled trees with which General Schuyler had thoughtfully obstructed their path, homesick to the point of yearning themselves to death, consoling their loneliness by lavishing affection on their many animal pets—black bears, deer, foxes, raccoons—the German mercenaries were really a pitiful, bewildered lot, but they were objects of especial hatred to the country-boy soldiers from the Hudson valley.

An added fillip was given to the whole strange rout by the presence of hundreds of women—camp followers for the most part. There were also the Baroness Riedesel, wife of the commander of the Hessians, with her three little daughters; Lady Harriet Acland, wife

IN THE SLATCHES OF BRIGHT SPRING WEAT

SON'S OLD MEN STILL TELL MELODRAMAS OF THE SEA

of the commander of the Grenadiers; and a commissary officer's wife who was making life pleasant for Gentleman Johnny Burgoyne. The whole army had thought the expedition from Montreal to Albany would be a pleasant walking trip in the clear early autumn weather. They had expected the Beckers and their farmer friends to do exactly what they were doing. But they had not anticipated the fierce opposition of men roused to fury by the British use of mercenaries and Indians, by the murder of poor Jenny McCrea, by love of their river farms. Before the Beckers had reached Stillwater an army was advancing from that very town, an army in which Hudson valley men commanded by officers named Van Cortlandt, Livingston, Nixon, Ten Broeck were marching to defend their homes. With the Virginian Morgan's picked riflemen, with the New Englanders of New Hampshire, Massachusetts, and Connecticut, they were determined to stop the British at the northern end of the Hudson valley.

The story of the next weeks has been often told. Though the British claimed victory, they were stopped by the battle of September nineteenth. When it was over the Americans were nearly out of bullets and a British attack would have meant disaster. While they waited in fearful suspense, the Dutchmen of Albany were wildly scrambling about their roofs and windows, stripping them of lead to be handed over to General Schuyler and made into pellets. The army was once more ammunitioned before the enemy moved.

No satisfactory word had come to Burgoyne of the progress of Sir Henry Clinton toward the Albany rendezvous. In a desk drawer in faraway London, forgotten by the fox-hunting Colonial Secretary, lay the order that would have sent him to the rescue.

Burgoyne was not a coward. He built fortifications and prepared for battle. On the seventh of October he was ready and General Horatio Gates obliged him. In a spectacular battle—high-lighted by the mad courage of General Benedict Arnold, who fought bitterly for the river he later tried to give away—the Americans defeated the invaders. Too late Burgoyne turned about. The weather, which had been, according to a young American officer, "charming" throughout the autumn, suddenly changed. A night retreat in a pouring rain bogged the wagons, including the thirty containing Gentleman Johnny's personal wardrobe. Where Schuylerville now stands the British Army was surrounded. It could neither advance nor retreat.

The weather had cleared by October fourteenth when a British emissary, Major Kingston, "well formed, ruddy, handsome," was admitted to the American camp and led blindfolded ("hoodwinked") to a pleasant spot overlooking the Hudson. An aide-de-camp, ambitious young Captain James Wilkinson, "in a plain blue frock without other military insignia than cockade and sword" awaited him. There, in the cool, sun-drenched October morning, the Britisher, with aplomb typical of his kind, "expatiated with taste and eloquence on the beautiful scenery of the Hudson's river and the charms of the season." Then he took up a discussion of such mundane matters as the surrender of Burgoyne's army.

The Indians, the redcoats, the Hessians had been stopped by an army in which hardly a man was regularly equipped and many a soldier was "in clothes he wore at work in field or tavern," an unhealthy army, "their disease being chiefly Fever Ague and Dysentery" which left scarcely a man unscathed.

The Beckers could come back to their farm beside the narrow, rippling river.

Down below things were not going so well. On September tenth, General George Clinton, now governor of New York, had told the legislature convened at the state capital in Kingston that the Hudson Highlands were "in so respectable a state of defense as to promise us security against any attack in that quarter. This, together with the several obstructions in Hudson's River has probably induced General Howe to alter his original plan."

It had done nothing of the sort, and the arrival of British reinforcements at New York seemed to prove that. All the further evidence necessary came a few days later. A crisp north breeze filled the sails of two great frigates, a half dozen smaller vessels, about forty clumsy flatboats, and Sir Henry Clinton was on the river with four thousand men. Tardily, on his own initiative, he had decided to create a diversion to help Burgoyne. The Americans would soon know whether their preparations of the past two years were sufficient.

Vainly General Putnam on the east bank and General Clinton on the west tried to outguess Sir Henry. With shrewd maneuvering the Briton kept them puzzled. He made a quick landing at Tarrytown—and was away. He did the same thing below Peekskill at Verplanck's Point—and Putnam dared not send any of his men upriver to the Highland forts. On the morning of October sixth there was a heavy fog. Before it had lifted, two thousand redcoats had landed near Stony Point and were somewhere in the mountains below Forts Montgomery and Clinton. American scouts found them two hours before noon near Doodletown. Brom Springster, Tory neighbor of the Orange County militia, had guided the invaders through the fog over the high pass called "The Timp," a latter-day Thermopylae which could have been defended by a few men if George Clinton had thought to station them there. A hundred Americans awaited the British at the "Hell Hole," a mile west of Fort Clinton. They fought bitterly as they were driven back into the forts.

Twilight was deepening when the overwhelming British force made its sharp quick attack on the twin forts. The American militia fought like the wildcats of their river mountains. The British casualties were three hundred—but there could be only one outcome. The forts were taken at the point of the bayonet and the Americans ran. George Clinton saved himself by a magnificent slide down the Hudson's steep bank—becoming a mighty human avalanche hurtling to the water's edge where a boat awaited him.

Two American frigates, unable to escape against wind and tide, were given to the flames that night by their crews. The steep sides of Anthony's Nose on the opposite side of the river reflected the yellow light. The river seemed molten with the still-glowing ashes of hope. Down below the captured forts there was a clanking of iron. Soldiers were working at the iron chain upon which George Clinton had depended so much. At eleven o'clock the next morning it gave way. There would be no stopping the British now.

After a week of preparation and reconnaissance, a fleet of thirty sail, commanded by Sir James Wallace and carrying about sixteen hundred troops under Major General Vaughn, continued on the journey upriver. Alarm guns boomed from the towns and signal beacons flared from the hilltops as the hated white sails moved steadily northward. Poughkeepsie was in a panic. Roars of the big guns on the frigates' decks echoed about in the hills and valleys of the Hudson. Cannonballs ripped through the fine houses of well-known revolutionary worthies as if the walls had been cardboard. Kingston guessed what was coming. It was the last refuge of the "government-on-the-run" which had been moved from Harlem to Kingsbridge to Philipse Manor to Fishkill to Poughkeepsie. General Vaughn had called the town "a nest of rebels . . . a nursery for almost every villain in the country." Kingston could hardly expect mercy.

At five o'clock the white sails were off Esopus Island and messengers were spurring lathered horses over country roads to warn everybody along the river. Across the Hudson at Clermont the Livingstons had been working feverishly. The precious books of the late Judge Livingston were carefully laid in the bottom of a big dry fountain on the grounds and covered with old sloop sails and a thick top layer of barnyard manure. Possessions not easily carried were hidden in a deep cave formed weeks before by felling trees across the top of a sharp little ravine. A train of wagons filled with silver, furniture, bedding, was on its way into Connecticut. In one of them sat stalwart Margaret Beekman Livingston, ancestor of many a distinguished York Stater, laughing heartily at her fat black cook who sat on a pile of kitchen utensils and directed her little grandson's driving efforts with energetic thrusts of a long-handled toasting fork.

The Livingstons might laugh. They would find warmth and food and friends where they were going. But the Dutch folk of Kingston were not laughing. Winter was only a month away, and the thought of a winter on the Hudson with no roof over the head is not a happy one. "Lope bei Hurley out!" came the cry through the starlit October night. "Lope younge Lope—die Roye komme!" All night frightened wives packed their belongings while burghers hurried to the woods to bury treasures they could not take with them. The road to Hurley, a little town three miles back from the river, was a channel of pitiful refugees, fleeing the wrath of the British.

In the morning at nine cannonading began. The American galley, *Lady Washington,* lay at the mouth of Rondout Creek and above it on the heights of Ponckhockie a hundred and fifty militia manned a battery of five guns. By noon the Americans had sailed the *Lady Washington* up the creek and scuttled her. A British force of four hundred was landing. A few moments later the militia had spiked their guns and fled. Then the British marched into the defenseless town and began a systematic campaign of pillage and burning.

Of the hundred and sixteen houses of the town only Tobias Van Steenbergh's was left standing. Some said afterward that it stood because the Van Steenbergh servants had rolled a number of barrels of rum from the cellar and insisted on treating any soldier who came near. Others said General Vaughn was sweet on a pretty Dutch girl who lived there. One barn out of the hundred and four in the town was left, possibly because, the legend goes, owner Ben Low had once been kind to an ill wanderer who turned out to be a British spy. Church, courthouse, schools, markets, all were devoured by the flames. Mary Crooke Elmendorf, believing with reason that none could resist her Dutch cooking, left a full meal on her table. When she came back it was gone, and so was her house. Mrs. Ben Low left her silver chest in the care of a British officer's wife who boarded with her. "I am a British officer's wife," cried the lady when the soldiers found it. "You'll all be saying that now," laughed one of the looters as he snatched the chest from her. He and his companions stole the silver, threw the chest in the street, abducted the lady's daughter only to tear the rings from her ears and let her go.

Three hours after the British had landed, Kingston was a smoking ruin. The standing stone walls of the Dutch houses emphasized the destruction and desolation. General Clinton, hurrying to the rescue with a command of militia, arrived at Keykhout Hill above the old town just after the invaders had gone. He and his men looked down on a ravaged waste that had once been a placid, beautiful river town.

Before they returned to New York the redcoats burned several houses above Kingston and made the journey the Livingstons had expected them to make, to destroy the two big houses at Clermont. General Vaughn had heard of Burgoyne's plight through the Tory messenger, Jacobus Lefferts, and had done his utmost to avenge it. But he did not dare stay so far upriver now, with no chance of uniting with the northern army. The Hudson had been saved again.

That winter many of the people of Kingston built lean-tos against the smoke-blackened stone walls of their old homes and lived in them. Others built roofs from one wall to another. A number lived with friends in near-by towns. Two companies of local militia were excused from service to help in preparations for reconstruction in the spring. Help came up the river from faraway South Carolina—money and food. Nothing could have done more to foster the idea of a unified and independent nation. At the town meeting in the unharmed Van Steenbergh house in March, trustees and officers were elected and one of their first acts was to authorize the transformation of many pounds of lead housed in Ben Low's barn into bullets for the Continental Army. That was Kingston's answer to its invaders.

Now that the British fleet had gone back to New York, and Burgoyne's captured army was on its dreary march to Boston, the Hudson valley was suddenly a happy place. From the Sterling Iron Works, thirteen miles west of the river near Sloatsburg, came the clang of hammers on anvils as the new chain that was to be stretched from West Point to Constitution Island was forged in links two feet long, two and a quarter inches square "with a swivel to every hundred feet and a clevis to every thousand feet." The rattle of iron and the jingle of harness sounded on the west river road as farm wagons brought the links to New Windsor, above West Point. There they were put together with logs attached to keep two strands floating parallel to each other, and allowed to drift downriver to the position intended. Here in April of 1778 the chain was anchored. Let the Britishers try to break through that! Rage over the burning of Kingston and joy over Saratoga produced a great exaltation in every American, except the Tories, in the river counties. "No king but God," shouted the men of the Hudson and dared the British to come again. But the theater of war had been moved and the valley was comparatively quiet for a year. The year 1779 came and in the summer and autumn the Continental Army was back on the Hudson keeping watch over the British in New York. The Americans wintered in Morristown, New Jersey. Then, in the spring, the enemy began to creep up the valley once more. They took Stony Point on the west shore and Verplanck's Point opposite—gaining control of King's Ferry, a valuable connecting link.

"I'll storm hell if you'll only plan it," said thick-set, theatrical Anthony Wayne.

"Perhaps we'd better try Stony Point first," said George Washington grimly.

Out of Fort Montgomery swung a column of four-teen hundred men who did not know where they were going. They marched inland and then to the south around Bear Mountain and West Hill, over the back of the Dunderberg, and down by the creek called Flora's Kill. At Springsteel's Farm they halted. The silence of the Hudson twilight was intensified that evening. No farmyard barking challenged the advancing shadows of the night—for every dog within a radius of three miles had been killed. It was nearly a half hour after midnight when the British sentries of the high fort cried out that the Americans were advancing. A half hour later the silent steel bayonets had done their work. The guns of the fort had been turned on the enemy and were bombarding Verplanck's Point and the frigate *Vulture* below in the river. The enemy's frowning fortress had been taken and the victorious troops were uniting in a wild, early morning celebration with the folk of the countryside.

Though Wayne had to evacuate Stony Point soon after his dramatic exploit, the valley was a channel of joy. The Hudson's patriots roared out gleefully the cocky folklore of the Revolution. Thirteen—the total of the states of the new nation—was a magic number. It had taken Wayne just thirteen hours to capture Stony Point; General Washington had thirteen teeth in each jaw, and since the Declaration of Independence he had grown three extra toes; Mrs. Washington had a mottled tomcat with thirteen rings around his tail; General Schuyler had a topknot of thirteen stiff hairs that stood up straight on the crown of his head whenever he saw a Britisher.

The feeling between noncombatants in the valley grew bitterer than it had ever been. Mounted bands of lawless men infested the neutral ground that extended for nearly a score of miles between the upriver Continentals and the downriver British. Claudius Smith, the "Cowboy of the Ramapos" who claimed to be a Tory, led one such group of outlaws. They made swift raids on the river farms, stealing cattle and livestock, which they sold on Manhattan. Sometimes an unlucky wagon train of supplies for Washington's army, too weakly guarded to withstand the attack of Smith's wild horsemen, would disappear mysteriously and completely. There were tales of the torture of old men and women in the effort to make them give up their savings, of sudden descents on little outlying communities and the murder of helpless inhabitants. Occasionally the Cowboys clashed with an equally dastardly gang of cutthroats called the "Skinners" who claimed to favor the revolutionary party but never troubled to ask the political beliefs of the farmers from whom they stole. Tory and revolutionary farmers alike heaved sighs of relief whenever these murderous bully-boys succeeded in destroying each other.

For his sins Claudius Smith danced at the end of a rope in his stocking feet before the war was over. He took his shoes off just before he swung to prove that his mother had not told the truth. She had said he would die with his boots on. Just to make him an ironic posthumous prop to law and order, the builders of the old courthouse at Goshen, west of the Hudson, used his skull as a brick over the doorway.

Meanwhile the British officers and men lived a gay life in the city at the Hudson's mouth, caring little for the threat of the army to the north. On Manhattan's boundary rivers lay prison ships filled to overflowing with miserable members of that despised military unit. A captured American poet, Captain Freneau, remembered them a few years after his release with bitter verses:

> Two hulks on Hudson's stormy bosom lie . . .
> There the black *Scorpion* at her moorings rides
> There swings *Strombolo,* yielding to the tides . . .
> Thou *Scorpion* fatal to the crowded throng
> Dire theme of sorrow and Plutonian song
> Requir'st my lay—thy sultry decks I know,
> And all the torments that exist below!
> The briny wave that Hudson's bosom fills
> Dripp'd through her bottom in a thousand rills
> Rotten and old, o'er filled with sighs and groans . . .
> Here doom'd to toil or founder in the tide

At the moist pumps incessantly we ply'd . . .
No friendly awning cast a welcome shade
Once it was promised but was never made.

In these boats and in others on the East River many
Hudson valley farm boys wasted away under the stern
eyes of the Hessian and Scottish guards. They ate moldy
bread and rotten pork, or nothing. They spent every
night in shackles. In the daytime they gazed from the
decks across the water at the stockade in Lispenard's
Meadows (now part of Greenwich Village), where, imported by one Jackson, three boatloads of gay ladies—
two white cargoes from England and one black from
the West Indies—made merry with the British soldiers.
It is scant wonder that so many men born to free life
among the fields and wooded hills beside the same broad
stream on which they floated, gave up reason, and often
life itself.

On a day of late September his Majesty's ship
Vulture sailed upriver and loitered about off Teller's
Point, seventeen miles below West Point. It was nearly
midnight before a boat put out from the shore toward
her. When it returned a slim erect man stepped ashore,
clad in a greatcoat under which gleamed the uniform
and trappings of a British major. A figure emerged from
the shadowed bank to meet him. All night the two men
talked in low tones, while the owner of the rowboat and
his crew waited near by. They were still talking when
dawn had spread over the river. The light revealed the
features of Major General Benedict Arnold, commander
of the West Point fortifications, and of Major John
André, an elegant of the British Army, poet, play-
wright, songster, embroiderer, beau. When farmer

Joshua Smith refused to take the major back to the *Vulture* in daylight the two officers decided to continue their talk at Smith's house. While they were closeted there during the day a few Americans on the east bank began a desultory fire on the *Vulture* with a small cannon incapable of doing the boat serious damage. Nevertheless, the *Vulture* dropped downriver, leaving its important passenger behind.

That night Smith gave André a civilian's coat and ferried him to the east shore. He rode with the young man the rest of the night and left him after a roadside breakfast at the home of a poor widow. Only neutral ground lay between the major and safety. Three countrymen who occasionally served in the Continental militia captured him near Tarrytown, stripped him, and found the plans of West Point in his boots. Whatever the balance of cupidity and patriotism within them— and there have been many debates on the integrity or lack of it evidenced by the trio—they surrendered André to Colonel Jameson in command of Continental troops at White Plains. That officer naïvely sent a messenger to General Arnold informing him of the capture of a British officer who had by some means obtained the plans of the fort. Arnold was having breakfast with his staff when the message came. He read it calmly, waited a few moments, excused himself and went to tell his wife what had happened. Then he strolled down to the river landing, boarded the six-oared barge that was kept at his disposal and ordered the crew to race downriver at top speed, for, said he, he was on a "mission of the greatest urgency for General Washington." Before he had climbed to safety over the side of the *Vulture*, General Washington was in West Point, the conspiracy to surrender the Hudson to the British had been at least partially revealed, and the name of the brave Benedict Arnold had been destined to become a symbol throughout America for treachery and ingratitude. New matter affording some reasonable interpretations of motives has been added from time to time to this story, but the British documents concerning the traitorous plan have not been read by historians. Recently purchased from the British government by the University of Michigan, they await in Ann Arbor a perusal that may radically alter the conception current in America for more than a hundred and sixty years, and may destroy more reputations than Arnold's.

The gallant British major was tried by a military tribunal of fourteen general officers at Tappan on September twenty-ninth. He was sentenced to be hanged at noon on October second, and hanged he was, while a Continental Army band played "The Blue Bird" and officers and men who would have gloated to see the hero of Saratoga so used were blinded by tears.

The rest of the American Revolution was fought far from the banks of the Hudson. Washington's army crossed the river at King's Ferry on its dash to join the French at Yorktown and compel the surrender of Cornwallis. When the news of that great event reached the North there were bonfires and salutes in all the up-river towns, and the state legislature, meeting in the Dutch church at Poughkeepsie, offered thanks to Providence for the good news. After that, during the years while the Peace of Paris was awaited, the great general, his staff, and his troops were lodged once more on the Hudson near Newburgh. There Washington received in a letter the so-called "offer of a crown" which he said he "must view with abhorrence and reprehend with severity." It was there, too, that he watched the growing bitterness toward the Continental Congress that culminated in the seditious "Newburgh Address" with its demand that the troops make use of their armed might to better their condition, and its fiery rhetorical questioning of the soldiers: "Can you, then, consent to be the only sufferers by this revolution, and, retiring from the field, grow old in poverty, wretchedness and contempt?" And it was in the New Building of the Newburgh camp that Washington stopped his pacific reply to Armstrong to put on spectacles and say to his officers, "You have seen me grow gray in your service. Now I am growing blind,"—two sentences that destroyed the effect of the notorious address more effectively than public burning of it could ever have done.

The great Virginian did not like staying on the Hudson while the banks of the Potomac were calling. He had written to Martha Washington at Mount Vernon complaining of his life "without amusements or avocations . . . amongst these rugged and dreary mountains." The first of these phrases may not be accepted literally, however, for the people of the Hudson outdid themselves in honoring the successful general and his officers. Count de Ségur, one of the many French officers who visited the valley to pay his respects to Washington, was overwhelmed by the beauty of the river—"a vast sea flowing between forests centuries old"—and delighted with the people who lived along its banks. "I should like to live in this country with you, my heart," he wrote to his wife, ". . . this is the only country for honest people."

There was skating on the river that winter and the

next summer gay parties rode along the banks. Baron von Steuben convulsed the headquarters family by returning from a few hours' fishing to announce that he had caught a whale and by not seeming any the less proud when investigation proved that his German pronunciation had given seeming enlargement to a Hudson River eel.

On the sunny last day of May in 1782, General Washington gave a great party complimenting his allies and celebrating the birthday of the French dauphin. Tall evergreen saplings cut and trimmed in the valley woods were brought to the river bank on the shoulders of the American troops and there cast down with shouts of "God bless the dauphin"—though some who had worked hard at the job and did not like the French were suspected of shouting less complimentary sentences. Other soldiers built a sylvan bower interwoven with valley flowers and with fleurs-de-lis cut from tissue paper. Five hundred officers sat beneath the green canopy, ate heartily of roasted ox and drank the thirteen toasts, eight of which honored the French alliance. There was a parade of troops and then a gander hop to the old tune of "Soldier's Joy," General Washington making a graceful figure in the stag affair stepping off with one of his officers. Late in the night a running fire laid by the troops in pyrotechnic design leaped into the sky, moving rapidly northward on the west bank. It seemed to jump the river to catch on the east bank and run southward. The hills on both sides of the water were black silhouettes and the Hudson's ripples gave back the dancing flames.

The autumn colors had faded in the valley on the happy November day in 1783 when General Washington left Newburgh and rode down the river road to meet Governor Clinton and General Knox with his troops at Harlem. Even as the British were withdrawing from the Battery, big Knox led the vanguard of the victorious American Army into New York. The whole line of the Hudson was free.

12

To Go—or Not to Go!

Dᴜʀɪɴɢ the long British occupation of the mouth of the Hudson, New York had been the asylum of thousands of loyalist refugees from all the rebelling colonies. Along the river many Tory families had been brave enough to try to live on their property and to protect themselves throughout the war though they were often severely dealt with. Sometimes the Tory men enlisted in the British forces and lost most of their lands through confiscation, although patriot committees usually left wives and children a pittance to live on. And sometimes the loyalist families took the aggressive as a note in a Hartford, Connecticut, paper—the *Freeman's Journal*—indicates: "We hear from Poughkeepsie that about a week ago, seven Tories were committed to gaol there, charged with robbing several houses and putting the families in fear. It is said, when taken they were all painted and dressed like Indian men, but that five of them proved to be women, three of whom are a mother and two daughters."

After Yorktown, however, these families found themselves in a pitiful situation. The bitterness of their patriotic neighbors was increased by success. On every side they heard condemnation and were given to expect persecution. The usually humanitarian General Washington was reported to have said that he could see no

course left for them but suicide. The patriot papers
were rabid in their jeering attacks.

Realizing that to stay would imperil their lives,
the loyalists appealed to the British government to find
them homes elsewhere. Some were allowed to go to England, others went to the West Indies, but by far the
greatest number were shipped to Nova Scotia. "Hell or
Halifax," they shouted defiantly as their transports set
sail from New York harbor. "Nova Scarcity," the patriots shouted after them, rejoicing that their enemies
were bound for a cold, barren coast and were leaving
behind pleasant homes and fertile lands.

"The country counties have engaged many months
ago, to hold the Toryes banished," wrote a Fishkill
citizen in a letter published in the New York *Morning
Post* on November 7, 1783; "the voice of the inhabitants
is so universally against them that they cannot hope for
a peaceful residence among us." And in the same issue
of the *Post* appeared a burlesque of a Hamlet soliloquy
beginning:

> To go—or not to go—is that the question?
> Whether 'tis best to trust the inclemency
> That scowls indignant o'er the dreary Bay
> Of Fundy, and Cape Sable's rock and shoals
> And seek our new domains in Scotia's wilds
> Barren and bare; or stay among the rebels!

The exodus from New York in the year 1783 was
the removal of a considerable part of the Hudson River
civilization. More than twenty-eight thousand refugees,
many of them residents of the New York region, left for
Canadian ports in that year alone.

13

Refugee Family

HANNAH INGRAHAM knew that there was
one of all her spring days in the valley which she would
never forget. It was the day her father told her he was
going away for a while and kissed her and her younger
brother John. Then he held their mother close before
he set out along the road downriver. Years later Hannah
told the story. Part of it went like this:

"My father lived at New Concord, twenty miles
from Albany. He had a comfortable farm, plenty of
cows and sheep. But when the war began and he joined
the regulars they (the Rebels) took it all away, sold the
things, ploughs and all, and my mother was forced to
pay rent for her own farm. What father had sown they
took away, but what mother raised after she paid rent
they let her keep. They took away all our cows and
sheep, only left her one heifer and four sheep.

"Uncle had given me a sheep, and when he found
we were like to lose all, he took it away and kept it
for me.

"Little John, my brother, had a pet lamb and he
went to the Committee men and spoke up and said
'Won't you let me have my lamb?' He was a little fellow, four years old, so they let him have it.

"My father was in the army seven years. They took

137

grandfather prisoner and sent him on board a prison ship.

"Mother rode fifty miles on horseback in one day when she heard it to go to see him and take him some money to buy some comforts. He had a paralytic stroke when he was there, and he never recovered, poor grandfather.

"My father was taken prisoner once but he escaped. The girl who was sent to take him his supper one night told him she would leave the door unbuttoned and he got off to the woods, but was wandering most two months before he found the army again. Mother was four years without hearing of or from father, whether he was alive or dead; any one would be hanged right up if they were caught bringing letters.

"Oh they were terrible times!

"At last there was talk of peace and a neighbor got a letter from her husband, and one inside for mother to tell her father was coming home."

Hannah's father arrived on Friday, September 13, 1783. But the little family did not have time to celebrate the occasion, for he said they must leave the farm at once. He read some sentences from the newspapers of a near-by town that called men like himself "abominable wretches, robbers, murderers and incendiaries."

"Let it be a crime abhorred by nature," he read, "to have any communications with them . . . they will carry their mark on their foreheads, let them be avoided like persons contaminated by the most deadly contagion and remain as their demeanor merits, as vagabonds on the face of the earth." And in another column of the paper he found a notice that said a boat was waiting at the mouth of the river that would take people away to a new country.

At once everybody had to start getting ready. Hannah's uncle came over. The two men killed the cow and sold the beef to another farmer. A neighbor cut off the tallow and took it home and made a sizable parcel of candles for the journey, putting in plenty of beeswax so that they would be hard and good. The uncle thrashed out twenty bushels of wheat and the grandmother, who had come over with him, made bags to hold it. Hannah and John helped pack a tub of butter and another of pickles and some bags of potatoes. By Monday night everything was ready for loading on the river sloop.

And then, on Tuesday, just as they were about to set out for the nearest landing a crowd of angry men gathered around the house. Some of them came in and shouted fiercely and took Hannah's father outside. Hannah's uncle stepped forward and promised that if they would let his brother stay with his family that night he would hand him over in the morning. The men paid no attention and took him away and Hannah cried all night. But in the morning her father returned. The men had decided to let him take his family out of the country.

Five wagons held all the household goods and provisions they took to the sloop. There were other sloops on the river and other grieving families in them. It was a sad last journey between the banks they all loved so well. Hannah was eleven years old when they left their home.

At the mouth of the river in New York harbor a big boat waited and very soon after the family had come aboard and stowed their belongings in the hold she was on her way north. Then came weeks of stormy weather. Many of the people going to the new country were very ill but no one died. Every few days, though, a new baby was born and all the families aboard tried to celebrate, but some of the older members looked sad.

The first snow of the northern winter was falling on the white tents provided for the boat's passengers by their new government when Hannah's father led his family ashore on the bank of a bleak river. They lived in the white tents for a few days, eating food which kind people brought to them and saving their bags of provisions. Then they rented a little boat and started up the river. It took nine days to reach the land that the government had given them and when they pitched their tent there they had been away from home just two months.

Then Hannah's father went up the bank and through the woods until he found a fresh spring. Hannah told about it later: "He stooped down and pulled away the fallen leaves that were thick over it, and tasted it; it was very good. So there he built his home."

One morning when Hannah and John waked up in the tent they saw their father wading through the drifts. He told them to call their mother and follow him through the trees. He picked up a wooden chest and started out and each one of the family picked up something useful and followed. He went so fast that they could not keep up but they were able to track him by his footprints in the snow. Soon they heard him pounding and they saw, through the woods, the gable end of their new house.

"There was no floor laid, no window, no chimney," Hannah said, "but we had a roof at last. A good fire

was blazing on the hearth and mother had a big loaf
of bread with us, and she boiled a kettle of water
and put a good piece of butter in a pewter bowl
to eat our breakfast that morning and mother said:
'Thank God we are no longer in dread of having shots
fired through our house. This is the sweetest meal I
have tasted for many a day.' "

Hannah's father said he would finish the house in
about a month. Then they could start the New Year
of 1784 in a fine Nova Scotia home and they would
come to love it and to forget the old farm beside the
Hudson.

14

Fireflies in the Rigging

THE big yachts that brought the Dutch across the Atlantic were unwieldy for navigable river waters. And so, while the Hudson was reflecting the glory of the spread sails of the *Bachelor's Delight* and the *Broken Heart*, the *Gilded Otter* and the *Spotted Cow*, the *Salt Mountain* and the *Seven Stars*, the *Good Bear* and the *Blue Rooster*, the *Glowing Oven* and the *Golden Shark*, the *Blind Ass* and the *Angel Gabriel*, water-wise boatmen on the shore were planning simpler craft for general river use. Out of their experience and shrewdness came the Hudson River sloop—a type that was to become known throughout the world and to dominate the river's traffic for two centuries.

The sloops the Dutch built were like their wives—well rounded in the bow and high aft. Their average length was about seventy feet, though ambitious masters in eager competition sometimes insisted on ninety or a hundred. At first sight the sloops seemed all mainsail. The mast was set well forward and the jib and topsail were small, while the big main sheet bellied out with more than a little bag from the long, heavy boom.

From these sturdy vessels the Dutch boatmen learned the ways of Hudson's "Great River of the Mountains." Through many a windy night they leaned on the heavy tillers, their eyes fixed on the points of

the high horizons where hill slopes end and stars begin.
White sails in the shadow of the Great Chip Rock
moved upriver while the moon rolled a salty tide
against mountain waters pouring down and cloud masses
to the north muttered grumbling protest. Through the
wide choppy waters of Tappan Zee the Dutch skippers
tacked with their eyes on the peak of Hook Mountain,
always so long in view that they dubbed it "Tedious
Hook." Then they scudded past Haverstraw, and
through the reach known as Sailmakers to the shining
curve of the Crescent. Above lay other reaches, Hoge's
and the high banks of Vorsen, Fisher's and the sweet-
smelling Clover with the long high wail of mountain
wildcats drifting over it. Then Bacerack, Playsier—the
almost endless waters of the Vast, and finally the jungle
banks of Hunter's.

Skippers learned to follow the tides as they glanced
off the bank at a bend and to go with them even across
midstream rather than sail shorter distances in straighter
lines and slower time. It was safer to anchor than to
lose ground when both wind and tide were set against
them. Voyages came to be measured by tides—"two
ebbs and a flood." When it was low water at Kingston
it was high water at the Hudson's mouth. The thunder-
storms and gushing brooks of spring could check the
northward rush of the moon tide forty miles below
Albany. They learned to take advantage of land breezes
that spring up off the Palisades even in weeks of summer
calm and blow a little while when the moon is waning
and dawnlight has not yet begun to grow. They found
out that in a southeaster the farther upriver they went
the stronger the wind blew. In a northeaster it was
better to begin reefing if Manhattan bound. Taking in

the topsail was generally enough of a compromise with a Hudson wind, but if it became very strong the mainsail was lowered a bit. Sudden squalls had to be watched for, too. These came strong enough to capsize any unprepared sloop when they came. But usually lowering the mainsail halfway and setting part of the jib would be a sufficient answer to wind and thunder.

Novices used to be afraid to watch an experienced skipper jibe—change his mainsail from one side to the other while running before the wind. It seemed suicidal, even after trimming down the sheet, to put the helm hard up and let her swing to an angle of forty-five degrees. The wind would hit the loose sail and send it across the deck, the heavy ninety-foot boom swinging as if it were a fishpole. The sail would go thundering over the taffrail, obviously about to yank the mast out by the roots when it fetched up. Calmly the skipper would hold the helm hard up, while letting the sheet run freely. Just as catastrophe seemed inevitable the sloop would have swung far enough around for the wind to catch the sail on the other side and blow it all aluff. Then the skipper would throw the helm hard over, and as gently as a disciplined pony the sloop would take to her course again. That trick had to be played "mighty careful," though. A latter-day sailor, Ben Hunt, tried it once when he was at the wheel of the sloop *James Coats*. When the mainsail came over the deck a loop in the sheet caught him around the neck and popped his head into the river without taking the rest of him along.

It did not take many trips upriver to convince a sloop skipper that he should wait in the lee of Thunder Mountain if a west wind was blowing, because it would be dead ahead once he had rounded the point into the

Race. When sloop commerce was at its height fifty sail might be waiting here, and when the wind changed or a flood tide came there would be a great fluttering of canvas as they came all together around Jones Point. Then thunderous curses echoed in the gateway of the Highlands as the sloops veered into the swift deep water of the Race, taking the wind from each other, running athwart their rivals' bows, bumping and scraping. An hour later, having passed Anthony's Nose at the end of the Race, they would be a dignified peaceful parade of shining white sails more than a mile long, all well on their way toward the safe waters of Newburgh Bay.

Soon after the Dutch came to the Hudson the sloops became the usual means of transport for the polyglot populations of Manhattan and Fort Orange and the occasional settlers between. David de Vries sailed his to Fort Orange and return in 1640 and several months after that he took it to the Tappan Zee to trade with the Indians. There he found that a government sloop had preceded him and was trying to collect a tax in corn from a group of spluttering redskins who advised him not to land.

Profane Jacob Klomp was the captain of the most generally used sloop between Fort Orange and New Amsterdam a few years later. He carried beaverskins and grain and lumber in cargoes so heavy that his vessel sat low in the water as she sailed downriver. On the return journey he sometimes brought hogs, butter, brandy. He had to pay a fine of 250 guilders for throwing in a generous portion of the last-named stimulant when he sold a kettle to the Indians of Catskill.

In 1654, as a result of a number of similar episodes,

all boatmen were forbidden by court order to sail from Fort Orange without permission and a rigid inspection of their vessels. In the same year the sloops of Klomp and Claes Thysz sailed to New Amsterdam bearing beaverskins and grain as the contribution of Fort Orange to the expenses of fortifying Manhattan. More than a score of years later, when the British had taken over the government of the river lands, Claes Lock's *Hester* had replaced Klomp's sloop as a favorite transport.

The Hollander boatmen were more skillful than the English and the language of most men who "followed the river" remained Dutch after English rule came, and for a considerable time after it had gone. Negro slaves, the Dutchmen discovered, easily adapted themselves to river life and it was not an unusual sight to see a sloop manned by blacks and commanded by a white captain— all carrying on loquaciously in excited Dutch.

As experienced builders and masters gradually improved on the early models, the sloops became gay boats. Dutch owners slapped vivid colors on them until they looked gaudier on the water than an Italian peasant's cart on its way to fiesta. Prettiest of all were the Nyack sloops—trim and fancy in gold and red and green and blue stripes—sailing palettes on the Hudson's mirror. Hudson River sailors have never held with flat sails. "Just don't hold the wind," they say. They have always loved to see the air at work—bellying the mainsail, keeping it rap-full when beating to windward. They have been wrong, as the yachtsmen of today know, but few sights could be lovelier than that of a river sloop with a bagful of wind, looking as if she might be lifted out of the water at any moment and become a many-colored magic carpet blowing down the channel between the mountains.

In the days before the big steamboats the packet sloops were roomy and had plenty of deck space. Passengers promenaded during the day, and on gala occasions danced to the music of fiddles under the stars. As the young republic grew and the river towns filled up, the stream was dotted with hundreds of sail day and night. Each town had its market sloops and on the way to New York the green of vegetables, the gold of hay and grain, the red of apples bobbed above the bright paint of the gunwales. In 1769, Albany claimed more than thirty such craft, each carrying four or five hundred barrels of flour on its eleven or twelve trips a year to New York.

The captains of these sloops were general agents for the whole town. They sold a farmer's produce in the city, bought him what he wished, and sailed back to deliver the purchases and the remaining money. They matched cloth for the housewives, took care of passengers young or old entrusted to them, hove to for a pleasant chat with the captain of a passing sloop when they felt like it. They sent ashore for milk to put in the tea or stopped so that passengers might take a walk and admire the "sublimity" of the river scenery. At the beginning of the Revolution they helped many a rebellious colonist and his family flee bag and baggage from the advancing British; at the end of the Revolution they piloted weeping Tory families downriver to the big boats which would take them to their new life in exile.

As more Yankee skippers took to the river at the beginning of the nineteenth century, new American

water lingo replaced the Dutch. Scholarly talk about
the moon's phases and their effect on the tides was soon
translated by the unlettered skippers into familiar idiom.
Apogee and perigee were easy for them. Flood tides were
weak when the moon hung far away "in the apple tree"
and were full when the moon hung near "in the pear
tree." They spoke of inexplicable "witch tides," so slow
that it seemed the moonlit brine was being held back
from its periodic race by some mysterious enchantment.
But cobwebs in the rigging were spell-breaking counter-
charms. Spider-spun traceries hung over the decks could
mean but one thing—a spanking breeze in the morning.

The Cruise of the *Experiment*

The Hudson River sloop waited to prove herself
all-time "queen of the world's singlestickers" until the
British armies had left the mouth of the big stream.
As the new nation's shipping began to seek far ports, a
wild dream grew in the minds of Captain Stewart Dean
of Albany and the owners of the 80-ton square-rigged
sloop *Experiment*. The captain was mighty proud of
the *Experiment*. Like the other captains of the river,
he had boasted that she could sail anywhere in the
world with himself to command and her crew to obey.
There were weeks of excited preparation while she lay
in her slip at Albany. Then one day in the autumn of
1785 tearful farewells were spoken at the foot of "The
Hill." Eight men and two boys, one black and one white,
saw the mainsail fill, felt the boat leap southward—
waved to the cheering crowd on the bank.

Through November and half of December the vessel lay at Murray's Wharf on Manhattan's edge while her dozen and more owners, the India Company of Experiment, met each Tuesday night to consume ever-increasing amounts of porter as they planned her great adventure. Thousands of pounds of ginseng were in her hold—they knew a land where ginseng was a treasure of high price. From up the river had come furs of many squirrels, of mink and foxes, muskrats and raccoons, a bearskin and four pelts of spotted fawns, and, for the wonder of people in a far land, the coats of three of those howling cats that had given the river mountains their name. More than four hundred gallons of Jamaica spirits went rolling up the gangplank and with them four fine casks of William Maxwell's best Scotch snuff. There was tar and turpentine, rosin and varnish to add to the pungent smell of the *Experiment* as she made ready to sail. On December eighteenth the *Experiment* cleared New York, and kept on south. "And so God send the good sloop to the desired Port in safety. Amen"—thus ended her bill of lading.

Word reached Albany in July that she had been reported at Antigua. After that there was a long silence. A year went by and another six months. The insurance companies that had refused to insure the boat congratulated themselves on their good judgment while they mourned her probable fate. Then on a late April day in 1787 a rumor ran about New York that sent all who heard it scurrying toward the North River wharves. The *Experiment* had been sighted. She was beating up the river at that very moment. A Hudson River sloop had sailed around the Horn, on through the Strait of Sunda, and still farther to the great Chinese city of Canton. She had been the first American craft to make a direct voyage from the United States to China, the second to reach Canton.

The big crowd cheered and waved as Captain Dean proudly gave orders to make her fast. Because he had commanded the *Enterprise* of the American Navy during the Revolution, he was in full uniform and had taken the liberty of uniforming his entire crew as well. A band was playing martial music and a boatswain's whistle was sounding as "with all the pomp and circumstance of war" six self-conscious men and two nonchalant little boys, Billy De Wever and Black-boy Prince, came ashore to be idolized. It was nothing, they said, smooth sailing all the way and not a day's sickness among the lot of them. The only real excitement had been that at some distant ports the people had mistaken the little *Experiment* for the tender of a fleet of men-of-war and had been frightened nearly out of their wits at the prospect of a bombardment. No, they had not been obliged to use any of the six carriage guns mounted on the sloop or any of the big collection of muskets, boarding pikes, and cutlasses they had taken along just "in case."

New York's *Empress of China,* first American ship to reach Canton, had been there when they arrived. While they lay at the Pagoda Anchorage of Whampoa, suburb of Canton, the *Truxton* of Philadelphia, the *Hope* of New York, and the *Grand Turk* of West Salem had come in. The harbor had been crowded with ships of England, Sweden, France, Holland, Spain, India, but the greatest harmony had pervaded the whole fleet, "all being ready to assist one another on every occasion." The *Experiment* had left Canton only four months and twelve days ago, and here they were.

And now perhaps some of the crowd would like to see the great chests of the finest bohea tea they had brought back, or hyson tea; or the eighty bales of striped yellow Nankeen silks; the incredible black taffetas and cinnamon-colored satins that all America was talking about; the thirty-one chests of exquisitely decorated porcelain, so beautiful that it had come to be known simply by the name of the place of its origin—China. Eagerly the New Yorkers trooped aboard. The *Experiment* and her crew were the wonder of the town.

A hundred and fifty miles upriver the homefolks went wild with joy. Captain Dean had brought great credit on Albany and that thankful town immediately named a water-front thoroughfare Dean Street, a title it still bears. He had given distant nations "an exalted conception of the enterprising spirit of the United States." Said the New York *Packet:* "The successful and safe return of Captain Dean has taught us that fancy oft times paints danger in much higher colours than is found really to exist and that by maintaining a spirit of enterprise, diligence, and activity we are enabled to surmount difficulties which on a cursory view are deemed fraught with dangers."

The captain sailed off to China seven times after that, but the *Experiment,* sold at auction to new owners, capitalized on her reputation by going back into regular New York-to-Albany passenger service. Hector St. John de Crèvecœur, Normandy-born farmer of Orange County, wrote an interesting reminiscence of a trip he took on her after her return from Canton. He said he and his companion chose the *Experiment* for their journey from New York to New Windsor because of "the beauty of its construction, the unusual size of its

cabin, and above all the expectation that the conversation of Captain Dean . . . would be very interesting."

The captain—who had evidently returned to the
command of the *Experiment*—told them that in all his
extraordinary voyages to Canton he did not make "a
piastre worth of repairs" and that "if the Chinese duty
at Canton had only required a sum in proportion to the
size of his sloop he would have made an advantageous
voyage."

He went on then, if Crèvecœur's memory is to be
trusted, to prove his conversation interesting by giving
a long stilted speech on the beauties of the Hudson and
to prophesy that "it is here that the rich, the idle and
the aged will come to find rest, freshness and health."

When the *Experiment* had entered the Highlands,
country of echoes, her skipper told Crèvecœur that
within the high hill walls the "wood-nymphs hear every
language and repeat with pleasure the songs of the
travellers." He said that once with the aid of his mega-
phone he had shouted out over the channel, "Hail, fair
wood-nymphs!" and that no less than seventeen of the
lovely forest creatures had answered, repeating his hail.

"With these words," wrote Crèvecœur, "the Captain shouted 'Hail, Passengers!' But the wind and the
noise made by the wake of the boat permitted us to
hear only the nearest wood-nymphs."

After the retreat cannon at West Point had sounded
and darkness had begun to dim the shore lines Captain
Dean took the passengers into the *Experiment*'s big
cabin, which was furnished and decorated in elaborate
Chinese style with many a memento of the great voyage,
all visible in the glimmering light of Chinese candles,
"each one inclosed in its glass bowl." On the wall hung

a big map of the Hudson drawn during the Revolution "under the surveillance and by the order of Washington." The captain said wistfully that he wanted to be a farmer. "I navigate only to become one some day," he said; and pointing out on the map the rich lands on the far side of the Catskills, he added that if he ever did he would prefer to live there, out of sight of the river.

At midnight underneath the moon the passengers of the *Experiment* were still trying out the echoes, making them repeat verses and songs. They heard great splashes "as if some giant, lodged on the top of the mountains, had thrown great rocks into the river."

"Those are sturgeons," said the captain, "which having jumped to a great height, fall back into the river. I am ignorant of the motive of such strange exercise."

After many years of voyaging Captain Dean retired to live on Arbor Hill in Albany, most honored of the old town's hearty sea dogs and a fitting predecessor to the tough upstate whalers and traders of the river ports. He was a very old man full of memories when he died.

Memory of Sloops

The voyage of the *Experiment* had immediate results. It popularized the Hudson River sloop as no other agency could have done. Hundreds of the single-stickers with big mainsails dotted the river throughout the first fifty years of the nineteenth century. Many of them were famous for their furnishings, their size, their achievements. Around 1795 Captain Andrew Brink

built the "very large and splendid" *Maria,* which for
many years carried passengers and cargo from Livingston Manor and the upriver towns. The *John Jay* was
her Poughkeepsie rival. Among the first of the distinguished upriver families to own their own sloop were
the De Windts who had made their money out of a
sugar plantation in the Virgin Islands. The *Caroline,*
named after the daughter who married the famous
landscape architect Andrew Jackson Downing, performed many errands for the new aristocracy of Fishkill. A trip to New York on a family sloop during the
social season was a greatly anticipated event and many
an upriver planter with a daughter saw to it that her
elegant conveyance "burned upon the water" like the
barge of Cleopatra. Fresh paint, new ropes, white sails
accompanied the Hudson heiress to the Manhattan marriage marts.

As the steamboats took more and more of the passenger trade, the sloops lost prestige and became freight
carriers. They bore to market Hudson River brick,
Rosendale cement, bluestone, hogs, and butter. Conservative travelers still used them as packets, however,
until late in the fifties, because bursting boilers continued to make steamboat travel perilous. As late as 1860
there were at least two hundred sloops on the river.
Those built early in the century were very sharp-
prowed, with deep keels and a considerable draught.
Many of the interiors were paneled in West Indian mahogany. The people of the valley remembered and loved
them long after the palatial steamboats had driven them
from the Hudson.

There was the *American Eagle,* swiftest in all Haverstraw, the lovely *Ariel,* and Cornwall's white-clad

Bride; the famous *Greene County Tanner* that later became a schooner, the slim *Huntress,* the *Jewel* and the *Linnet,* and New Hamburg's *Little Martha* with her black captain and crew of his two black brothers. From Peekskill came the wide-winged *Mohican,* fit rival to the *Mad Anthony,* the *Zenobia,* the *Rising Sun.* From Rondout sailed the *Phœbe Jane Minnerley* and from Lewisburg the *Flying Cloud.* The *Twilight* was a graceful sloop—no lovelier, though, than the *Ophelia.* The *Victorine* of Cold Spring was swiftest of the lot when she was new but not even she could show her heels to the sturdy old *Canaan* beating up the river in a northeast blow. "Old Horse" her captain called her because once she had felt a nor'easter in her bones she was mighty hard to blanket. Everybody knew the *Samsondale* and loved to pass her at night because Captain George Woolsey, standing at the tiller on the quarterdeck, lifted a rich baritone in sentimental melodies through the dark hours.

The Hudson sloops had experienced much before they left the river. Their skippers and their passengers had seen many things that once were beautiful and that, like the sloops themselves, have gone from the river now. They had seen clouds of pigeons so thick that the sunlight of a fair day had been shut out and the big shining surface had been turned to sullen gray. In the early days they had beheld the great autumn bushburnings when—to clear away the dead underbrush and make hunting and berrypicking easy—the Indians had set forest fires on both sides of the river and the sloops seemed to be drifting through the golden nave of a high cathedral pillared with towering flame. On some nights while they were scudding in mid-channel sailors saw by the black pine torches' flare Indians and whites hurling spears into the twisting flanks of leaping 200-pound sturgeon whose scales were aglitter with reflected light. Perhaps most beautiful of all were the quiet clear hours when the blue hills and bluer mountains of the twilight had been lost in darkness and a little breeze brought swirling clouds of fireflies to dart downward and give their evanescent imitations of the distant stars.

Young Peter Kalm, sensitive Swedish naturalist, on an American journey saw fireflies invade the dusk of crooked streets in Albany and dare to crowd into the open doors and windows of the Dutch river town. And once on a warm June night he lay on the deck of a packet sloop anchored just above "Danskammer" to see swarms of the little flying lamps descend upon the rigging, making each rope into a shimmering chain of light.

15

Rolling to Hyorky from the Catskill Shore

A SNOW-WHITE whale curvetting with its
brown mate in the swirling waters of the Hudson
startled the settlers of Fort Orange in the rainy spring
of 1647. A group of Dutch, Irish, Swedes, and Germans lined the banks, fearing the pale beast as an omen
of evil. Assurances of those "who had been to Green-
land" that the two visitors were natural sea dwellers
did not comfort them. Only when the dark one ran
aground on an island at the mouth of the Mohawk and
died, thereafter permeating the air for six miles in all
directions with an intolerable odor, would they accept a
realistic explanation of what they had seen. Then, with
practical thrift, they descended on the fat corpse and
broiled out of it a great quantity of oil, but not so much
as escaped them, for the whole surface of the river was
covered with grease for three weeks. This was the first
profitable whaling venture of the Hudson valley dwellers, but far from the last.

Although a "considerable large whale" made a tour
of Manhattan Island in October, 1773, making itself
visible in both boundary rivers, nobody seems to have
done anything about it. It was not until more than a
decade later that the packets and sloops of the Hudson
became accustomed to the stinkers of the whale trade
as they tacked up the reaches of the river bound for

home ports under the Catskills. In the spring of 1783, Seth and Tom Jenkins, brothers native to Nantucket, left Providence, Rhode Island, with $100,000 in their pockets. They wanted a practical place to locate seagoing folk: it was to be as suitable as Nantucket but less vulnerable. The constant threat of attack by the British Navy had caused islanders many a worrisome night during the past few years and the Jenkinses decided they would lie awake in their beds no more. They had a look at a possible site in Connecticut and almost bought the Henry Rutgers farm on the East River above New York. Colonel Rutgers wanted $200 more than their price and the brothers were willing to split the difference but the colonel was not, and so the searchers went up the Hudson. They liked Poughkeepsie and would have settled there had they not, with Yankee thoroughness, gone farther and seen Claverack Landing. Here was water for boats of any draught and here was a kindly Dutch settlement of busy farmers who needed seafaring neighbors to trade with for mutual profit.

In July Tom and Seth bought land at Claverack and went back to Nantucket. Seth brought his family to the new home almost immediately, arriving in early autumn with his wife, four children, and his mother-in-law. The next spring Tom and all the good New England salt-water folk he and his brother could convert sailed up the Hudson in a fleet unlike any the farmers along the shore had ever seen. The Yankees came in a parade of sturdy whalers that were ready, as soon as they had landed the score of families, to come about and set sail for the South Seas. And to make sure that the time would not be long before they did just that, their owners had brought with them, ready built, the frames of tall, new houses, Nantucket style, soon to stand so close to the placid river that high tide sometimes sent the bowsprit of a moored whale ship crashing through a window. Immediately after these Nantucket, New Bedford, Martha's Vineyard people had landed, they flaxed around and did things. Boats were sent downriver to fill their water casks, for it was already known that Esopus waters not only made the best ale but would not "rope" in the distasteful manner of most fresh water carried on long sea voyages. Then the voyagers left for Hyorky—their name for any far-distant shore—and the men who were left muckled right into building houses, a Quaker meetinghouse, a school, and more whalers. They changed the name of Claverack Landing to Hudson and in less than two years it was an incorporated city with a proud fleet of twenty-five sail on the high seas—more than the big city of New York could boast. The Hudson River whaling business was running before the wind.

Now the Jenkinses, the Paddocks and the Macys, the Bunkers and the Folgers and the Coffins, the same families that made Nantucket an island to be loved and respected, were prospering as they had hoped. Captain Robert Folger returned in the *Hudson* with a stinking cargo of sperm oil for the Jenkins candleworks. Captain Judah Paddock came back with another. Captain Pinkham scudded off to the Falklands after seals and returned with hundreds of hides and a tale of turtle eggs the size of a man's head and turtles so large no man could turn them over. Down off the ways just south of the town slid whaler after whaler—*Liberty, Volunteer* and *American Hero, Juno, Diana* and *Helvetia, Harriet, Huron* and *Namina, Martha Beaver* and *Uncle*

Toby—while the band played and cannon roared and everybody—school children, farmers, shopkeepers—cheered themselves hoarse between bites of old Mrs. Newberry's gingerbread. "Greasy luck!" they shouted to the proud captains waving from the decks as they started downriver on their search for whales. Captain Solomon Bunker came back in the *American Hero* with the largest sperm cargo ever brought into the United States. Let Nantucket match that!

The Dutch were doing their part too. At first the newcomers had thought them as odd as huckleberry chowder and made fun of their dialect. But as the store houses filled with ready cargoes of beef and pork and staves and leather and country harvest, the Yankees decided that they had better not try any cornstarch airs. These Dutch fellows understood everything that was said in English and then cooked up their shrewd deals among themselves, jabbering crazy language.

So Hudson grew. In 1790 it became an official seaport with customs officers and government seals, and in 1797 it lost to the upriver town of Albany by only one vote the honor of being the capital of New York State. Within five years it had recovered, however, for on the first day of March, 1802, twenty-eight hundred loaded sleighs entered the city and, as soon as the ice broke in the river, vessels began setting out southward at the rate of around fifteen a day. More boats had been added to the fleet—*Alex Mansfield, Eliza Barker, James Monroe,* and *Edward*. Tom Jenkins bought a gold-headed cane so that he could direct launchings better, and redheaded Squire Worth, who had come to the river country with Tom in 1784, had his portrait painted and scolded the artist for making him look "like a one-story house with the chimney afire."

Then when the young city was bowling along with a fair wind and an even keel a smear blew up. The British declared contraband any ships trading with France and her allies, and Napoleon replied that France would seize any ships entering or leaving a British port. Thomas Jefferson mixed up the whole business further with his embargo act forbidding all commerce with foreign countries.

So tar barrels hung over the mastheads of the Hudson whalers and traders to keep the wood from rotting. Business was struck with the dry wilt and the whole city of Hudson was sunk in the mollygrumps. The sea dogs of the Catskill shore might as well stay home and tend the kitchen halyards.

The War of 1812 did not help matters any—except that Hudsonians were glad they lived a hundred and twenty miles inland and not, like their Nantucket cousins, thirty miles out in an ocean infested by the British. Hudson was shrinking. Its once proudly boasted limits began to fit like a shirt on a handspike. The Bank of Hudson failed and there was no longer any stir along the wharves. Those farmers who had invested in shipping—and there were many—got no returns. For twenty-five years the upstate whaling trade lay becalmed.

But a man with Nantucket blood in him usually lands on his feet. Around 1830 Captain Laban Paddock, his brother Judah, and some of the other salt-water men decided they had been fooling around long enough and they would go back to whaling. They sent out some boats which returned with hundreds of barrels of oil in the holds. They sailed again, and more ships followed them. One came back with a cargo worth $80,000. That was having your gingerbread cut the right way, said the Paddocks. Hastily they and their associates organized the Hudson Whaling Company. There followed a decade of "greasy luck" and Hudson was a rich and busy city once more.

This time the town did not have the river's whaling trade to itself. Both Poughkeepsie and Newburgh had smelled rich cargo passing their wharves. Newburgh had a whaler on the way to the Pacific in 1832 before the Poughkeepsie Whaling Company was organized "for the purpose of engaging in the whale fisheries in the Atlantic and Pacific oceans and elsewhere and the manufacture of oil and spermacetti candles." Among the directors of the enterprise were the wealthy brewer, Matthew Vassar—who founded a college; euphoniously named Paraclete Potter, and Alexander J. Coffin (no whaling company could be complete without a Nantucketer). A crowd at the dock cheered lustily and a cannon, booming from a high rock overhead, made the echoes fly back and forth between the October-tinged banks of the Hudson, as the 300-ton *Vermont,* first Poughkeepsie whaler, set sail. Less than a month later the company had bought a second boat, the *Siroc,* and enthusiasm for the trade grew so rapidly that in the following spring Poughkeepsie and Troy businessmen incorporated a rival organization—the Dutchess Whaling Company.

The combined fleets of the four Hudson River companies soon numbered about thirty ships and great quantities of oil were returning to enrich the investors of the valley towns. Captain Norton of the *Vermont* was stabbed by a member of his crew and put ashore at Charles Island in the Galápagos Group where he died; the *Siroc* was wrecked at Valparaiso, Chile; Captain Glasby of the whale ship *Meteor* of Hudson got entangled in the line after harpooning a whale and was dragged overboard and drowned. But oil was still a golden flood along the river front.

More men were needed for crews, and many an upriver farm boy signed on for a voyage to the waters off Hyorky. A smart Harvard College boy named Richard Henry Dana, Jr., working his way on the brig *Pilgrim,* wrote in his journal of a two-year voyage that the *Pilgrim's* crew had sighted the Poughkeepsie whale ship *New England* off Patagonia and had been honored by a visit from her captain—six-foot, garrulous, Job Terry, "known in every port and by every vessel in the Pacific Ocean." While Terry spun a yarn that lasted through his entire visit, supercilious young Dana looked over the crew that had rowed their captain to the *Pilgrim* and reported them "a pretty raw set just out of the bush" who "hadn't got the hayseed out of their hair." One of them "seemed to care very little about the vessel, rigging or anything else, but went around looking at our livestock and leaned over the pig sty and said he wished he was back tending his father's pigs."

Generally the long-sparred Dutch farm boys made good sailors, though. They learned to eat potato scouse, salt horse, fu-fu, and dandy funk, and to sleep on a "donkey's breakfast" mattress. The Yankees could not fool them more than once by admonishing "Cast hot water and ashes to windward!" The new crew got a little nervous the first time a whale was raised, but it was not long before they could take a Nantucket sleigh ride behind a harpooned whale with the nonchalance of the best of them. On the lee days they carved out scrimshaw for their upriver sweethearts, and shouted "Thar she blows! Thar she white-waters! Thar goes flukes!" on the busy ones. When they returned they sneered at the frosted-cake, gilt-trimmed passenger steamers that passed them on the Hudson and laughed loudly when the villa dwellers on the banks lifted perfumed fingers to aristocratic noses as the whale stench came ashore.

The sailors and the captains and their landlubber employers had the time of their lives for ten years. Sails caught the wind on many seas, because now New York was offering the upriver whalers competition with her sturdy boats—*Autumn, Dawn, Hesper, White Oak, Desdemona, Shibboleth*—but there seemed to be enough business for all.

Then suddenly the bottom dropped out of the whale trade. The great panic of 1837 was much to blame, for all prices dropped to a low level and stayed there. Some of the captains said the upriver businessmen would not put enough money into the trade and that they were too stingy with their pay to officers and hands. The businessmen replied that the river towns were too distant from the whale produce markets and complained because their fleets were crippled for three months every winter when the river was frozen over. Modern inventions began to presage the end of the use of whale oil for illumination.

Whaling died out as a Hudson River industry—but the fascination of far shores remained. The dreamland of Hyorky and the vision of big profits marching in quick-time still enchanted the valley sea dogs. The whal-

ing captains turned traders and their boats knew distant
rivers—the Amazon, Congo and Manhissa, the Orinoco,
the Plate, and the little streams of the Mosquito Shore.
To Catskill, Athens, and New Baltimore, to Peekskill,
Hudson, and Poughkeepsie, to Newburgh, Kingston,
and Marlboro the sloops and schooners of the Hudson
brought rich cargo—ostrich feathers and elephant bone,
tortoise shell and ebony, gold dust, rum, and Spanish
dollars.

And with almost every voyage came a new tale of
adventure in Hyorky. Sometimes the captain wrote
down the story for his neighbors to marvel at. The
York State seamen apparently were a little more articulate than the New Englanders, for there are a number
of printed "narratives," probably more per capita than
the Yankees can boast. Newspaper accounts, taken from
the lips of survivors, provided other evidences of the
tough fiber and unflinching courage of the boys from
the river farms and towns. These melodramas of the
sea are still told beside the river, in the slatches of bright
spring weather before the sun gets too hot, by old men
who had them from their fathers and their grandfathers.
Not so long ago Hudson folks buried an old-timer who
remembered the fine solemn funeral of a young Hudson
naval lieutenant, whose body was brought to his home
town five years after he was killed fighting pirates of the
Windward Passage. And there are many men in the
valley today whose grandfathers recalled a taciturn old
man, Captain Benjamin Lawrence, who once commanded the whale ship *Huron* out of Hudson. When he
was only a boy he had been a boat steerer on the tragic
1819 voyage of the *Essex* out of Nantucket. Captain
Lawrence was so silent, they say, because most of the

time he couldn't forget the open boat, the starving and the thirsting, the day that Isaac Cole went mad and died, or the next day when they cooked and ate him.

These and many other Hudson River stories speak of strength and endurance. They tell of foreign places but they also have something to say about the kind of people who once lived in the valley.

Here is a group of them—one from each of four seaports along the Hudson.

1. The Flowered Tabinet

The Tale of the Wreck of the *Oswego* of Hudson and What Happened Afterward

Just a month before the nineteenth century began, the Quaker captain Judah Paddock interrupted his long series of whaling voyages by sailing from Hudson with the ship *Oswego*—bound for Cork with a cargo of flax-seed and staves. There were thirteen in the crew, and some have said that the unlucky number accounted for what happened. First mate Dan Hussey was from Nantucket and black Sam was from Philadelphia but most of the rest, including second mate John Clark, two young boys, one of whom was the captain's nephew Gorham Paddock and the other a Negro—Jack, were from Hudson or near by. The *Oswego*, 260 tons and four years old, was a fast sailer and the voyage to Ireland was so successful that Captain Paddock infringed upon his Quaker principles a bit by buying in Cork two gay pieces of flowered tabinet, one dark and one light, and each large enough to make his pretty young wife a dress. Light of heart, with many gold coins in his wallet and 1,200 Spanish dollars from the sale of his flaxseed hidden in the middle of a barrel of beef, the captain set out for the Cape Verde Islands to pick up a load of salt and skins and bring them to New York.

Then somehow things went wrong. Captain Judah's navigation reckoning turned out not to be worth a Hanna Cook, as Hudson sailors used to say, and it was no straight wake the *Oswego* plowed toward the Cape Verdes. On the dark night of April third the sudden cry of "Land ahead!" came almost at the same moment as the stunning jar which told everybody aboard that the *Oswego* had run aground. The hours seemed endless until daybreak and the terror of the crew was pitiful. Dawn came at last, showing the *Oswego* hopelessly wrecked near a sandy shore extending in a white plain far back to wrinkled barren mountains against the hot blue sky. Captain Paddock calculated, rightly this time, that this was the coast of South Barbary, and, recalling tales of American seamen enslaved by Arabs, advised against leaving the boat. He was finally persuaded, however, to go ashore and march his men toward Santa Cruz, which he reckoned a hundred and eighty miles away.

So the Quaker captain put on his best and set out, very brave in a new beaver hat, a "nearly new superfine broadcloth coat," silk vest, soft corduroy pantaloons, fine worsted stockings, and new half boots. In one pocket was his shiny gold watch and in another $600 in gold coins. In his hands were a spy glass, an umbrella, and a copper teakettle filled with water. One other property he still possessed. Jack, the black servant, while packing extra shirts for his master into his own knapsack discovered the two pieces of flower-covered tabinet and added them saying, "Master, my mistress shall wear those gowns yet."

By the end of two days the marchers realized that few of them could ever reach Santa Cruz, for many of the water bottles were broken and food was scarce. So Captain Paddock decided that he and his fellow towns-man John Clark would go on with the two black serv-ants and the rest would return to the *Oswego*. The four had gone only a short distance when they were cap-tured by a group of seven Arabs led by a short, old man whose copper color contrasted strongly with the white-ness of his short hair and long beard. The Arabs drove their captives back to the *Oswego* and made the rest of the crew prisoners. They left four of the Americans behind and began a long journey inland, driving the others ahead of them. Five days of almost incredible torture followed. Lashed on over long wastes of hot, glaring sands and up over the steep crags of stony mountains, their tongues dry and cracked from thirst, their bodies weak from hunger, the Americans became broken beggars, clinging to life for no reason that they knew. From the ninth to the fourteenth of April they staggered along in front of their captors with not more than four ounces of food apiece during the whole time and less than a quart of water—except for some grains of raw barley in a field and one long drink from a stagnant, stinking pond. Then they came upon a wandering Arab tribe.

At once the white-haired old man held a sale—shouting that his captives were "as good as any Christian dogs he had ever seen." Although the tribesmen dis-agreed, they looked at Judah Paddock and his country-men and bought them all except the Negroes. The white

slaves heard the black ones crying bitterly as the old
Arab and his companions drove them off into the desert.
Judah Paddock realized that he had seen his loyal Jack
for the last time and with him had gone the pieces of
flowered tabinet.

The eight Americans found themselves in a group
of about twenty men whose tribe was ruled by a sheik
named Ahomed. Three English boys also were slaves of
the group. Captain Paddock, having justifiably little
faith in the foreign influence of his own country, told
Ahomed through an interpreting English slave-boy that
he and his crew were British. He said that the English
consul at Santa Cruz would ransom them. Ahomed decided to try them out first at cutting grain but the
men were smart enough to be wasteful and inefficient.
Finally they refused to cut any longer and marched
from the field in a body, although the Arabs threatened
to shoot them if they did not halt. After that Ahomed
concluded that the men would be more profitable to him
if taken to Santa Cruz and ransomed. As they entered
the city after a week's march, hoping to find their freedom, one of the English boys said to the deeply moved
Judah Paddock, "Captain, the water runs off your face."

But their adventure was not quite over. There was
no English consul at Santa Cruz. So the governor kept
the men of the crew in the town while Ahomed and
Paddock rode on to Mogador. There his Majesty's consul
was generous and obliging. A ransom of $1,700 was
advanced at once and the Americans were free. Captain
Judah Paddock, after having been for six weeks a slave,
dressed himself in a suit of the consul's clothes and
allowed an English sailor to bathe and shave him. He

then looked in a mirror, seeing there "such ghastliness as I never saw in a body that had life and motion."

One day at the British consulate Paddock sat and listened with somewhat grim enjoyment to the story of how a group of Arabs had come upon the stranded *Oswego*. They divided up everything into equal parts, even to little equal piles of the ballast dirt. But several of them were knifed to death in the fight over the 1,200 Spanish dollars in the barrel of beef—and they had to divide the loot all over again.

As the story ended a wild Arab peddler entered the consulate, quickly opened his pack and began to show his wares. Spread before his eyes Captain Paddock saw the two pieces of flowered tabinet that Jack had carried so faithfully. He could scarcely restrain his tears.

While the captain looked on the consul and another English gentleman bought the pieces for two dollars. After he had told the story of Jack and his prophecy they begged to be allowed to give the cloth to him. Penniless, with Quaker integrity, he refused.

It did not take Captain Paddock long to reach his river home. The English consul arranged for him and the two young Hudson boys to sail for Lisbon. There Captain Herman of the *Perseverance* of Baltimore offered them free passage to the States. Once in Baltimore, Captain Paddock found a Nantucket Islander who was glad to lend him money enough to pay for the rest of the journey. The three stopped off in Washington to tell their story to Secretary of State John Marshall and urge him to reimburse the British for the ransom. From New York the boys and the stalwart captain took a river packet to Poughkeepsie and from Poughkeepsie they took a stage up the river road to their homes. On December 1, 1800, they climbed down into the arms of their families, after an absence of exactly a year. That evening Captain Judah Paddock unpacked the trunk which the English consul had given him; at the bottom, where his friend had hidden it, he found a piece of flowered tabinet, the light-colored piece. Eighteen years later when he wrote down his memory of the wreck of the *Oswego* and what happened afterward, he told of finding the gay cloth and presenting it to his wife. With proper Quaker pride in thrift, he said she "wears the gown at times to this day."

2. The Bloody Flag

The Capture of the *Combine* of Catskill by the Pirates of the Yucatán Channel

When Captain Jacob Dunham of Catskill was over seventy he and his one-man crew eased the heavy-laden coal sloop *First Consul* into a small slip at Poughkeepsie very early in the morning. Then he and his crew went to bed. Sometime later they were wakened by the cry, "Come out, come out! You're sinking!" They had to swim for it but they reached shore while the *First Consul* sank in thirty feet of water.

Captain Dunham felt that this experience was humiliating to an old salt who had been "rudely driven by winds and storms, captured by enemies, robbed by pirates," and so he sat down and wrote his reminiscences, ending them with the touching statement: "I have now brought my poor old sheer hulk to anchor in the harbor of Catskill."

The memoir proved that the captain had been an old hand at adventuring before the *First Consul* disappointed him. Twice he and his Catskill sloop had been captured when he tried to run the British blockade during the War of 1812 and each time he had talked himself out of a tight place. In 1816, with a Hudson River captain who had never been out of sight of land and two broken-down sailors, he had sailed the sloop *Biddle* to the Mosquito Shore where he had hobnobbed with that bloodthirsty pirate of educated and gentlemanly airs, Captain Mitchell, and with his elegant and genteel companion, Miss Sarah Taylor.

"I'll never die in peace until I've killed a hundred Spaniards," said the handsome dark captain.

"How many left to go?" asked laconic Dunham.

"Seventeen, by God. I've killed eighty-three so far with my own hands."

There was another bit of excitement in Captain Dunham's life when, in command of the former pirate ship *Allen*, "a small sharp-built schooner well fitted for the sea," he was pursued by a strange schooner in the Windward Passage.

Dunham's boat had been named after the brave young officer who had captured her at cost of his life from pirates in the Bay of Leguapo—Lieutenant William Howard Allen of Hudson, New York. With only a few men in an open boat of the navy gunboat *Alligator*, Lieutenant Allen had dared attack a fully manned 80-ton schooner flying the bloody flag of no quarter. Shot through the head and breast, Allen had lived to see the pirate vessel captured and five American boats rescued. According to Francis Adams, then representing the United States in Cuba, while Allen was dying "his conversation evinced a composure and firmness of mind and correctness of feeling."

When Dunham took command of the *Allen* he knew he had better not let her be retaken by her old owners. And so his state of mind was far from calm when, in the lee of Santo Domingo, a large vessel fired a 32-pound ball at the *Allen*. In Dunham's own words, it "struck the after leach of the mainsail, cut off the bolt rope and after-cloth of the sail and glancing downward struck the trunk deck [within six feet of the captain] and entered the cabin, passed through my bed and then followed the ceiling into the hold, cutting away the plank and three timbers, and landed in a bale of cotton." The shot proved the high point of the adventure, however, for the pursuer turned out to be English and the day ended for Dunham over a pot of cider in her cabin, with her captain exclaiming, British fashion, "Curse me if you ain't game."

Most exciting, however, of all the events of Captain Dunham's career happened in the spring of 1821 when he and his friend, the Catskill merchant Apollos Cooke, purchased the seventeen-year-old schooner *Combine* for a trading voyage to Haiti. The *Combine* sailed from the mouth of the Hudson on August tenth, and four weeks later was beating into the Haitian harbor at Jeremie. After one of his typical bargaining periods in which Dunham sometimes sold horses of the Hudson farm region to the Haitian president at $240 a horse, the *Combine* set out for Catskill. On October thirteenth, as Dunham was doubling Cape San Antonio in the Yucatán Passage, the *Combine* was suddenly the center of attention of three schooners, a sloop, and a large open boat. As they bore down on the helpless trader one of the schooners fired a shot across her bows and Captain Dunham had no choice but to heave to. A small boat put out from the largest schooner and its occupants were soon clambering aboard the *Combine*, dark men with fierce eyes who shouted Portuguese curses at their captives. Each carried a musket in his left hand, brandished a drawn cutlass in his right, and wore at his side a long knife and a short dagger. Beating Dunham and his crew with the broad sides of their cutlasses, the pirates forced them to work the *Combine* near to shore and anchor her. They told the trader captain in sign language that he and his men might go free if he would hand over his money. Dunham gave up $480 in gold and silver, all he had, and bade them keep their part of the bargain. Their answer was to bring the largest schooner alongside and to break out from her masthead the blood-red flag—signal of death.

With the point of a dagger already piercing the skin of his breast, Dunham insisted that he had no more money and pleaded with the pirates to let him and his crew depart as they had promised. The pirates replied by stripping the *Combine* of everything movable. Swarming aloft, they cut loose her squaresail, topsail, and topgallant. They even took her kitchen pans to their own galley and set the captive cook to working with them.

Dunham and his crew were driven into the forecastle of the pirate ship and the scuttle was closed. As the Americans sat there in semidarkness, they heard someone outside calling the name of the first mate. The scuttle opened and as that officer went out into the glaring sunlight men seized upon him. Once more locked in, the prisoners heard for seemingly interminable

moments the sound of the broad side of a cutlass cracking bare flesh. It stopped and there was a silence, then one
sharp command, "Fire!" and a ragged volley of shots.

"Heave him overboard!" came the same voice, and
they suddenly realized that it was speaking in English.

In the forecastle one of Dunham's sailors frantically felt about for his razor. "I'm damned if I'll be
murdered by them rascals," he said, but a pirate had
already stolen the razor.

"Seaman Brown," called the voice.

"I suppose I might as well die first as last, captain,"
said Seaman Brown, and he shook hands with Dunham
before he went out on the deck.

Again the group in the dark forecastle heard blows
—a silence—the cry "Fire!" and the voice saying
"Heave him overboard!"

"Captain Dunham," said the voice, and the commander of the *Combine* crawled out of the forecastle.

"Tell us where the rest of your money is or you'll
get what the others got."

"I have no more," said Dunham.

They forced him to stand within a chalk circle
that had been drawn on the deck while one of the
pirates beat him cruelly with the flat side of a cutlass.
When the blows stopped he saw standing a few feet
away two pirates with muskets aimed at him. At the
word "Fire!" they pulled the triggers and the explosions
from the guns almost deafened him. He looked down at
the deck for blood, believing that the shots had so
stunned him that he could feel nothing. As he did so
he felt the cutlass on his back again and heard the order
to go aft to the cabin. In the cabin he found the first
mate and Seaman Brown, badly bruised but otherwise

unharmed, and the motionless figure of his cook, un-conscious, perhaps dead. After cruel ordeals, other members of the crew joined them. Then all were ordered back aboard the *Combine* and told to get going. Captain Dunham hung what canvas he had left and set the course for Cuba. Trying to revive the cook, he discovered that the senseless fellow's state was due only to his having broached more than one of the demijohns in the pirate schooner's hold.

"Oh, captain," he said, suddenly waking from his stupor, "it was the best Jamaica rum you ever tasted."

3. The Roasted Captain

The Story of the Wreck of the Newburgh Trading Schooner *Colonel Crockett*

When Captain George Austin and first mate Daniel Wood returned to Newburgh on the whale ship *Portland* with an oil and bone cargo that sold for only $40,000 they decided that there was more money in the African trade than in whalers. They had made several successful voyages for the Newburgh Whaling Company on their ships *Portland* and *Illinois* and both men were very popular with the citizens of the river town. Obtaining financial aid for a trading voyage was easy for them.

Captain Austin and Mr. Wood fitted out a schooner named for a stout fellow, *Colonel Crockett,* and they hired a stout lot of Newburgh boys for crew. Among them were Robert McTurk and Robert Blainey, seamen; black John Fowler, cook; and young David Baker, cabin boy. Second mate David Reed they picked up in New York on their way out, and later at a foreign port they added seaman Charles Wilson. On June 20, 1839, they left Newburgh bound for Hyorky—wherever its waters might be. A year later they were off the coast of Africa, skimming past Elephant's Island into Delagoa Bay. Between the tropic banks of the Komati River they sailed a hundred miles among the crocodiles, and dropped anchor. They were soon trading with the natives, and the hold of the *Colonel Crockett* of Newburgh began to fill with ebony and ivory from the banks of the Tembi and the Umbelozi. When they had $30,000 worth of cargo Captain Austin ordered the anchor hoisted and the sail set for the home journey. Next day first mate Daniel Wood came down with a tropical fever. In a few hours most of the crew were glassy-eyed and dry-tongued, suffering fearful chills beneath the blazing African sun. Then, in the mouth of Delagoa Bay, with the open sea ahead, the *Colonel Crockett* slid to a sickening stop. She had run onto a sand bar. Captain Austin ordered his men into shallow water with ropes. Gasping, shaking, too weak even to stand, they could not haul the schooner off. Austin ordered the yawl lowered, and he and the strongest seamen tried to launch it in the pounding surf. If they could get out beyond the line of breakers they could reach a Portuguese settlement sixty miles away on the English River and summon aid. Again and again they took the little boat to meet the seething waves, until they could try no longer.

Captain Austin and second mate David Reed proposed then to walk overland through the jungle to the Portuguese. They decided that they would be safer if they went unarmed, for the natives on the shore might be provoked to attack them if they carried guns. But the natives seemed friendly enough. A number of them even went along to guide the two ship's officers to the English River. The party had covered thirty-five miles and African twilight was descending when, without warning, the savages attacked. A volley of spears brought both white men to the ground. Fortunately Reed, who had seen the treacherous motion of his assailants, had quickly turned his side toward them and most of the spears aimed at him struck him in the arm. One hit near his eye, however, and knocked him unconscious. He came to a few hours later, lying beside a big fire, and his captors were merrily carving the roasted body of the slain captain and eating it. The mate lay still, realizing that they thought him dead and were saving him for their next meal. When the cannibals, gorged with the feast, had fallen asleep he rose, tiptoed over them, and raced back toward the boat. Suffering terribly from his wounds, he reached the *Colonel Crockett* the next morning.

While he lay fighting for life, first mate Daniel Wood died of the fever, leaving Reed in command. Then Robert McTurk, Robert Blainey, and John Fowler died. Now, with the strength of desperation the few survivors tried again to launch the yawl. This time they succeeded. They sailed to the Portuguese settlement and told their story. Immediately the governor dispatched a boat to salvage the valuable cargo. In their eagerness the Portuguese loaded the boat too heavily and on the return trip it capsized with the loss of all aboard. This left only three members of the crew of the *Colonel Crockett* alive, and of these only one, cabin boy David Baker, had been of the group of Newburgh stalwarts who had set out from home at the beginning of the voyage. Charles Wilson and young David left Reed at Delagoa Bay to recover from his wounds. They were fortunate enough to get passage on the English iron steamer *Nemesis* from which they were later able to board a whale ship of Stonington, Connecticut. On the first of March, 1841, young David Baker walked up the steep little street that leads from the river wharf into Newburgh.

4. The Trampled Crucifix

The Tale of the Survivors of the Wreck of the Poughkeepsie Whale Ship *Lawrence*

On the night of May 28, 1846, the crew of the whaling ship *Lawrence* of Poughkeepsie felt the dread sudden grating that meant they had run on a hidden rock reef. Hurried calculations showed them to be three hundred miles east of the islands of Japan. All night long they manned the pumps while the water crept inexorably, inch by inch, into the hold. In the morning they divided their provisions and launched their three small boats in a rough sea. Then they set out on the long row to the Japanese coast. Gradually the crews lost sight of each other in the towering waves. To this day no one knows surely what happened to the captain's boat or that in charge of the first mate. In the boat commanded by second mate George Howe were three upstate seamen—the brothers Tom and Peter Williams and Henry Spencer, and the ship's carpenter,

Murphy Wells of Poughkeepsie. For a week, while their food and water diminished at frightening rate, the men rowed to the westward. Then came the overwhelming joy of the sight of land. It was short-lived, however, and followed by sudden despair, for as they dragged the boat up on the beach a horde of natives surrounded and overpowered them. Straightway they were thrust into a big wooden cage "similar to those used to exhibit wild beasts." Then began a life of such horror that it would seem their minds must give way. For eleven and a half months the men lived in the big cage, half starved, tortured by the curious stares of the natives who treated them like dangerous animals. One night after they had been in the cage so long that all hope of rescue seemed vain, Tom Williams could stand the monotony and hopelessness no longer. Despite his brother's frantic objections, he succeeded in bending the bars of the cage far enough apart to let him through. Then there was the long silent wait, the prayerful suspense, and in the morning the result that they all knew in their hearts was inevitable. Beaten and broken, Tom Williams was rushed back to the cage by a mob of natives who threw him in with angry cries. He slumped in a shapeless heap on the floor, bleeding from a deep gash on his forehead that no efforts of his companions could stanch. For six hours he lay there, crying out deliriously, and then he was quiet. In the late afternoon some Japanese came carrying a coffin. George Howe and Harry Spencer and Murphy Wells had to hold Peter Williams with all their strength when the natives lifted his brother's body into the box and took it away. The four companions never found out what was done with Tom.

More months went by. One day several men in

elaborate costume came to the cage to look at the captives. Later other men came and bound their arms and marched them down the coast. The sailors knew there was hope when they reached a group of houses inhabited by blond, big men who turned out to be Dutch settlers. Now they waited two more months in a Japanese prison. Then a Japanese official who spoke English informed them that they were to be beheaded because they were British and the Japanese hated the British.

"We are not British," said second mate George Howe. "We are Americans. We have fought and beaten the British."

The official seemed doubtful over that. Finally he said: "If you are Americans, what is your religion?"

"Christians," said George Howe stoutly.

The Japanese went away. After some time he returned with companions. One of them carried a wooden crucifix. He hurled it to the floor of their cell and said:

"We do not like Christians any more than we like the British. Since you are Americans, we will allow you your freedom on one condition—that you stamp upon this Christian idol. If you refuse you will be beheaded."

The four sailors debated for a while. They did not want to die. Finally George Howe said that since Christ had come into the world to save people he was sure that they would be forgiven if they stamped on the cross. And so, praying forgiveness, each one of them jumped upon the wooden figure and stamped it into the earthen floor of the prison.

A few days later Japanese guards marched the four York State sailors to a Dutch boat bound for Batavia, on the island of Java. There, in December of 1847, they were released. From Batavia they had to work their way home as best they could. In five years Murphy Wells, the Poughkeepsie carpenter, had got as far as the island of St. Helena. There he met and talked with Captain Baker of the bark *Eureka* of Canton. On his arrival at the port of New York around the middle of June, 1852, Baker dispatched to Poughkeepsie folks the news of the wreck of the *Lawrence* and the strange story of the later adventures of her crew.

No one knows whether any of the other three ever returned to his Hudson River home. No one knows surely what happened to the men in the other small boats that took them away from the *Lawrence* after it was wrecked that rough May morning in 1846. A few weeks ago a white woman, returned after fifteen years of residence on a South Sea island, told a legend that compels speculation. She said that to this day natives on various islands tell the tale, claiming that it happened on their own coast. They say that toward the middle of the last century swimmers saw a strange cratelike something bobbing up and down in the white surf. They brought it ashore and found it to be a cage with strong wooden bars. They saw inside it a water-decayed body which they assumed to be that of a large wild animal of the monkey variety. A Dutch trader told them that their animal was a white man.

16

River of Lost Dreams

As THE eighteenth century ended, the Hudson ran through a smiling, free land of peace to a flourishing free city. To the west lay lands of incalculable wealth, awaiting development. Now a man might take his wages, buy a farm, and in a land where the only ruler was the people become as independent as any foreign king. Though imperialistic Russia would not recognize a country devoted to the radical ideals of democracy, the experimental republic called the United States of America would get along.

The farmers who had fought under George Clinton for their homes in the Hudson valley exulted. Thousands of confiscated riverside acres that had belonged to Tories were to be divided and they were the boys to divide them. In the wave of patriotic fervor that swept the new nation there were probably few who realized that the men of small means who had counted on slices of Tory land were not getting them. The story of the holdings of the Tory De Lancey family is the story of most of the confiscated properties. Organized cliques of land speculators descended upon them and swallowed them. "Suffering no qualms of conscience in stripping the exiled James De Lancey of his possessions," writes Harry Yoshpe, a recent able historian of the period, "the Livingstons, the Gouverneurs, the

Roosevelts, the Beekmans, and other representatives of distinguished families contrived to get the bulk of the estate into their possession and remained for many years among the foremost in the social, political and business life of the new republic."

As the great land boom got under way the manor lords and their kin were ubiquitous—not only in the bargaining along the river, but in the land exploitation to the west. Refugees from the French Revolution, many of them of distinguished birth, were finding asylum in America and the river families found association with aristocrats both congenial and desirable. The Schuylers and Van Rensselaers were delighted to welcome to a valley farm the Marquis de La Tour du Pin and his beautiful and accomplished wife.

And Peter De Labigarre, who arrived on the Hudson in 1793, had by 1795 become husband to a Beekman old maid, brother-in-law to a Livingston, and entrepreneur of a scheme for establishing a model town on Livingston property. De Labigarre had apparently begun his American career as a merchant on Whitehall Street in New York City but the excitement of the land deals soon had him in its grip. He bought about one hundred and fifty acres on the east side of the river in two purchases from Robert R. Livingston, and collaborated with one Charles Balthazar and the distinguished French soldier and engraver, Julien Fevret de Saint-Memin, in making plans for a community to be called Tivoli. Two prints from Memin's copperplate of the plan still exist.

De Labigarre built his own home, the Château de Tivoli, on a beautiful site above the river. It was an imitation of a moat-surrounded French château with a high octagonal tower. There, during the years that his children—Amaryllis Laura, Julius Agricola, and Louisa Maria—were added to his family, he tried to make his dream of a river town materialize. Around the large central Zéphyre Square he grouped the streets named Chancellor (after the most important Livingston), Diana, Flora, Peace, Friendship, Plenty, Commerce, and Bargain. He planned a "Public Basin" and a "Pleasure Ground" with a circular drive at the north end of town bordering the river. Then he sold several lots, to people who began building homes, and waited for riches to flow in upon him. But something went wrong. Riches did not flow. By 1807 the Livingstons had foreclosed the mortgage, the Château de Tivoli had been sold to the staccato accompaniment of an auctioneer's hammer, and De Labigarre was dying in New Orleans a defeated man. A high brick wall, Memin's two prints, and two imported Empire urns on the gateposts of the estate now occupying the site of the château are the only visible evidences of the Frenchman's dream.

The Livingstons were not discouraged. They had witnessed the amazing success of the Nantucket Quakers in establishing the prosperous town of Hudson at Claverack Landing and they wanted to profit by similar processes. Three of them—Edward, Brockholst, and John—saw great possibilities in founding a rival city on the west bank, a city which would be a market for west-country produce and might eventually be a terminus for a great east-west canal which would give Great Lakes commerce an outlet into the Hudson. The metropolis might even, through its business importance, become the capital of the state. This was a greater dream than Tivoli. With swelling enthusiasm the Livingstons planned the city on the shores opposite Hudson, calling it Esperanza. They laid out along the river the great Esperanza Key which in visions they saw crowded with commerce of the seas. They offered lots 25 feet wide by 100 feet deep. They named the streets Liberty, Equality, Love, Happiness, Beer, Cider, Eliza, Mary Anne, Art, Science, Montgomery, and Livingston. They sold many lots. Houses sprang up. Business was brisk. And then the town of Athens sprang up beside Esperanza and eclipsed it. Today Esperanza is a lovely rural village that does not dream of big docks and crowded shipping and city streets.

Development and profits were not the only compelling ideas of the first years of the nineteenth century in the Hudson valley. Eastern America was teeming with creative thought. Prophets announced themselves and immediately disciples gathered about them. The movement of the idea frontier seems to have been from New England westward through the Mohawk valley. This would account for the progress of Shakers, Mormons, Spiritualists, Oneida Perfectionists, and some other advocates of unconventional practices. The Hudson was to have its share of earnest experiments, however.

By 1825 the ideas of Robert Owen, the English philanthropist and communist-reformer, had so fired the imaginations of people along the river that they had established on its banks at Haverstraw the Franklin Community, based on the same startling principles as those the Owenites had been trying to put into effect at New Harmony. On their jointly owned Rockland County acres the communists strove manfully to support themselves through farming and to live rationally, avoiding "absurd and irrational systems of religion— and marriage combined with some one of these irra- tional systems." They brought down upon themselves the wrath of neighboring Christian communities by their beliefs, by their adoption of a costume for the ladies "similar to that of an Indian" (the gown reaching to the knees with pantalettes on the legs), and by their gay recreations. "Ye who love the music of the stirring fife," wrote James M'Knight, a former member who had resigned in bitterness because he had been asked to work on Sunday, "ye who love to trip the 'light fan- tastic toe' and gamble away the hours which ought to be devoted to reflection and religious contemplation, go to the Franklin Community, there, undisturbed by thought, or religious melancholy, you may pass your evenings in threading the giddy mazes of the ball, and laugh at the stirrings of remorse, and the upbraidings of a guilty conscience."

The Franklin Community lasted less than six months, chiefly because its members found it difficult to resign their interest in personal property and to abol- ish the use of "mine and thine." When it broke up, some of its more seriously devoted members went upriver to Coxsackie to join another group of Owenites in estab- lishing a new community which they called the Forrest- ville Commonwealth. There were good names among them—Macy, Quimby, Dickinson, Fosdick, Weeks— but most of the visionaries who made up the several radically minded farm communities in America at the time preferred expounding their theories to plowing, milking, and building. "We wanted men and women who would be willing to live in simple habitations and on plain and simple diet and be contented with plain and simple clothing and who would work together for each other's good," said one of the Forrestville group. Apparently its members were incapable of living up to its program, for the commonwealth lasted but a year.

Aside from a Vegetarian Colony which was attempted at Highland, the only other early experiments in community living along the line of the Hudson came up the river to Ulster County in 1838. In the township of Wawarsing, some miles back of Kingston, eleven New York City Jews bought five hundred acres from the early settlers, and on a wild and barren plateau in the Shawangunk Mountains they established a colony which they hoped might become a new Jerusalem. They called their upriver refuge Sholam (Peace). With a bad example to profit by—Major Mordecai Noah's attempt to colonize Grand Island at Niagara Falls with Jews in 1825—they made their first practical efforts successful. They let contracts to an upstate builder to erect their houses, a store, two factories, a synagogue, a museum, and an art gallery, and before many months their community was ready for occupants.

When the settlers came up the Hudson to their new homes they seemed to their neighbors to be people of education and culture with belongings that proved them once to have been well-to-do. Possibly some of them were of Portuguese origin since there is a record of their appeal for aid to a synagogue of Portuguese Jews in New York. As soon as the colonists had arrived the new factories were put into operation and all went to work with characteristic racial enthusiasm. Perhaps here, they said, the ancient glory of their race might be revived.

One of the factories was given over to making quill pens. Big loads of goose quills were brought up from New York to Kingston on Hudson River barges and taken inland by wagons. At Sholam they were boiled in oil, scraped, split, separated into bunches of a dozen quills each, tied with bright red ribbons. Then they were sent back to New York.

The other factory made fur caps. The trappers of the Catskills found the Jews ready customers for the skins of wild beasts. Soon all the river towns and the towns to the west were invaded by distinguished-looking Jewish gentlemen in fur caps carrying packs filled with other caps and goose-quill pens. The peddlers were so successful that they soon added another line of goods. They sent their wives down the river to New York to buy secondhand clothes. These they brought back to Sholam and made over skillfully. Many an upriver lad's "new city-bought suit" was made possible by the re-tailoring and low prices of the Jews of Wawarsing.

Sholam had more vitality than the Franklin Community or the Forrestville Commonwealth. There were happy times when its residents felt that the new Zion might truly be in the river county of Ulster beside the Shawangunks. Visitors, many of them prospective customers, came to see the colony and to buy. They were cordially welcomed to a large reception room where they sipped tea and ate cakes and chatted with the colonists. After that little social ceremony was over they might mention the subject of trade.

For four years the Jews of Sholam worked to make their vision of a new home for thousands of their race a reality. Then they realized that they had failed. The profits of peddling goose quills, fur caps, and made-over

clothes were not enough to feed them, pay their traveling expenses, and pay off their mortgages. Sadly they
sold their lands and dispersed.

And so all the dreams that had been dreamed along
the Hudson of little democracies within the national
democracy proved false. There were no further important attempts at similar communities for nearly a hundred years. Then in the middle thirties of the twentieth
century a little black man who said his name was Major
Divine appeared in Kingston with a satchelful of paper
money and began buying lands on which to establish
"heavens" for his followers. "Father Divine" now holds
twenty-four properties along the Hudson—his last
purchase near Highland being a five-mile stretch of
river front just across from the residence of Franklin
D. Roosevelt, President of the United States.

The early nineteenth-century communists and
vegetarians and Jews failed to create their practical
utopias. The twentieth-century Negro whose many
thousands of followers believe he is God himself, may
have succeeded. Now the mid-Hudson west bank is a
refuge for earnest, pleasant black people who believe in
paying their debts, in avoiding alcohol, gambling and
other dissipations, and in trusting Father Divine to take
care of them. Forsaking their earthly names for those
the prophet has given them—Faithful, Joy, Reverence
—they say "Peace" to one another in greeting as they
walk happily about their Hudson River homes. No one
except Father Divine can tell how long these river
heavens will last, for no one except Father Divine, and
possibly not even he, knows exactly how they are fi-
nanced.

17

The People's Warrior

THOUGH the early nineteenth-century utopian democracies on the river failed of survival, democracy itself was not failing. George Clinton was fighting the fight of the people as well after the Revolution as he had before it. Federalist Alexander Hamilton had defeated him in his efforts to prevent state adoption without amendment of the federal constitution at the Poughkeepsie Convention in June of 1788, but the old war horse had just begun to fight against the dangerous aristocratic tendencies which he believed the younger man to represent.

He beat Hamilton's candidate for the governorship the next year and soon after his election Senator Rufus King reported him as having declared that since the Tory De Lancey party had been extinguished by the Revolution "all the great and opulent families were united in one Confederacy; that his politicks were to keep a constant eye to measure of this Combination, and thought the people should be on their guard." From 1795 to 1801 he had to suffer the humiliation of standing aside in political retirement while Federalist representatives of these families, John Jay and others, ruled the state. He still maintained political control of the democratic west bank of the Hudson, however, though the great estates and the Federalist towns of the east bank were against him.

He came out of his retirement in 1801 to defeat Hamilton's candidate—Manor Lord Stephen Van Rensselaer—with the support of Manor Lord Livingston and his family. Then, in 1804, at the end of his seventh term as governor he bought a river estate at Poughkeepsie and lived there the rest of his life.

His emotions must have been mixed when in July of the same year he heard the shocking news from Weehawken. There on a little level patch of grass above the Hudson his archenemy Hamilton had fallen in a duel with his former supporter turned renegade, Aaron Burr. The democratic ideal which George Clinton had unswervingly supported all his life lost two of its most dangerous foes that day. Hamilton lay dead and Burr's political power had been drilled by the same bullet.

Though he deplored these facts, George Clinton must have looked out over the river from his new home with satisfaction in the days that followed. His nephew, De Witt Clinton, would carry on his fight for the people. Already there was talk of his becoming governor. De Witt was a man of ideas. He would think of ways of helping the people of the Hudson valley.

18

Upriver in a Teakettle

WHEN his new steamboat rounded Kidd's Point and entered the windy channel between the Highlands, tall brown-eyed, curly-haired Robert Fulton began his favorite song:

> "Ye banks and braes o' bonny Doon,
> How can ye bloom sae fresh and fair?"

and the eight Livingston girls around him joined in, raising their soft voices in the misty mid-August afternoon:

> "How can ye chant, ye little birds?"

The three Livingston men, putting their heads close to the heads of pompous Dr. Samuel Latham Mitchill, learned Dr. McNeven, and the very English, very Reverend Dean of Ripon Cathedral, offered baritone support as Fulton swung into a high sweet tenor:

> "And I sae weary fu' of care!"

Above the loud splashing of the circling paddles that sometimes threw water aft and too close rose the tenuous melody of the love song:

> "Ye break my heart, ye little birds . . ."

Little Sarah Barker, whose father had kept in his warehouse for months the engine that was now performing so valiantly amidships, must have wondered as she sat on a plank across the stern of the boat, with her legs sticking straight out in front of her, why they sang so sad a song when they were so happy.

There could be no questioning the joy of all the singers. But happier than tiny big-eyed Sarah, happier than noble Mr. Fulton as he sang tenor and turned upon Harriet Livingston eyes "glorious with love and genius," happier than Harriet who delightedly returned the ardent gaze of her long-haired, broad-browed suitor, was that shrewd opportunist, Chancellor Robert R. Livingston of the state of New York.

A ride on a steamboat was no novelty to the volatile, redheaded chancellor. He knew that the idea had been in the air before the close of the Revolution. He knew that John Fitch—now sleeping in a suicide's grave in Kentucky—had been running a regular if profitless steam packet service on the Delaware with landings at Trenton, Bordentown, Bristol, Burlington, and Philadelphia seventeen years before, in 1790, when Fulton was painting miniatures. The chancellor had even ridden in a little steamer of John Fitch's on the Collect Pond in New York City in 1796, and in the same year Yankee Captain Morey in a steamboat of his own devising had taken him up the Hudson to Greenwich Village and back and obtained from him expression of "great satisfaction" in her performance. His brother-in-law, John Stevens, puttering with horticulture, real estate, and education at Castle Point, Hoboken, had found time to cooperate with his sons John and Robert in the building of a number of steamboats. The boys had run one of them, the *Little Juliana,* across the Hudson and back in May of 1804, using twin-screw propellers instead of paddles. Yet the chancellor chose to regard the maker of the boat on which he now rode, named *Clermont* for his Hudson River country home, as the inventor of the steamboat.

The distinguished gentleman's cheerful mood could be attributed to many causes. One of them was that before this present successful venture Nicholas Roosevelt, who had been associated with him, had lost interest in steamboating on the Hudson and had set his agile mind to considering other schemes—keeping only a negligible interest in the patent rights of Fulton's boat. Another was that John Stevens had refused an invitation to become a partner a year ago. To make the triumph of the Livingston family more complete, dear Dr. Mitchill, now being transported by the *Clermont,* had that very spring in his capacity of state senator secured repeal of the privilege previously granted by the state legislature to miserable, defeated John Fitch— that of making and operating the only boats "urged or impelled by the force of fire or steam" in all New York waters. And then the legislature had, with considerable ridicule of the practicability of steam travel, granted to the chancellor and his young partner the rights just revoked. Now Robert Fulton had had the brains to put together most of the good ideas that had already been used in other steamboats and had constructed a packet which, if properly handled, would make money. So would other packets like it. There was even more need for steamboats on western rivers than on the Hudson. The prospect opened by the steadily chugging paddles had no horizons. And the chancellor knew a secret. Fulton was to become a member of the family. The Pennsylvania farmer's son was to marry the daughter of Walter Livingston and Cornelia Schuyler—pretty, harp-playing, picture-painting Harriet. The chancellor was to give out the good news just before they left the boat at Clermont and then they would all go ashore for the betrothal feast.

Fed by the black cook, Richard Wilson, and attended by stewards both black and white, the joyful party whiled away the night of August seventeenth and enthusiastically expressed their delight when the chancellor made announcement of the engagement of Harriet and Robert a little before one o'clock the next day. While they refreshed themselves with wines and food that afternoon, Andrew Brink, once commander of the good sloop *Maria* and now captain of the steamboat *Clermont,* rowed across the river to fetch his wife so that he might keep his promise to "take her to Albany on a boat driven by a teakettle." "Toot" Fulton had not had to hire a whale to pull his boat after all, as Thomas Paine had once suggested. Whether the *Clermont* looked like a "backwoods sawmill mounted on a scow and set afire" or like a "monster moving on the waters defying the winds and tide, and breathing flames and smoke," the important idea was that she moved against the current at about five miles an hour. On realization of that fact in Albany next day, her Scottish chief engineer fittingly celebrated it by getting so drunk that he was discharged.

And when on her return trip Chancellor Livingston left her at Clermont Landing and, standing on his own pier, watched her dwindle from his sight downriver, he knew that at last, more than a score of years after a

steamboat had first been contrived, after fifteen steamboats had been built and operated on American waters
by eight different inventors, a sixteenth boat made by
Robert Fulton had established steam packet service under his control on the Hudson.

Both the chancellor and Robert Fulton died believing that their monopoly had many years to run,
Livingston in 1813 and Fulton two years later. While
the western rivers swarmed with bigger and better
steamboats the partners had so hampered the development of steam travel on the Hudson that they had not
even profited greatly themselves by the few boats they
had built. The price of a ticket was high and so was the
class of passengers. Travel on the *North River*—the
new name of the *Clermont*—during the next few years
was pleasant and socially charming. The Van Rensselaers, the Roosevelts, the Van Tassels, the Ten Eycks,
the Duers, the Brevoorts, the Stevenses, the Schuylers,
Matthew Vassar found travel by steamboat interesting
and convenient. For seventeen years after the first voyage of the *Clermont* the Livingstons continued on their
selfish way, still claiming feudal manor tribute from
the farmers on their vast holdings along the shore, and
squeezing monopoly tribute from any steamboat owner
who ran his vessel on Hudson water.

Through the willing legislature the Livingston interests claimed rights over the entire width of the Hudson to the line of the New Jersey shores. Vainly New
Jersey protested that she controlled the waters on her
side of mid-river. Finally, in the spring of 1811, encouraged by William Thornton, clerk of the Patent
Office in Washington, who was fully aware that Living-

ston and Fulton had not invented anything but were
with doubtful justice forcing every man who built a
steamboat to pay them royalties, an Albany company
built the *Hope* and the *Perseverance,* steam-propelled
vessels. Fulton complained bitterly of the "twenty-two
pirates who have clubbed their purses and copied my
boats and actually started my invention in opposition
to me." A few months later he had the satisfaction of
knowing that by order of the courts the two vessels had
been destroyed within sight of their despairing builders.

Eagerly expecting great profits, the monopolists
went ahead with the building of the *Car of Neptune,*
the *Firefly,* the *Paragon,* the *Lady Richmond.* After the
chancellor's death Fulton began supervising the building of the biggest and most elaborate Hudson steamer
yet contemplated and he gave it the name of his late
partner. Before it was completed Fulton, too, died. He
had lived but eight years after his first triumphant voyage and the monopoly he had fostered was allowing the
operation of only eight boats on the Hudson.

The Livingstons did not have things their own way
as long as they expected. Americans do not like monop-
olies. They never have. And so before long a typical
American monopoly fighter was raising hell on the
Hudson. A big towheaded, blue-eyed Dutchman with
all of a Dutchman's poetic gift for inspired profanity
was swaggering the decks of a little steamer called the
Mouse-of-the-Mountain and the *Mouse* was running
from Elizabethtown, New Jersey, straight through the
sacred waters of the Livingstons' Hudson to dock at
the Battery. The squawk of the monopoly was heard
all over the nation. Vainly it tried to get at the owner
of the audacious boat. He turned out to be a southern

gentleman of means, one Thomas Gibbons, who was living very comfortably outside of New York State's jurisdiction.

Meanwhile the *Mouse* was doing so well that her trade had outgrown her and the Dutch skipper was cursing the delay as hurrying builders made a bigger boat, the *Bellona*. By the time the *Bellona* was on the water her enemies were beside themselves. They dared not confiscate her when she landed at the Battery for fear New Jersey would seize one of their boats at a west-bank landing. So they procured a warrant for the arrest of the Dutchman, a Cornelius Van Derbilt, and sent officers down to the Battery to serve it. With cold blue eyes the skipper watched them come aboard. As soon as they were on their way to his cabin he went ashore. No one seemed to know just where he was when the officers asked for him. And no one seemed to have observed him return to the *Bellona* before she cast off unless he was the man who was seen to make a flying and successful leap for her afterdeck as she got under way. Daily for two whole months the officers descended upon the *Bellona*. Before that period was over the captain had wearied of his jumping and had built in the hold a secret closet with a sliding panel. There he rested while the deputies searched.

After a few weeks of this the lawyers for his enemies obtained writs against the whole crew for contempt of court in protecting the captain from lawful arrest. When the officers triumphantly hopped aboard from their picket boat, however, they found neither crew nor captain; only a lone young female stood at the wheel and guided the *Bellona* on her way. The wily captain had dropped his crew in New Jersey and had

himself kept things shipshape until the moment when
he was obliged to take to his secret closet. The deputies
had no writ for the girl and finally had to disembark
while the passengers laughed them down the ladder and
asked how they liked the new self-servicing boat.

When the deputies saw Captain Van Derbilt loiter-
ing conspicuously about the Battery on a bright Sunday
some days later they should have known that something
was up. Nevertheless, with cries of vengeful delight,
they fastened upon him and took him upriver to
answer to a contempt charge before the formidable
Chancellor Kent. There, while the chancellor lowered
in dignity over the proceedings, Cornelius Van Derbilt
produced a paper proving that on the Sunday he had
been arrested, and for that day only, he had hired himself to old D. D. Tompkins who held a proper license
from the monopoly. Out he went, a free man, while the
Livingston attorneys cringed under the lash of Kent's
tongue.

Van Derbilt's boss, Thomas Gibbons, was so pleased
with this exploit that he got the New Jersey legislature
to pass a law stating that any New York officer who
arrested a citizen of New Jersey for operating a steamboat against the monopoly was liable to see the inside of
a Jersey jail. Van Derbilt awaited his chance and when a
deputy strode aboard the *Bellona* to arrest him he suddenly cast off and set out for New Jersey, scaring the
kidnaped officer into panic-stricken protest.

By this time the whole country realized that the
place where the real battle between the people and the
monopoly would be fought was the United States Supreme Court. The case was entitled *Gibbons* v. *Ogden*,
but everybody knew the name Gibbons meant any plain

American who wanted to build a steamboat to carry
folks on New York waters, and the name Ogden meant
the monopoly because Ogden was a former governor
of New Jersey who held special permits from the Livingstons' North River Company.

Gibbons said there was just one man to get to
represent the rights of the people of the nation as a
whole and he got him. And so, when Chief Justice John
Marshall nibbed his quill pen, drew back the sleeves of
his gown, and nodded for the argument to begin, he
knew and the whole country knew that the city of
Washington was in for some real New Hampshire thunder. In those days there was no need to identify the
thickset lawyer with the Indian-black hair, the "fellow
with an eye as black as death and as heavy as a lion's—
and no lion in Africa ever had a voice like him." Let
Tom Oakley, attorney general of the state of New York,
show off his clear cold logic. And let his hotheaded,
silver-tongued helper—Thomas Addis Emmet—cry out,
"The happy and reflecting inhabitants of the States may
well ask themselves whether, next to the Constitutions
under which they live there is a single blessing they
enjoy from the art and labor of man greater than that
they have derived from the patronage of the State of
New York to Robert Fulton." Everybody except the
monopolists knew they were finished before they
started, licked by a "man with a mouth like a mastiff,
a brow like a mountain and eyes like burning anthracite." They were up against Daniel Webster, and Daniel
Webster was in his prime.

The New Hampshire roarer said years later that
his speeches in the "steamboat" case and the Dartmouth
College case were the best he ever made, and he named

the steamboat case first. There in the Supreme Court of the United States he stood and his deep rolling voice was like the eternal warning in the piled-up clouds that are mirrored in Hudson water. And above him sat John Marshall, the greatest of all the great chief justices the country has known, taking it in—Daniel Webster himself said so—"as a baby takes in its mother's milk."

There were rivermen on the Hudson that day who said the sky was inky and the water black until just about the time Daniel Webster way down there in Washington was saying a sentence that crackled like lightning: "The people of New York have a right to be protected against this monopoly." Then suddenly, the rivermen said, there was a sun in the sky and the water leaped and sparkled, because the great stream knew that once more it was free to all Americans. The river must have known what was in John Marshall's mind when Daniel Webster said that, for the decision upholding the argument came weeks later. The chief justice had taken his time just to be sure there was no mincing of words. It took no Philadelphia lawyer to interpret what he meant when he wrote that the state laws giving the monopoly exclusive privilege were "repugnant to the Constitution and laws of the United States."

At those words hundreds of hammers took up a rapid beat along the river from New York to Albany. There were going to be a lot of steamboats on the Hudson.

19

Never Was Mountain More Truly Portrayed

ALMOST every fair day of an autumn in the middle 1820's a delicate, melancholy, blue-eyed young man played on his flute in a forest mottled by the shadows of the Catskills. Before him an easel held a little canvas; beside him lay a palette and brushes. To travelers of the river road who were curious enough to seek the source of liquid echoes in the rocky glens above them he said in gentle British accents that he was Thomas Cole, an artist, and that after two years of peripatetic trading of flute solos and oil landscapes for bread he had at last found in the Hudson valley the subjects which, of all subjects in the world, he most wanted to paint. "From the moment when his eye first caught the rural beauties clustering around the cliffs of Weehawken," wrote the young man's biographer a few years later, "Cole's heart had been wandering in the Highlands and nestling in the bosom of the Catskills."

When the cold winds of approaching winter had begun to pierce the cloth table cover Thomas Cole's mother had given him in lieu of an overcoat on the day he set out from Steubenville, Ohio, a few years before, he folded his few belongings and plodded down the river to the big city at its mouth. New York was more than ready for the arrival of an artist with American

landscapes under his arm. Her merchants had been making money and they were feeling proud of themselves
and their country. America had the stuff, they proclaimed. America's crops were bigger, her mines richer,
her trees taller than those of other countries. America's
ships had stormed the seven seas, their skippers sailing
rings around the foreign captains. The men on her
frontiers were rough and tough. They could lick their
weight in wildcats and they were the bravest in the
world except the honest, roaring, bully-boys of her
city wharves and streets.

Less sure of supremacy in the lists of culture, the
New Yorkers who might be expected to champion it,
the prosperous bourgeois merchants with social pretensions, shouted very loudly. They quoted the great
French painter, David, who asked, "Why are all the best
English painters American?" and they pridefully
pointed to Benjamin West, Washington Allston, and to
two famous resident New Yorkers—William Dunlap
and Colonel John Trumbull. But from the only important painter their own river valley had produced,
poor John Vanderlyn, Kingston born and Kingston
bred, they turned self-consciously away. They had seen
his nude "Ariadne" and they wanted it known that
Americans yielded to no refined foreign society in their
abhorrence of painting neither elegant nor sublime.

And so when pale, religious, wavy-haired Thomas
Cole appeared in New York with his careful reproductions of Catskill scenery, the patriots cheered again.
Americans yielded to no refined foreign society in their
country, they boasted. The Hudson, barring a regrettable lack of castle and ruins, was more beautiful than
the Rhine. Crotchety old Colonel Trumbull bought one

of Cole's landscapes for $25. So did famous William Dunlap. Indeed, that artist was so impressed by the idea of displaying reproductions of Hudson scenery that he spent the next year inventing and exploiting his "Eidophusicon, or Moving Diorama." While a lecturer delivered an accompanying travelogue, this first of American moving-picture machines showed the entire Hudson valley painted on rolling sheets, two hundred and fifty thousand square feet of canvas, that gave the spectator the illusion of traveling on the water.

A painter introduced under such auspices could not fail. At once genteel, shrewd Philip Hone, remembering his early training as an auctioneer, offered to buy the Cole landscapes from the painters who had purchased them and he got them for $125. (A quarter of a century later, on being informed of Cole's death, he exulted in his rightness of taste.) Other patrons, eager to see the breath-taking beauty of America's "Great River of the Mountains" transferred to canvas, presented themselves. English-born Mr. Cole, who had been before his sojourn in Ohio a Liverpool wood engraver, became in a few months one of America's most noted artists.

"The painter of American scenery has indeed privileges superior to any other," Cole wrote. "All nature is here new to art," and he rejoiced in stern Catskill peaks "never beheld by Claude and Salvator, nor subjected to the canvas by the innumerable dabblers in paint of all past time." He did not realize, not even when his friend, Asher B. Durand, a skillful engraver brought up on the Jersey side of the Hudson, "attacked" a landscape, that he was sounding the keynote of a movement which was to establish the only "art school" America has ever harbored.

The representatives of America's new nineteenth-century culture divided the arts with a glib and firm didacticism into adjectival categories. Portrait painting they considered a matter between the patron-subject and the artist, involving justifiable personal vanity, but they spoke with offhand assurance of two other classifications in the art of painting—the historical and the landscape. They had a preference for the former, basing it on canvases like West's "The Death of Wolfe" and Trumbull's "The Battle of Bunker Hill." "It is usual to rank landscape as a lower branch of the art, below the historical," wrote Cole, and it was soon evident that he and Durand and the artists who were following their lead were determined to reverse this judgment. For a half century they succeeded. No sooner had these two founders of the Hudson River school expressed themselves than the woods were literally full of artists. Studios sprang up along the length of the river. Earnest, bearded young men set out in twos and threes on long walking tours. Stopping for days at a time to put semblances of the Hudson's scenery on canvas, they sometimes aroused the antagonism of armed, masked, calico-robed farmers who suspected them of being in some way in league with the hated manor lords. On the big stream's banks during the next years sat the easels of Albert Bierstadt, John Kensett, Worthington Whittredge, John Casilear, Sandford Gifford, J. F. Cropsey, Frederic E. Church, Thomas Moran, John Bristol, Jervis McEntee. They were an unorganized group brought together in the beautiful valley by mutual interests, and all culture-loving Americans took them to their hearts.

At once the well-to-do began to buy the canvases, priding themselves on the prices they paid for them. No group of artists ever fared better materially. Few homes that claimed culture and means were without at least one Hudson River scene. Americans were fairly bursting with pride over the big river. Those who could not afford to own even the cheaper canvases of the school found consolation in purchasing the charming prints of Disturnell and later of the spirited and beautiful Currier and Ives Hudson River Series. Having discovered that the landscapes of Cole, Wall, and others could be transferred in blues or reds to china dishes, American housewives kept English potteries busy manufacturing plates, bowls, cups and saucers on which were stamped the Pine Orchard House, Jessup's Landing, Military School at West Point, Iron Works at Saugerties, Albany Theatre, Hope Mill, Entrance of the Erie Canal into the Hudson, A Pass in the Catskills, View from the Ruggles House at Newburgh, Little Falls at Luzerne, and hundreds of other scenes that gave American eaters glimpses three times a day of the glories of the Hudson.

The principles upon which the Hudson River School of Painters based their work were simple. Eagerly they acclaimed the "noble subject." To them the most beautiful objects in the world were the blue Catskill crests at ruddy twilight, the dramatic pines on their misty slopes, the wide glimmering river at their feet. But the beauty of these natural things was not its own excuse for being. It inspired man's noblest thoughts, as their American friend, William Cullen Bryant, and his English contemporary, William Wordsworth, kept repeating in their verses. Let the painters, then, reproduce on canvas as nearly as possible the images of the Almighty's greatest handiworks and they would create "great moral impressions." To do this was the end of all good painting. Just as the good, bearded Bryant could not in his verses let a wild duck disappear into such a sunset sky as they loved to paint without pointing a moral lesson, they could not depict a mountain without feeling that, if the work was successful, whoever looked upon it would feel awed and humble in the presence of divine sublimity. And so with reverent hearts they chose to paint rocky glens and lofty crests, streams plunging through wild forests, crystal lakes mirroring the tragic gestures of dead trees.

The world-felt spell of the romantic movement was upon these painters but the most important individual influences were those of the already named European painters, Claude Lorraine and Salvator Rosa. With characteristic passion for generalization and category Cole announced that he had discovered "the law of congruity in nature" and associated it with these artists. "When the region is one of savage character," he wrote, "the trees in their predominant traits correspond; in places where the aspects of nature are more gentle then the expression of the woods is soft and pleasing and the general outline of the trees graceful and beautiful." With Salvator's dramatic and gloomy glens Cole identified the first section of his law, to Claude's classicism and his serenity of trees and skies he related the second. Only a few years after he had pronounced the dictum the inevitable adjectives had been affixed and Andrew Jackson Downing, the Hudson valley's most distinguished landscape gardener, was dividing his own art into two parts—the Picturesque as illustrated by

Salvator, the Beautiful as influenced by Claude. Though Cole carried his admiration of the latter artist to the extent of arranging to live in his house while visiting Rome, he believed himself more capable in the field dominated by Salvator. "I believe I am best in the stormy and wild," he wrote, and his belief found utterance in paintings that gave expression to the romantic spirit which Sir Walter Scott's novels of dark heaths, rocky ravines, frowning castles were creating abroad and James Fenimore Cooper's tales of wild American background were spreading at home.

Since Nature was herself the greatest artist, producing effects that inspired noble contemplation, the Hudson River painters displayed great indifference to formerly accepted ideas on composition. All one needed was a point of view, a place of vantage for his easel, and the natural scene spread in a wide panorama before the eyes supplied the arrangement. By 1847 critic Tuckerman, who had established himself as the group's most ardent champion, was writing condescendingly: "Time was when a landscape was painted by a kind of mathematical formula; rules of composition, far more than observation of fact, formed the basis of the work; one side must be higher than the other, here must be light, there shade; and academic precedent fairly usurped this most unconventional branch of art." For interesting variations the Hudson's painters, like today's photographers, sought new subjects or a different point of view. They knew that once the Hudson's scenic possibilities had been exhausted, varied material lay beyond it, lavishly displayed in other American rivers, lakes, and forests, "each possessing characteristic traits of beauty and all cast in a grander mould and wearing a fresher aspect than in any other civilized land." The important principle was to stick close to nature. "You say Mr.— has failed in his compositions," wrote Cole to a friend; "perhaps the reason may be easily found—that he has painted from himself instead of recurring to those scenes of nature which formerly he imitated with such great success." The true painter could afford to take no liberties with the great natural phenomenon which was his mighty theme. He must suit the canvas to the subject instead of making the subject fit the canvas. Since the subject was grandiose, canvases were usually large. Mr. P. G. Stuyvesant, ordering two pictures from Cole, said that as he "preferred having something very valuable" he would like to have "two pictures of the size of Mr. Van Rensselaer's." An architect, dissatisfied with a canvas Cole sent him, demanded in its place another composed of "rich and various landscape, history, architecture of different styles and ages, etc., or ancient or modern Athens." Tuckerman in ecstatic admiration of a picture by Cole's disciple, Church, wrote that "four or five pictures might easily be cut out of this one."

The Hudson River painters were almost incredibly skillful. Since the aim was to create as nearly as possible the illusion of looking upon the subject itself, they applied themselves with all diligence and talent to portrayals "so true and natural as to win ardent praise of the most scientific and artistic lovers of nature." The leaves of the Catskill trees seemed so real that they might be plucked. Kensett's literal minuteness won even the admiration of England's Pre-Raphaelites, who yielded to none in insistence upon accuracy of detail. Critics recommended that those who wished to enjoy Church's "A View of Niagara Falls" to the utmost should provide themselves with a long tube to be held on a level with the eye, stating that the picture, when gazed upon through this device, established a complete and perfectly satisfactory illusion even to persons who had actually seen the real falls.

In their efforts to create just such illusions the painters took their big canvases directly to the spot where the views they wished to duplicate could be observed, and painted them outdoors. This occasioned patient waiting for approximately the same dramatic light that had shone on the day a painting of a storm in the Catskills or a sunset in the Highlands had been begun. They made efforts, too, to catch in paint something of the quality of the summer mists that hang above and about the river.

All the painters were seeking almost the same subjects. George Inness, who began with them and soon broke away, ridiculed in his later years the type formula of the school, speaking in exasperation of the inevitable and everlasting "foreground plant" on which the artist might exhibit all of his startling virtuosity. Anyone who has studied the school comes to look for this, and he may well admire the careful delineation of the different trees, the silvery birches, dark hemlocks, gnarled chestnuts, the amazingly true representations of white lichens on the gray rocks. Beyond the foreground plant in a typical picture, a panorama of vast extent and realism stretches far away.

As the years moved on, Thomas Cole found that the limitations he and Durand had at first set for their work could no longer contain him. His sensitive soul, expressing itself sometimes in mystic poetry as well

WHITE CLOUDS RIDE ON SOFT AIR . . .

SILVER-BACKED SHAD ARE RUNNING

as in paint, compelled him to transcend realism and
to impose on his natural backgrounds emphatic evidence of his great moral purposes. Durand continued on
his meticulous way and with him went Casilear, Cropsey, Kensett, Whittredge, and others. They believed
that their exact depictions of nature were enough, that
if an artist painted "not in the spirit of a mere copyist
but as a lover and worshipper of his subject" his work
might become not imitation but a vehicle of moral
instruction. Cole's nature was too creatively inspired
to stop here. And so, though he painted the Catskills
with as much care for perfection of detail as ever, he
could not see a beetling summit without wishing to show
upon its painted image a ruined palace to prove that
life is transitory, glory fleeting. As poor Charles Fenno
Hoffman, a poet crippled in boyhood by being crushed
between a river steamboat and a wharf, consoled the
valley dwellers in his "Moonlight on the Hudson":

> What though no cloister grey nor ivied column
> Along these cliffs their sombre ruins rear?

so Cole consoled them by painting into his reproductions of the Hudson's banks false evidences of human
antiquity. In the spring of 1838 he was working on a
picture whose subject could equally well have been
chosen by almost any of the painters he influenced.
From a craggy promontory, gaunt above still waters,
rose a tumbled, solitary tower. About it birds were
flying in the light of a pale, new-risen moon. A few
high clouds caught ruddy light from rays of the de-
parted sun. Standing lonely on the shore, a shepherd
looked out over the gleaming liquid surface.

Such sentimental conceptions were part of the general attitude of mind among the cultured folk of the valley in the middle years of the century. It became so strong that, two years after Cole's picture was painted, John Church Cruger tried to create in real materials on his magnificent island estate just such an atmosphere by building stone arches—still standing—in imitation of a time-broken ruin and settling weird Mayan figures in them. For eighty years these carved limestone figures, gifts of the American explorer, John Lloyd Stephens, who had found them in Yucatan, kept their vigil over Hudson waters.

The Clews family at Hyde Park emulated the Crugers by building at a high point over the Hudson a ruined arch. Still further to solace the mourners for romantic man-made scenery on the river, the great actor, Edwin Forrest, built at Riverdale in 1838 a castle which combined "the best features of both Norman and Gothic design." The Cunninghams built another. The Stevenses lived in a castle at Hoboken. Only the growth of enthusiasm for the pillared Greek revival houses and the fancy Italian "villas" saved the Hudson from being one vast stage-set in emulation of the Rhine.

"The Fine Arts," Cole wrote, "are an imitation of the Creative Power." And so, with the teachings of Christianity in his mind he planned his first series of big paintings entitled *The Course of Empire*. From Catskill he wrote to Durand asking his friend to send him by the next sloop a rearing plaster horse or a fighting gladiator, a ramping lion "or a roaring one" to become figures in the vast landscapes which should tell how vain is earthly pomp and human ambition. During the days when the studios of the Hudson River school

dotted the banks of the Hudson, from Bierstadt's, overlooking the Tappan Zee and the Palisades, to Durand's
at Newburgh—to which Cole objected as having "little
rich forest scenery near . . . and as for mountains,
where are the Catskills?"—on up to Cole's and Church's
near Catskill, many a sloop bore picturesque plaster
freight to the nearest landings. The five paintings de-
picted the progress of human power from early idyllic
savagery through great civilized days of triumph to
decadence, destruction, and a final melancholy night
in which one may see by the light of the moon a solitary heron nesting on a crumbling column beside a
tranquil ocean. When the series was done, America
was prouder than ever of her native culture. James
Fenimore Cooper hailed it as "one of the noblest
works of art that has ever been wrought" and he went
on to say that the day would come when it would command a price of fifty thousand dollars. Encouraged,
Cole went on to other like mystical conceptions, leaving
Durand and his followers to "mere description of wild
nature" while he painted pictures poetically expressive
of himself.

Gradually, however, the Hudson became a story too
often told by the painters on its banks. Cole had painted
most of the valley scenes that appealed to him. He had
made a journey to the river's headwaters "in search of
the picturesque" and had even betrayed his first love
by traveling across the state in order to paint parts
of the valley of the Genesee into another series, *The
Voyage of Life*. New Hampshire's White Mountains
lured many members of the school to snowy peaks.
Some looked for material farther away among the natural glories of the European Alps. A few even joined

the expeditions of the western explorers that they might paint for the first time the great American West. While Bierstadt was busy on vast works like "The Domes of the Yo Semite" and "Storm in the Rockies," Church was traveling over the world seeking subjects worthy of his tremendous canvases—"The Heart of the Andes," "Cotopaxi," "The Icebergs."

Cole died in 1848. He was only forty-seven and at the height of his popularity. He had found the broad Hudson kindly, despite one early experience: an up-river patron had taken him to his home, humiliated him at table and nearly froze him in a cold studio. The river families—the Van Rensselaers, the Verplancks, the Wards, the Hones, the Coldens and many others—had paid generous prices for his paintings. Yet he some-how suspected that he had failed. "I am content with nature; would that I were with art," he said, and he wrote to a friend, "I am not the painter I should have been, had there been a higher taste."

Durand lived to be an old man; he saw attitudes change and the young artists laughing, as they always do, at the old. Before he died in 1886, the naïve con-ceit of the new America, which had given his work and Cole's its impetus in the eagle-screaming days of the thirties, had been lost in the disillusioning years of Civil War and its sad aftermath. He saw painters who had been born on his loved Hudson, George Inness at Newburgh, Homer Martin at Albany, begin to paint "from themselves," scorning his careful, painstaking realism and shaping their materials into synthetic ar-rangements to suit their own ideas of composition. He saw them forsake the monotonous browns, with which many of the Hudson River school had painted shadows, and abandon the satinlike final surface which he and his fellows had thought essential to an elegant and finished work of art. He saw them strike out boldly with colors which they admitted they had not tried to make identical with those their eyes beheld. Like Cole, Durand felt misgivings and wished that when he was young he had had the opportunities and advantages painters were now enjoying. But he remembered happily the fellowship of the other Hudson River painters, the walks with poet Bryant in the Stevens private park, "Elysian Fields," on the river's bank at Hoboken, the long excursions afoot in the wooded Catskills with Casilear and later with Kensett and Cranch and other young admirers, and he was content.

The love of the grandiose paintings of the Hudson River school died out gradually. It was still alive in the eighties and nineties but it was weak before newer and stronger ideas. The big canvases had a long heyday of nearly a half century. Some of them are now to be found in New York City public buildings—the new home of the New York Historical Society, the Brooklyn Museum, the Metropolitan Museum of Art, the New York Public Library. Many lie forgotten in the attics and auction rooms of America. For gradually intimacies defeated mighty austerities, poetic reveries routed exact illusions. The light that had revealed steep cliffs and august hills as language translatable by the artists of America withdrew.

20

The Marriage of the Waters

THE *Seneca Chief*, elegant packet, moved from Lake Erie into the new canal, "Hellespont of the West," at ten o'clock on Wednesday morning, October 26, 1825. At once a battery five hundred miles long began to fire. The gunners of Rochester heard a booming in the west and pulled their lanyards. The Syracuse cannoneers sent the sound echoing over the hills to Utica. The valley of the Mohawk gave it channel toward Albany. Spurts of white smoke crowned the high promontories of the Hudson, and the Catskills resounded with sharp explosions. Man-made thunder shattered against the columned walls of the Palisades. The first message ever carried on sound waves from Buffalo to New York had arrived in eighty-one minutes. The answer was back in Buffalo eighty minutes later. The whole state knew that by a new channel Erie water was running to the sea.

"Who comes there?" shouted the captain of *Young Lion of the West,* waiting beside the stone aqueduct at Rochester.

"Your brothers from the West on the waters of the Great Lakes."

"By what means have they been diverted so far from their natural course?"

"Through the channel of the great Erie Canal."

"By whose authority and by whom was a work of such magnitude accomplished?" called the catechizer.

"By the authority and by the enterprise of the people of the State of New York."

With that the whole valley of the Genesee shook with the cheering of crowds and the salute of guns and the explosion of fireworks.

Then the *Young Lion of the West,* with its cargo of two eagles and two wolves, a fawn and a fox and four raccoons, swung in behind the *Seneca Chief* of Buffalo, the *Niagara* of Black Rock, and the *Noah's Ark,* whose passengers included two Seneca Indian boys and a black bear, and moved on eastward. At Weedsport the next day two gunners enthusiastically ramming home a second charge to express their emotions at the sight of the flotilla were blown to small bits— but their coincidental deaths were not allowed to dull the spirits of the voyagers.

The after-midnight stars were paling as the boats approached the big lock which would set the procession down on the surface of the Hudson. There they waited through the night hours, and in the morning of November second they sank slowly to the river level. "At 10 o'clock," said the Albany *Advertiser,* "the *Seneca Chief* with the governor, lieutenant governor, the Buffalo, Western and New York Committees on board came down in fine style and the thunder of cannon proclaimed that the work was done! and the assembled multitude made the welkin ring with shouts of gladness." As they floated free from the lock the *Seneca Chief* and the *Young Lion of the West* were each taken in tow by ten yawls, manned by crews of four rowers, with sloop captains as coxswains.

Through a double line of canalboats they moved down the Albany basin and through the sloop lock into the Hudson. They were towed up to the east side of the pier beside the steamboat *Swiftsure*. Then the ceremonies began. All day the Albany militia marched and countermarched in their fancy uniforms, bonfires lighted the city hilltop, there was feasting and singing on the Hudson's wharves.

At ten on Friday morning, November third, the banner-hung steamer *Chancellor Livingston*, a hundred and fifty feet of gleaming white paint and gilded tracery, led off the greatest procession the surface of the river had ever borne. In her tow plowed the *Seneca Chief*, repository of western produce and culture. The brand-new *Constitution*, fastest of river packets, was next, bringing the *Young Lion of the West* in her wake. The *Chief Justice Marshall* towed the *Niagara*. Then came the swift *Constellation* and, on the towropes of the *Olive Branch* and the *Swiftsure*, the safety barges *Richmond* and *Matilda*, bearing precious ladies at a discreet distance from the danger of exploding boilers. The little *Saratoga*, "sporting like a dolphin," sped from ship to ship. Beneath the colored streamers and fluttering banners of each vessel a brass band poured out its collective heart in patriotic airs. The artillery companies at Albany fired one great volley as the fleet moved away and the people on the crowded wharves and piers yelled and waved.

As the river widened, the procession assumed a squadron formation and there was much calling of messages and offering of toasts between passengers of different vessels. Soon Hudson was in sight and the long single file was resumed. Engines were ordered stopped and the big boats drifted slowly downstream while salvos from Prospect Hill sounded out above the heads of thousands massed upon the riverbank, and the salty sea dogs of Hudson looked curiously at the *Seneca Chief,* freighter from fresh-water oceans to the north-west. The guns of Athens answered the fusillade from the east bank and the *Young Lion of the West* answered both with a single shot from the little brass cannon at her prow. At Catskill a military company was paraded at the wharf, firing volley after volley into the clear warm air of early afternoon. Signal guns along the banks warned the smaller towns of the passing of the "fleet from the dominion of fairies." Cheered by imported wines and "sumptuous fare," the passengers hailed Germantown and Saugerties, Barrytown and Kingston. One of them wrote a few days later: "After Alexander of Macedon had carried his arms into India he did not descend the Indus with greater triumph or make a prouder display."

The light grew softer on the green water and the hills began to turn blue. As darkness settled, the *Chancellor Livingston* suddenly became a great triangle of burning lanterns. The other vessels were atwinkle. Staatsburg was a dark splotch of trees and white houses but just beyond it, at Hyde Park, James Livingston's big colonial mansion stood in light. Down by the water tar barrels burned fiercely, throwing out tongues of red flame. Rockets from the *Chief Justice Marshall* ascended in streaks of fire and burst into showers of stars drifting down to meet their own reflections in the water. Poughkeepsie was one red glare and a thunder of many cannon.

Midnight had come when the fleet reached West

Point but a salute of twenty-four guns greeted its arrival, setting strong echoes playing among the mountains. Stiff and fresh as on morning parade the cadet band marched aboard the *Chancellor Livingston,* bass drums pounding, brasses blaring to the stars. The twenty-four guns gave them a rousing farewell as their music faded downriver. After that there was a long silence while the night shifts went on duty and the passengers slept and the big steamers chugged along toward New York and its great day.

"The face of Nature was illuminated with a smile from Heaven," as the steamboat *Washington,* moving up the Hudson at sunrise, met the fleet "between the State Prison and Weehawken" (off West 10th Street, Greenwich Village).

"From whence came ye?"

"An escort from Lake Erie."

"Whither bound?"

"To the Atlantic—what vessel is that?"

"The Yacht of the City of New York having on board a Deputation from the Honourable the Corporation to welcome you into our waters, congratulate you on the great event, and offer the hospitalities of the City."

"We highly appreciate this mark of civility on the part of the City and request the Deputation from the Honourable Corporation to come on board."

After the deputation was safely delivered to the *Chancellor Livingston,* the *Washington* came about to join the procession. As it did so, from the towers of the shore hundreds of bells began a clamorous pealing and all over the city bands began to play. Cannon roared salutes "and their reverberations from the rocky shores and romantic cliffs of New Jersey, added, if possible, new glories." The Hudson was so crowded with small boats that there was scarcely room for the parade to move downstream. At the foot of Whitehall Street the shining steamer *Commerce* towed into line the safety barge *Lady Clinton,* a floating island of green boughs, brilliant blossoms, and distinguished ladies. The steamer *Fulton* moved up beside the *Chancellor Livingston* to share with her the honor of towing out to the ocean the first canalboat ever to make the voyage from the Great Lakes to New York. Behind the trio the pretty boats of the Watermen of Whitehall, the *Sylph* and the *Lady of the Lake,* gleamed in sunlight, moving slowly over placid, windless waters. There were fourteen steamboats in line now. The sailing packet *Hamlet,* strung with pennants, had been taken in tow by two steamers because no air filled her canvas.

Just within Sandy Hook the United States schooner *Porpoise* and her crew, "a Deputation from Neptune," awaited the procession. As the vessels approached they veered about her into a great circle three miles in circumference.

On the *Seneca Chief* two bright green kegs ringed with gilded hoops were brought to the deck and the commodore of the fleet, Mr. Rhind, had an idea, apparently sudden. He asked that a portion of the Lake Erie waters which they contained might be saved and sent to General Lafayette in "bottles of American fabrick" made by Mummer and Company to be conveyed in a box made by Duncan Phyfe from a cedar log brought by the *Seneca Chief* from her home port. The request having been granted, tall, majestic Governor De Witt Clinton lifted one of the kegs and poured water from Lake Erie into the Atlantic, saying, "May the God of the heavens and the earth smile most propitiously on this work, accomplished by the wisdom, public spirit, and energy of the people of the State of New York and may He render it subservient to the best interests of the human race."

Then that champion speechmaker of the era, "Nestor of American Science," Dr. Samuel Latham Mitchill, continued the formalities of the marriage of the waters with a speech so eloquent, so learned, so full of symbolic meaning that all were satisfied though few understood. As he spoke, the great man opened phial after phial of rare waters, sent to him by admirers from all over the world, and emptied them into the waves off Sandy Hook. The pure flood of the Elbe fell from his hands in a glinting stream; the "sacred waters of the Ganges, overflowings of the Nile," dippings from the Amazon, the Neva, the Plate, Columbia, Tagus, Orinoco, Seine, and Thames, all united with the ocean "as an emblem of our commercial intercourse with all ports of the world."

In conclusion Dr. Mitchill said: "Sir! He who now accosts you has no contrivance to conjure up new associations of ideas nor to utter them in phrases novel or unheard before; yet if he did possess that power he would tell you how recently imparted influence of republicanization would henceforward cooperate with the sea's phosphorescence to render it luminous, and with its salinity to continue it wholesome; he would portray freedom pervading the billows and rolling with every wave to the shores, and trace its workings upon the compacted continents and scattered islands comprehended within its embrace. Had he the ability he would observe that this renovating and regenerating would rise, by exhalation into the atmosphere, and impart some of its qualities; that it would impregnate the clouds and descend in rains and dews; that it would enter the vegetables and animals which constitute the food of the human race; and that finally, the frame of man himself would be gradually so modified and mended by it, that at length even the sable and savage tribes dwelling in the tracts bordering on Senegal, the Gambia, and the Congo, shall lay aside their ferocity and enjoy, as we ourselves do, Liberty, under the guidance of the Law."

After that speech the procession moved off again, returning from the deep to the festivities ashore. As the *Porpoise* passed the English sloops of war *Kingfisher* and *Swallow* in the harbor she manned her yards and gave the Britishers three cheers. His Majesty's men heartily responded and the British band struck up "Yankee Doodle." The West Point musicians answered with "God Save the King." International amity was further encouraged by a breakfast party on the *Swallow,* at which Lieutenant Baldock, in command, showed his American guests his own water colors picturing the Eagle and the Lion—Columbia and Britannia—in affectionate embrace.

Meanwhile, the landlubbers of the city had not been idle. At the Battery bugles were calling the five-mile parade into formation before eleven in the morning. Four mounted trumpeters rode out in front and a band marched briskly after, playing a march "composed expressly for the occasion." The grand marshal rode in advance of his aides, all wearing white satin collars with colored rosettes and carrying short white batons tipped with gold. Sturdy foresters followed on foot bearing on their shoulders axes, symbolic of their conquest of the thick western woods, and after them farmers and gardeners with spades and hoes. Then came the almost endless line of social and trade groups headed by the Horticultural Society.

The tailors marched proudly, carrying out the bridal idea of the occasion with two large banners, one depicting Adam and Eve under a tree in the Garden of Eden, with the inscription "United We Are," and the other reading "I was naked and ye clothed me." Tiny white-clad Master Hatfield led the men of his father's trade, the hatters, bearing in his youthful arms a flag on which was printed a couplet:

> Rocks and hills can't now restrain
> Erie's waters from the Main.

The journeymen coopers, on a large-wheeled stage, manufactured as they rode a sixty-gallon cask and knocked together a forty-gallon job as an encore. The combmakers, as their car moved along, cut, manufactured, and finished fifty dozen shell and horn combs which they tossed to pretty lady spectators. Many fire companies were in line and the silver trumpets of the captains caught the sun, the horses stepped proudly, the engines shone, the uniforms were brilliant and romantically cut. The stage of the Typographical Society was drawn by four horses. On each side of it, operating at full speed, was a newly invented gilded printing press and between them, in Dr. Benjamin Franklin's old armchair, sat James Cram, most venerable printer of the city. Two men costumed as heralds and two as Mercury helped him fold and toss to the crowds broadsides on which the busy presses had printed an ode composed for the occasion by printer Samuel Woodworth. It ended with symbolic stanzas that were nevertheless realistic enough to bring blushes to the cheeks of female readers along the way:

> 'Tis Done! the monarch of the briny tide
> Whose giant arm encircles earth
> To virgin Erie is allied
> A bright-eyed nymph of mountain birth
>
> Today the *Sire of Ocean* takes
> A sylvan maiden to his arms
> The goddess of the crystal lakes
> In all her native charms
>
> She comes attended by a sparkling train;
> The Naiads of the West her nuptials grace
> She meets the sceptred father of the main
> And in his heaving bosom hides her virgin face.

The great parade lasted until late in the afternoon. The sea procession landed at Pier Number One on the East River and all the men participants joined the marchers. Throngs lined Greenwich Street, Canal, Broadway, and Broome, cheering the bakers and butchers, the brewers and booksellers, the millers and music dealers, the tallow chandlers, the students of Columbia College, the soapmakers, the tin-plate workers.

The thousands who crowded about City Hall that night soon realized that the spectacles of the day were only a preliminary to the glories after sundown. Though City Hall was lighted "by twenty-three hundred and two brilliant lights—1,542 wax candles, 450 lamps, and 310 variegated lamps," making fireworks difficult, Richard Wilcox, pyrotechnic artist, succeeded in completely overwhelming this flood of illumination by the use of thirteen gerbes, or sheaves, "each six inches in calibre and containing fifty pounds of composition, alternately changing into Chinese, Diamond and other fires." Auxiliary works placed behind these were fired simultaneously to give background. At the same moment fifteen hundred large fireballs rose, crossing and recrossing in intersecting arcs of concentric circles. A gleaming willow tree, decorated with yellow stars, hung for a moment in the night sky and then a poplar lifted boughs of flame. A shower of golden rain descended, and suddenly the rain was silver. Three hundred and twenty rockets of four pounds each, thirty of nine pounds, twenty-four of twenty pounds, hurtled upward from both wings of the composition and, as their arcs crossed, burst into fiery serpents, scrolls of light, the delicate tracery of snails. The largest rockets, fired at a 40-degree angle so as to fall into the Hudson, left behind them wide peacock spreads of colored lights that drifted slowly down to meet the water.

Everybody went home then, happy that after eight years of waiting, Clinton's Ditch was finished and that, through its confluence with the Hudson, the West and the East were one.

21

Hudson River Aesthete

OLD BARON DE LIDERER, wandering the Hudson's banks on a summer day, came upon a tall thin boy whose brown eyes were deep and full of light and whose glinting dark hair tumbled about his collar. Before they had returned to Newburgh in the evening —the baron, Austrian consul general, to his summer residence; the boy to a red cottage in the Highlands— they had talked about many things and they knew that they would walk together again. Andrew Jackson Downing, a good name for a boy born in the autumn of 1815, had found a friend whose mind was stored with knowledge of stones and flowers and trees. The baron had found that treasure to the experienced, an eager listener.

The old man and the young one explored the river country often after that. Andrew's schoolmates at Montgomery Academy and his four older brothers and sisters would have been surprised at the animated face, the quick tongue of the dark boy whom they knew to be usually silent and expressionless.

It was not long before the baron had walked his protégé up the river to the flat rock, which has been called "Danskammer" ever since Henry Hudson saw savages prancing there, and had presented him to Edward Armstrong, beau idéal of the west bank, deity of a granite temple of his own devising which was the wonder of the near-by countryside. Puffing steamers had dragged barge after barge up to the Armstrong wharf, all loaded to the water line with slabs of dark-gray Breakneck Mountain granite from downriver and of pearly granite brought over from Quincy for the trim of the columns. As for the big columns them-selves, yokes of oxen in long double line had strained and heaved at the sharp cries of the teamsters but no column had moved, until someone had the idea of mak-ing each into a roller with holes at the ends to receive an impromptu axle so that it might be revolved slowly up the bank.

Inside the granite temple all was black walnut, for mahogany was "out" now. There were a billiard room, a gun room, and many nurseries, because billiards, shoot-ing, and the begetting of large families were activities that current fashion approved, and handsome Edward Armstrong was current fashion's darling. With his vivacious wife, who could be fluent in both Italian and French and painted in water colors the fruits and flow-ers he gathered for her, he lived the life of a cultured American country gentleman as he and many of his fel-low countrymen conceived it. He wrote poetry and he played upon the violin and he danced "better than any young gentleman between New York and Albany," cutting perfect double pigeonwings. Southdown sheep nibbled his meadow grasses, thoroughbred horses neighed in his stables, his wharf ran out into deep water where even the biggest of river steamboats might stop, his shore line was a wide crescent of white and shining sand.

Young Andrew Jackson Downing's visits to Dan-

skammer set the current of his life. Sensitive and lonely,
child of a poor nurseryman-gardener who had died
when he was seven, he found in the river temple a
life more perfect than he could have dreamed. Edward
Armstrong affected him profoundly. Many years later
an intimate wrote of Downing: "The workman, the
author, the artist were entirely subjugated in him to
the gentleman. That was his favorite idea. The *gentleman* was the full flower of which all others were suggestions or parts. . . . His social tendency was constantly toward those to whom great wealth had given
opportunity of ameliorating culture."

The young man's progress toward this sort of snob-
bishness was hardly delayed by Mrs. Armstrong's eager
acceptance of his suggestion that she plant a double
row of locusts along the "avenue" leading to the door
or by the attentions of Charles Augustus Murray, English travel writer, and Raphael Hoyle, English landscape
painter, who found their visits to Danskammer the
more pleasant for his company. Impatiently he put
aside his mother's insensitive request that he become an
apprentice-clerk in a dry goods store and announced
that he would be a horticulturist like his brother
Charles, who had inherited their father's nursery. His
new friends understood and valued such a profession.

Charles made him a partner when he was nineteen
and Andrew went to work. Soon he had visited every
estate for miles up and down the river to study its
planting and arrangement. He had put aside now the
cabinet of mineral specimens which he and the old
baron had gathered in their walks in the Highlands.
And, since college was financially impossible, he would

try to educate himself by reading and by observation of the manner of life of cultured people.

Nowhere on the Hudson, not even at the Armstrongs', was there a greater emphasis on the joys of the cultured life than across the river in Fishkill Landing at "Locust Grove," the low, many-gabled Dutch homestead of the De Windts. The old trees that gave the place its name interlaced above the approach in fan vaulting so perfect that the "avenue" was called the "Cathedral"; creepers and roses and honeysuckle clambered over the long piazza; horse chestnuts and weeping willows shaded the big garden. John Peter De Windt had married Caroline, daughter of that Abigail Smith Adams who had been born of Abigail Smith Adams and John Adams, second president of the United States. Eleven children were born to John Peter De Windt and his delicate spouse, and the eldest of these was birdlike Caroline.

It was inevitable that Andrew Jackson Downing should find his way to Locust Grove, that the De Windts, living gaily in an atmosphere of luxurious decay, their house a rendezvous for all the young people of the neighborhood, for West Point officers, for lovers of the arts, should be impressed by his dark, glamorous person and by the quiet, polished manner learned at Danskammer. As for Downing, he must have been pleased by a home where guests and the family sat on the veranda and "listened to the tale of fiction." This habit was expressed in the hostess's own rhythms:

By Dryden and Pope the breakfast is graced
At the close of the meal to the garden they haste,
And with congenial powers
Beguile the fleeting hours.

He was even more delighted with piquant daughter Caroline. There was many a chaperoned row on the moonlit Hudson, many a piazza promenade, many a visit to a near-by river estate where, again to resort to his future mother-in-law's inimitable verses:

Statues and paintings, Dianas and fauns
Embellished with flowers, and garnished the lawns;
The mansion displayed with delicate skill,
Refreshed by the fountain and cooled by the rill.

On June 7, 1838, Andrew Jackson Downing and Caroline De Windt were married. "It was a grand affair, a dance and supper," wrote Rose Armstrong in a letter from Danskammer. Andrew had bought his brother's interest in the nursery now, business was prospering. He began to build a dwelling for his bride among the Downing Botanic Gardens and Nurseries. From Locust Grove through a long telescope Caroline watched her new home across the river grow stone by stone. She saw no pillared shrine. It was a "Tudor Gothic villa" of sepia-colored sandstone with two small towers projecting high above the roof just over the wide entrance, and it was designed to prove "that a beautiful and durable and convenient mansion could be built as cheaply as a poor and tasteless temple." Despite his happy memories of Danskammer, Downing had concluded that a copy of a place of worship was unsuitable for human living.

"Highland Gardens," as they called their new home, lay above the water and looked out over strange treetops. The Hudson River whalers and traders had been bringing green booty home and Downing had profited by their voyages and those of many another

American ship. Sophora, Deodar and Gingko, Jezo and Judas and Tree of Heaven, Nezo, Nana and Incense Cedar, Weeping Cypress and Stinking Yew were neighbors of Baffin's Bay Borealis, Patagonian Fitzroya, African Tamaris and Taurian Pine. In the greenhouses down below, Chinese Rice Ropes, New Zealand flax, aloes, palms and Arundo made the Hudson's bank seem the edge of a tropic river. Just above the water a path went past rockwork covered with alpine plants and a pond filled with water flowers. And at one end of the velvet lawn before the house stood a great Warwick vase, rich arabesques looping the bowl in fantastic design.

The interior of the house was dark. The woodwork and furniture were heavy and deep brown. A visitor wrote: "Even the daylight is dusk—or, more properly speaking, pregnant with light . . . a sort of imprisoned sunshine, something warm and deep like a reflection of the man's brown eyes." In Downing's library, on small bookcases shaped like Gothic windows, white busts of Linnaeus, Franklin, Newton, and other scientists were ghost-heads in the gloom.

Among these plaster portraits Downing sat down to write a book which should tell what he had been thinking about building and planting in America. The earliest professors of landscape gardening were correct, he wrote, in dividing the art into two variations—the Beautiful and the Picturesque. The first of these was marked by undulations of turf melting into each other, gently flowing brooks, smooth-stemmed trees with full round heads, walks and roads that bent in easy arcs, smooth still lakes with flowered margins widely curving. Only houses of classical mode—Italian, Tuscan, or Venetian that would "readily admit of the graceful ac-

companiment of urns"—should stand in such surroundings. And "such a scene should be of the most polished
kind—grass mown into a softness like velvet, gravel
walks . . . firm, dry and clean . . . the most perfect
order and neatness should reign throughout."

If the reader would discover in the fine arts an
artist who epitomized in his paintings the Beautiful, let
him look upon the graceful and flowing forms, the
noble and chaste qualities in the pictures of Claude Lorraine.

As for the Picturesque in landscape gardening,
Downing said that it aimed at "a certain spirited irreg-
ularity." Surfaces should be comparatively abrupt and
broken with growth of a "somewhat wild and bold
character." The trees should have rough bark and be
planted close together as in the thickets of undisci-
plined nature. "Against the sky outline breaks the wild
and irregular form of some old half-decayed tree. . . .
If water enlivens the scene . . . let the stream turn the
ancient and well-worn wheel of the old mill in the middle ground and we shall have an example of the picturesque."

The house suitable to such a background would be
a Gothic mansion, an old English or a Swiss cottage.
Nowhere in the field of painting would one find so
many of the elements of the Picturesque as among the
bold rocks and wild passes, the vigorous rugged scenes
—robbers, banditti and all—that came from the brush
of Salvator Rosa. The romanticism of Sir Walter Scott
and of the Gothic novel had struck deep into Andrew
Jackson Downing. With his arbitrary theory as a basis,
throughout the rest of his book he showed how building
and planting might be made to conform to it. Preju-

diced in favor of the Picturesque, possibly by the fact
of his own residence in the wild Hudson uplands, he
told how deciduous and evergreen trees might be
planted to give free natural effects, how walks should be
formed, how water should be treated. Then he was
ready for "rural architecture." "But how shall we desig-
nate that singular perversity of taste, or rather that total
want of it, which prompts the man, who, under the
name of a villa residence, piles up in the free open
country . . . a stiff modern three-story brick which
. . . only serves to call up the exclamation

> 'Avaunt stiff pile! Why didst thou stray
> From blocks congenial to Broadway!' "

Objecting strenuously to "stables built after the
models of Greek temples and barns with elegant Venetian shutters," mansions with concealed chimneys and
"without porches or appendages of any kind to give
the least hint to the mind of the doubting spectator
whether the edifice is a chapel, a bank, a hospital, or
the private dwelling of a man of wealth and opulence,"
he admitted to favorable consideration Gothic castles
in romantic scenery or "where the neighboring mountains or wild passes are sufficiently near to give that
character to the landscape." This approval apparently
led to such a plethora of castles on the mountainous
shores of the Hudson that he was obliged to reprove
their builders in a later book for the use of inappro-
priate materials. "We could point to two or three of
these imitations of Gothic castles with towers and battlements built of wood. . . . If a man is ambitious of
attracting attention by his house and can only afford
wood, let him (if he can content himself with nothing

appropriate) build a gigantic wigwam of logs and bark
. . . but not attempt mock battlements of pine boards,
and strong towers of thin plank." And he added a further word of warning to the castle-dweller: "Unless
there is something of the castle in the man, it is very
likely, if it [his home] be like a real castle, to dwarf
him to the stature of a mouse."

Further approving villas in the Italian style and
in the varied Gothic styles of England, Downing moved
on to a concluding chapter recommending "embellish-
ments." In this category he included urns, conserva-
tories, covered seats, summer houses, weeping fountains,
prospect towers, pavilions, bridges, and rockwork. Most
curious of these were a moss house, an octagonal gatehouse, a rustic seat in which the central structure was
circular and intended for a collection of minerals, shells,
and geological specimens of the immediate neighborhood, a prospect tower three stories in height with a
double thatched roof and a spiral staircase leading up
to a platform "whence a charming *coup d'œil* or
bird's-eye view of the surrounding country is obtained."

Downing had written truly when in the Preface
to this first book—*A Treatise on the Theory and Practice of Landscape Gardening Adapted to North America*—he had said: "A taste for rural improvements of
every description is advancing silently but with great
rapidity in this country." No sooner was his book off
the presses than the culture-hungry East pounced upon
it. It went through edition after edition. While western
pioneers were building their cabins out of logs cut to
make a clearing, the prosperous merchants of the Hudson River country talked learnedly of Tuscan villas,
Tudor mansions, Mansard dwellings, Gothic cottages,

always referring to *Landscape Gardening* as authority. The book became a favorite wedding gift and no young couple thought of planning a home without thoroughly perusing it. Horticultural societies elected the author to honorary membership. Letters came from European enthusiasts. The big estates on the Hudson and in Connecticut and Massachusetts bulged with full-rounded curves or took on the rough defiant angularities of a scene from *Marmion*.

It was all very heartwarming, and Downing was so pleased by his recognition that he retired at once to the little dark room with the bookcases and the busts to compose a companion volume, *Rural Cottages,* in which he showed how his ideas could be applied on a less expensive scale. In this book he added to his list of acceptable architectural styles America's one contribution, "Hudson River Bracketed," a mode that met with such general response that the Hudson is still lined with cottages, mostly yellow (for he disliked white houses and green surroundings), their gables trimmed with vergeboards cut in mad scroll-saw patterns, poetic fancies of thousands of carpenters let loose in an orgy of quick carving, their sidewalls battened, their roofs set on brackets visible from without and within, brackets that offered a gentle compromise between the sharp upward angle of the pointed Gothic and the flatness of the Italian mode.

In two years Andrew Jackson Downing, twenty-six years old, had achieved fame. Now rich man and peasant sought his advice either in person or through his books. The Hudson River folk were proud of him. They pointed out that he gave fine proof of the opportunities the young democratic republic offered to the

humble poor. He was "self-made," he had overcome his
lack of formal education, he had leaped social barriers
to marry a girl who was both great-granddaughter of
one President Adams and niece of another. But no one
would have dared suggest these things to the tall Span-
ish-looking young man who walked slowly and spoke
with easy elegance, whose "perfect *savoir faire* would
have adorned the Escurial," who seemed to be watching
his companions constantly and keenly from behind
the pleasant mask that was his face.

Now that Downing's success had given him more
opportunity to do what he wanted, it was at once no-
ticeable that there was an objective he more ardently
wished to achieve than fame as a landscape gardener.
It was a way of life. The yearning that beset the poor
gardener's son when he had first visited Edward Armstrong in his granite temple would not be stifled.

But he wanted something better than the empty
catering to fashion he had seen at Danskammer. The
new way of life was to be aristocratic and at the same
time worth while. It would be such a life as went on
at his father-in-law's home across the river—carried
to a higher degree of intellectuality and with much
of the frivolity left out. All about him on the Hudson
he saw gropings toward this kind of living, in Edward
Armstrong's poetry and his wife's painting, in the verses
of his mother-in-law whose mother and grandmother
had written poetry before her. It was a logical development and carrying out of the nation's new cultural
ideal. Now that he had time for leisure, like his neighbors in the river estates, now that he was recognized
as one of the country's most gifted men of art, he

wanted to live as America's men of means and background should live.

It did not take Andrew Jackson Downing long to make his idea into a reality. In proper living there must be no evidence of anything so distasteful as work. His library seemed "the retreat of an elegantly cultivated gentleman." There were pens, portfolio, a desk —but no evidences of labor. Though he constantly produced more written work, it was impossible, said his friends, to believe him a diligent worker. The attitude that work was unpleasant and should be withdrawn from attention was carried so far by Downing and his friends and pupils that they urged keeping the entire machinery of an estate out of sight so that flowers might bloom, lawns be mowed, walks swept, "by invisible hands," at night or "at such hours as the family is supposed not to come out."

The hours at Highland Gardens passed in a synthetic haze as real in its artificial way as that which lay along the river on the summer mornings or shrouded the blue Catskills at twilight. Life was a planned idyl. To Caroline Downing's younger sister Elizabeth the villa was "a paradise where friends met congenial friends and where the feast of reason and flow of soul mingled with delicately seasoned meats, fruits and wines." Elizabeth's fiancé—young Christopher Pearce Cranch, who had come to Fishkill as minister—was persuaded to give up preaching for writing verses and painting pictures.

There were always guests at Highland Gardens, and more and more distinguished ones as time went on. Downing became known as the most perfect host in the river country—where hospitality was studied as an especial art. By day there was boating, botanizing, archery, painting, reading, conversation, lying on the lawn—with an occasional excursion into the mountains across the Hudson or a visit to a neighbor's highly decorated estate. In the evening by the lamplight in the bust-studded library Andrew and Caroline Downing took turns in reading aloud to their guests Lowell's new "Vision of Sir Launfal" and other poems which they liked.

In the mild twilights of summer there were charades on the lawn beside the Warwick vase, but the taciturn host who kept them going, directing them delicately, did not laugh at the antics of the players, and no one could guess the syllables he enacted because he performed so self-consciously and with such forbidding reserve. There was music—fine playing and fine singing of "Oh, Fly to the Prairie" and, for the baritones, "Rocked in the Cradle of the Deep." There was even a male trio, of which the distinguished writer George William Curtis was a member, who "made music in the moonlight on the lawn." Inevitably there was "some slight violation of the Maine law," a tasting of the soft sweet wines of the Ohio valley sent to Mr. Downing by his friend Nicholas Longworth, in Cincinnati.

At breakfast each guest at Highland Gardens saw beside his plate a blossom, a flower he was known to love or one his host had judged most fitting to his character. The tenderhearted found tea roses and honeysuckle; the modest and shy, violets and pansies; the brilliant and gay, marigolds, asters, or carnations.

Time seemed to stand still in the ordered world that Andrew Downing had created. When he was thirty-five he looked but thirty, and Caroline seemed younger and prettier with the passing of the years. In 1845 Andrew was editing the American edition of Mrs. Loudon's *Gardening for Ladies*. In 1846 he had accepted the editorship of the *Horticulturist* and soon thereafter he had begun to write articles and editorials urging that New York City provide itself with a large central park.

In 1849 came the greatest triumph of the career of living which seemed so much more important to him than professional success—the visit of Sweden's famous novelist, little gray, blue-eyed, red-nosed Fredrika Bremer, whom Hawthorne called "maiden aunt to the human race." She came directly from her ocean voyage by the river steamer *New World*, "a little floating palace, splendid and glittering with white and gold on the outside and splendid and elegant within."

Now all the machinery was put in operation and it all worked. By the library fireplace on the first evening Andrew and Caroline wooed their distinguished visitor with readings from the most esteemed American poets. Miss Bremer's incorrigible sentimentalism was encouraged by the opportunity of seeing a morning wedding in the neighborhood. Catherine Sedgwick, best known American woman novelist of the age, came over from Connecticut bringing her niece Susan to join the house party. A picnic was arranged, the spot to be the top of South Beacon Mountain. Downing, Miss Bremer, and Miss Sedgwick were to ride together, but the vigorous fifty-three-year-old American woman walked "as usual" and played havoc with the capon and champagne, while the Swedish guest of honor thought the party "too large and too merry for me." Later she wrote in her journal: "One little moment partly alone and partly with Mr. Downing, who knows how to be gay and jocular with the gay, and silent with the silent was to me the crowning luxury of the excursion."

To make matters even more perfect, invitations began to come in from neighboring villas. The very rich Mrs. Donaldson, whose grounds at her estate "Blithewood" Downing thought the best example of his landscaping ability, asked them over for a day. It was misty Indian summer, October on the river, when they set out. "The Indians are smoking their pipes in their great powwows," said Caroline Downing. There were sixty or seventy neighbors for breakfast at Blithe-wood. The meal ended with a dance, and Miss Bremer could observe that the American young girls were lovely and lively with "delicate figures though deficient in strength," and she complained of their lack of facial expression.

In the evening the gracious Mrs. Donaldson, for whose silken gowns three hundred silkworms were spinning their cocoons upon the Donaldson mulberry trees, played upon the harp in her darkly lustrous parlor. Then all of them went for a night stroll beside the river. Fortunately Mr. John Church Cruger's estate bordered on Blithewood. Mrs. Donaldson's guests were rowed out to look upon its recently built ruins from the shimmering water that they might grow silent in sadly ecstatic reverie. On the farthest point of land stood the huddle of tumble-down stone arches, dark and beautiful beneath the moon. Miss Bremer was amazed at the resemblance between the Mayan figures among them and Egyptian statues she remembered. One had a sphinxlike countenance and a head like that of a priest of Isis. "The ruin and its ornaments," she confided to her journal, "in the midst of a wild, romantic rocky and wooded promontory was a design in the best of taste."

From Blithewood, Downing and Miss Bremer took a railroad coach down the river. A rough young man spat on the floor in front of them and Fredrika, remembering Dickens's comments on American boors, said, "That gentleman needs a Dickens."

"Dickens would have mistaken him for a gentleman," said the elegant Mr. Downing with hauteur.

They paid a visit to another river house before Miss Bremer set out on a long tour of America. It was to the home of Mr. Hamilton, "the son of the general of that name, the contemporary and friend of Washington." There Fredrika was triumphant because elderly Washington Irving sat next to her at dinner and did not fall asleep as was his custom. After dinner she and one of the young ladies played duets on the piano and had just finished an overture for four hands —"which we played so that they who heard us cried 'bravo!' "—when Downing said it was time to go. Fredrika would have liked to continue but was compensated later: "I sat silent in the railway carriage beside my silent friend, the music of whose soul I am always conscious of though he speak not a word, so that after all there was no interruption of the music."

From her journal it would appear that the middle-aged Swedish virgin had quite unconsciously fallen in love with the brown-eyed, long-haired, haughty young man. She longed to see him again and after nearly two years of travel in America she eagerly awaited their reunion. Meanwhile, in 1850, Downing's growing interest in building expressed itself in a volume entitled *The Architecture of Country Houses* in which he divided all rural dwellings into three categories: cottages, farmhouses, and villas. He defined a cottage as a small dwelling in which the family might employ at most two servants, stated that a farmhouse should not be expected to display architectural ornaments any more than the farmer himself would be expected to wear "garments made by the most fashionable tailor in Broadway or to drive to his market town in one of Lawrence and Collis's most modish carriages," and described a villa as a house requiring a serving staff of three or more. In the same year he went to England, where he was flattered and feasted by a British society which saw in him its own champion in the States.

He returned to add a few perfecting Anglophile touches to his precious way of life which, more than any of his writings, he had come to look upon as his masterpiece. That Christmas, to the singing of fiddles, Downing and all his guests danced on the marble pavement of the great hall at Highland Gardens. Antlers and pikes, helmets and breastplates gave back the yellow light from rustic chandeliers wreathed with holly and the dancers were the gayer for looking upon the plumed hats of cavaliers hung upon the walls.

"He seemed to me handsomer, more manly," wrote Fredrika Bremer when she was allowed the boon of seeing Downing again. "His beautiful eyes beamed with self-conscious power."

She was delighted with his material progress. "He works as Jenny Lind seems to sing," she said. President Fillmore had appointed him to lay out the grounds for the Capitol, the White House, and the Smithsonian Institution in Washington. He was carrying on a voluminous correspondence. Persistently he urged the establishment of a great park in New York, the park which his young pupil and assistant, Calvert Vaux, was eventually to plan and achieve. Indeed, the idea had caused some wavering in his attitude toward society, much to Fredrika Bremer's delight for she had often playfully rebuked him for being "more exclusive and aristocratic in his beautifying activity than became an honest downright republican."

"It is indeed both curious and amusing," he wrote, "to see the stand taken on the one hand by the million that the park is made for the 'upper ten' who ride in fine carriages, and on the other hand by the wealthy and refined that a park in this country will be 'usurped by the rowdies and low people.' Shame upon our republican compatriots who so little understand the elevating influences of the beautiful in nature and art."

Though admitting the improving influence of landscape gardening on people of the class into which he was born, Downing still wanted it clearly understood that he was no believer in complete democracy, for a few months later he wrote pompously of "the inextinguishable rights of superior organization in certain men and races of men which Nature every day reaffirms, notwithstanding the socialistic and democratic theories of our politicians." He undertook at about this time a campaign against men of inferior organization in Newburgh who were allowing their pigs to wander the public streets and, despite threats and appeals for pity on the poor pig-owners, succeeded in having the pigs banned. Nathaniel Willis, dude poet and neighbor in the town of Canterbury, wrote "Now *we* want such a pig-apostle."

Fredrika Bremer said good-bye to Downing at the

Astor House, where she had first met him. "I felt that we parted forever on earth." And on the last day of the following June, in 1852, Highland Gardens opened its doors to a gay company as its owner prepared what was to be his final tribute to the ideal of perfect living. It was a festival of roses. Music drifted above the exotic greenery that lined the lawn, faltered out over the moonlit water. Melodious voices sounded in the regular rhythms of Lowell and Longfellow. There was discreet giggling in the games beside the great Warwick vase. The Ohio wines were sweet and clear. The perfume of the roses seemed to thicken the air. When the moon was high the host and all his guests rowed across the river to the Verplanck house to see the room in which officers of the Revolution had formed the Society of the Cincinnati. Downing spoke of swimming across the river and back when he was a boy and said he believed he could do it again. If one had to leave life, he said, he would rather drown than die in any other way.

A month later he and Caroline and their lovely young friend—the widowed Matilda Wadsworth, Mrs. De Windt and two of her children, stood on the dock at Newburgh in the sunny heat of early afternoon awaiting the arrival of the steamer *Henry Clay*. The boat swung sharply in to the pier and the passengers hurried aboard. A few hours later the *Henry Clay* was a smoldering wreck on the bank at Riverdale, and of the little party only Caroline and the De Windt children were alive. Downing had been drowned.

The news of the great gardener's death filled all lovers of homes and flowers and all his fellow worshipers at the shrine of aristocratic living with deep and genuine mourning. They made word-laments for him.

One said: "There lay the lifeless form of Nature's own gardener, protected from the burning sun only by leaves and shrubbery gathered from the banks of that river which, in the words of another, 'had he lived he would have made a river Rhine.'" Another wrote: "His name shall be perpetuated by fragrant flowers and delicious fruits, by gushing fountains and murmuring streams." From Sweden came a cry of anguish for "My American brother . . . whose image is forever pictured on my soul along with its most beautiful scenes, its romantic life, its Indian summer, and, above all, its highland scenery on that magnificent river where he had built his home and now—has his grave."

In Washington some of his friends erected a monument to his memory—a vase like the great Warwick vase at Highland Gardens, its base decorated with acanthus leaves. On one side the first lettering of the tribute reads: "He was born and lived and died upon the Hudson River." On another is a quotation from one of his essays: "The taste of an individual as well as that of a nation will be in direct proportion to the profound sensibility with which he perceives the beautiful in natural scenery.

"Open wide, therefore, the doors of your libraries and picture galleries, all ye true republicans! Build halls where Knowledge shall be freely diffused among men and not shut up within the narrow walls of narrow institutions.

"Plant spacious parks in your cities, and unclose their gates as wide as the gates of the morning to the whole people."

The dwellers in the Beautiful and in the Picturesque villas along that stream, those who understood

Andrew Jackson Downing best and shared his love of ordered, artificial, luxurious living, felt a chill about their hearts. It was as if the rumble of an upriver thunderstorm had silenced for a moment the festival of roses and all the guests knew they would be scattered soon. Only for a little while longer the ladies of the river houses looked out from the belvederes and gazebos that crowned their undulant acres of lawn and trees and sighed for the proud dark man who had made them beautiful. A little while longer they played sad songs upon their harps, remembering him in their moonlit pavilions.

22

Palaces Afloat

THE streets of the river towns were a color-poster fair as the fight for passengers began. Long blasts from tin horns, echoing from wall to wall, summoned eager travelers to the landings when a steamboat was approaching. Runners excitedly shouted the praise of their employer's packet and decried that of his opponent. Brass-mouthed and cunning, they claimed speed and safety for the boat they worked for, and denounced her rival as a slow tub with boilers "like to blow up any minute." The runners for the new boats with copper boilers pleaded with prospective patrons not to risk their lives on the older boats with iron boilers. The *New London* overcame this objection in record time with a few coats of copper paint and her runners shouted "copper boilers" with the loudest. One runner made it a practice to tell nervous old ladies his boat had "no boilers at all."

If passengers hurried to the landing at the sound of the horns they might see the white steamer puffing toward them, hear the distant voice of her bell, see her little boat lowered to the water and passengers and luggage dumped into it. As with slow and dripping paddles the big packet moved majestically by, skillful boatmen in the small craft beside her sheered off, reaching the dock by the imparted impetus. Arriving passengers were hastily deposited and newcomers as hastily embarked. The thin rope connecting the long vessel in the channel with the landing boat was being paid out longer and longer. Suddenly it tightened as deck hands on the steamer began to wind it on a hand winch. Swiftly the embarkers were bumped over the water to the still moving packet. In a moment they were on board and the paddles were roaring again. While the onlookers watched, the big gilt-trimmed steamer became a far white speck on hill-shadowed water.

Once on board, a passenger found himself engulfed in a maelstrom of his fellow countrymen. Everybody talked to everybody else and a man had but to raise his voice to express an opinion and he would be surrounded by a circle of eager listeners. "Speechifying is a very favorite species of exhibition with the men here," wrote the vivacious young English actress, Fanny Kemble, after a day of listening to Hudson steamboat orators. "The gift of gab appears to me to be more widely disseminated amongst Americans than any other people in the world. . . . As to privacy," she wailed, "at any time or under any circumstances, 'tis a thing that enters not into the imagination of an American."

Indeed, the presence of the unrefined and impecunious masses of the democracy offended the aesthetic sensitivity of distinguished foreign travelers and the new Hudson River aristocracy alike. One young snob, who took a day boat instead of a cheaper night boat because on the latter "you lose the pleasure which even common minds must feel when gazing on the glorious scenery," complained bitterly in his journal that he was forced to witness the "grand Pallisades,

the Highlands, and the abrupt sinuosities of this noble
river . . . without having a single friendly bosom with
which I might reciprocate those impressions of pleasure
which the occasion was so aptly fitted to inspire." And
the polite mayor of New York City, Philip Hone, confided to his diary: "Our boat had three or four hundred
passengers and such a set of ragtag and bobtail I never
saw on board a North River steamboat." So popular
did Sunday steamboat excursions become that the min-
isters of New York held a conference to denounce them
for emptying the churches.

At mealtimes in the big dining salons the crowds
jostled elbows at long tables covered with gleaming
white napery while black waiters in white jackets
rushed frantically about. Though table manners varied,
most Americans agreed that the measure of a gentleman was his politeness to females, and servants and
male passengers alike went to great lengths of sacrifice
to please them. Food was hearty, abundant, well cooked.
A steamboat breakfast one morning in 1829 consisted
of English beefsteak, French fricassee, towering piles
of American buckwheat cakes, and a delicacy aesthetically announced as "Baptized Toast" but recognized by
passengers as toast of the ordinary "milk" variety.

As competition increased the desire for speed grew.
Stronger piers were built and the captains and pilots
became more expert. Boys who had begun to "follow
the river" by learning the old place-rhyme

> West Point and Middletown
> Konnosook and Doodletown
> Kakiak and Mamapaw
> Stony Point and Haverstraw

could now nose a long steamer up to the big piles of a dock and hold her there while passengers and luggage were pitched aboard. "Commodore" Vanderbilt, "Uncle" Daniel Drew, "Live Oak George" Law, and the rest of the bold, hard river bullies began their ruthless battle of price cutting and chicanery. The North River Association, the largest boat-owning company on the Hudson, was so badly beaten by Vanderbilt that they bought him off the river. But he refused to stay off. Daniel Drew forced the association to take him in, then secretly started a rival boat against the company, using a fictitious owner's name. He finally persuaded his fellow directors to offer his dummy owner $8,000 more than they were at first willing to give for ownership of the boat. "I'll see if he'll accept," said Uncle Daniel. He went out and took a walk around the block and returned to say that it was a deal. The price of a steamboat ticket from Albany to New York, which had started at $7, dropped to $2 in 1840 when there were a hundred steamboats on the river, and eventually went down to 50 cents. At the height of the rate war some boats were charging no fare at all and passengers were paying only for meals and a stateroom.

Gradually the *Olive Branch,* the *Constellation,* the *Chief Justice Marshall*—the great boats of the thirties —gave way to the new and elaborate "floating palaces" of the forties. Enormous crystal chandeliers hung from the rococo ceilings of salons two decks high and surrounded by galleries. Corinthian columns vied with Gothic arches to express new ideas of elegance and splendor. Carved figureheads stared out over the river from ornately gilded bows. Gold eagles, balancing full-

spread on gold balls, topped slim white shafts on the
forward decks.

The Hudson River people were very proud of their
steamboats, "the most elegant in the world." Despite
the great crowds encouraged by low prices, they
thought of them as social assets. Orchestras had been
introduced in 1821, and the *Chancellor Livingston* had
immediately upheld its aristocratic tradition by holding
cotillions on the main deck. All important foreign
guests were taken for steamboat rides soon after their
arrival in New York. The private steamboat docks of
the big Hudson River estates, at which even the largest
packets would stop on signal, were evidence of high
social rank and great wealth.

More important than their social advantage, the
people felt that the big boats were proper conveyances
at public events of dignity and pomp. The Marriage of
the Waters had proved that. But even before that
August ceremony, a military band had played a dead
march aboard the *Richmond* as, with engines stilled,
she drifted past Annandale on July 6, 1818. On her
deck, "canopied with crêpe and crowned with plumes,"
lay the coffin of General Richard Montgomery, and in
the pillared portico of the old house, "Montgomery
Place," stood a lone woman, widowed at Quebec
forty-three years before. Canada had surrendered the
remains of her young husband and the *Richmond*
was carrying them to honored burial in New York.
While the minute guns were sounding along the
shore, while the muffled drums were beating over the
water, the old lady stood there as everybody thought
she should. When the *Richmond's* paddles were revolv-
ing again she fainted, and the people of the valley

sighed in a mournful ecstasy and were very sorry for her.

Six years later, on August 16, 1824, the *Chancellor Livingston* and five other steamers, with bands playing and banners flying, dropped downriver to give the returning hero of the Revolution, the old Marquis de Lafayette, his first sight of steam-propelled vessels. Late in September the *James Kent,* gleaming in the mist "like an enchanted castle upon the waters," gave him a ride after the Castle Garden ball in his honor. It was two o'clock in the morning and the moon was down when the marquis went aboard, but a throng of ladies in evening dress and wearing sashes which bore "a likeness of the General entwined with a chaplet of roses" rushed after him and refused to come ashore. The *James Kent* ran aground at Tarrytown but the persistent ladies would not leave her until the military band at West Point lured them to land. Their attentions were almost as embarrassing to the old man as Albany's attempt next day to drop on his head a stuffed eagle whose beak held a crown of laurel and immortelle for his noble brow.

More than a quarter of a century later the steamboat escort was still the valley's greatest mark of favor. On a summer day in 1851 the swift and lovely *Reindeer* proudly bore Jenny Lind from New York to Albany while great crowds along the banks cheered the "Swedish Nightingale," never dreaming that in a few months the great steamer on which she rode so happily would meet its end in a holocaust of bursting boilers, flaming woodwork, and shrieking, dying passengers.

Other visitors, distinguished but less honored, found the Hudson steamboats exciting. Mrs. Basil Hall

—who, after being entertained by the flower of New York's aristocracy for two weeks, complained that she had yet to see *one* American gentleman—admitted that the steamer on which she and her husband and child journeyed from West Point to Albany was "the most magnificent thing of its kind I have yet seen . . . and the dinner the best and the most neatly served that I have seen in any hotel in this country." The tart Mrs. Trollope, even more outspoken than Mrs. Hall against American ways and manners, had nought but good to say of the steamboats. Captain Marryat preferred the moonlight and solitude of the upper deck to the "whimsical sight" of five hundred people in the immense cabin below, sleeping in five long rows of triple-tier beds, "lying in every state of posture and exhibiting every state and degree of repose." While Harriet Martineau, from a West Point piazza, watched "gallant cadets and their pretty partners" dancing at a ball and listened at the same time to the band, the laughter of Negro servants, the rumble of a coming storm, two great steamboats below her were "constellations on the water" and rockets, veering from them like shooting stars, rivaled the lightning overhead.

In 1840 came the introduction of anthracite coal burned under forced draft, a practical invention by the distinguished president of Union College, Eliphalet Nott. A Hudson River steamer, hitherto accustomed to using between fifteen and thirty cords of fat pine each trip, now began to look less like "a horrible monster marching on the tide and lighting its path by the fire it vomited." Fat pine was still carried to bring up pressure for racing. Captains began tying down safety valves and using other illegitimate devices to attain speed. The boilers of the *Aetna* exploded and killed many passengers. So did the boilers of the *General Jackson*.

Steamboat racing on the Hudson began soon after competition was established. The *North America* and the *Champlain* and the *Nimrod* took to spurting whenever one drew alongside the other. Live Oak George Law bet Commodore Vanderbilt a thousand dollars that his *Oregon*, which had come into the river with a broomstick tied to her smokestack as a symbol of her ability to "sweep the river," could beat the *Cornelius Vanderbilt*. He won the wager, though his crew, faced by fuel shortage, had thrown into the furnaces all the carved wooden furniture and most of the fancy woodwork. The commodore in his excitement had wrenched the wheel from the hands of his pilot and had forgotten to slacken speed to make the upriver turn at Croton Point. The *Oregon* beat him back to the Battery by twelve hundred feet.

In 1845 the *Swallow*, racing with the *Express* and the *Rochester*, ran into the little island off Athens called Noah's Brig and more than a dozen lives were lost. Again and again the editorial pages of the newspapers denounced the flagrant disregard of human life. "The passenger walks and sits and sleeps almost in contact with a volcano that in an instant may blow him to atoms," said the *Republican Telegraph* of Poughkeepsie as early as 1824. Yet the racing continued for more than a quarter of a century—until there occurred a disaster of such magnitude that public opinion called a halt.

23

"Hear Me, Heaven-sent Stranger!"

A GREAT North River Opera House, said a February issue of the *Spirit of the Times* in 1845, would be opened on the Hudson in the spring. It would be patronized, the newspaper continued, by New York's "around the town aristocracy" and would "be ready in the early summer to sail up the river and amuse the people of the interior whose residences lie along the banks of the Hudson and so on up the line of the canal and perhaps to the Great Lakes themselves."

Showboats had already brought hair-raising melodramas to the landings along the inland rivers and the prospect of a floating theater delighted many New Yorkers. Nearly a decade before, some of them had read in Tyrone Power's *Impressions of America* the English actor's description of Elder Chapman's Mississippi showboat with its troupe "composed of members of his own family which is numerous and, despite alligators and yellow fever, likely to increase." Others had themselves beheld the garish banners and heard the brassy trumpets of the gilded boats of the West.

And so, with the coming of moderate weather the banks of the Hudson between Spring Street and Canal were lined with curious idlers gazing raptly at the magnificent preparations. The producers had obtained an old southern passenger packet as a basis for

their project and had brought her up the coast into the
Hudson. Then the tarnished letters of her name, *Virginia,* disappeared from her mud-stained prow and in
their place against the new white paint stood the shining golden legend—*Temple of the Muses.* Eagerly her
new owners set about remodeling her into a watergoing
play palace that would rival any like vessel on the
Father of Waters. She was a boat of 385 tons, 90 feet
long, 22 feet wide, flat-bottomed, with a 42-foot beam.
She housed a 90-horsepower engine, had a draught of
about seven feet.

Early on the soft spring evening of April second,
the members of "as respectable and well pleased an
audience as we could desire to see" set out from their
New York homes to attend the city's first showboat
performance. They had no difficulty in finding their
way to the *Temple of the Muses,* for a monstrous
"Drummond light" on the vessel's high bridge made
the Canal Street neighborhood for blocks around as
bright as day and sent its rays far out over the black
water. When, at six o'clock, the gangplank was opened
to patrons, an eager crowd trooped aboard to obtain
hasty refreshment in the great bow salon, 36 by 40
feet, with one bar for liquor and another for food, and
marble-topped tables at which one might sit while
listening to the nine-piece orchestra or staring at the
"elegant paintings, splendid mirrors, cut ground glass
lamp-shades."

An hour later the salon was deserted. When the
curtain slowly rose in the theater on the big boat's stern,
every seat in the $3 private boxes (of which there were
four in the proscenium and a tier in front of the stage)

was filled, as well as the majority of the 50-cent dress circle seats and the 25-cent parquet seats.

Pretty Mrs. Sutherland, in her costume of the forthcoming play, stepped from the wings to speak the "Opening Address written especially for the occasion by C. H. Saunders, Esq.," and the whole glittering horseshoe of the auditorium burst into hearty applause. After she had bowed and smiled her way out of sight again came the presentation of the play, also composed for the event by the prolific Mr. Saunders and obviously fitted by him to a nautical and patriotic presentation, since it was entitled *Our Flag, or Nailed to the Mast, An Original National Drama*. It may have had some claim to being termed international as well, for the cast, besides an Old Patriot and his son, consisted of two English Officers, a French Cook, an Irish Servant, and three ladies—Mary Adams, Jemima Baxbone, and Cleopatra.

When this drama had reached its satisfyingly na-tionalistic conclusion the audience was coaxed into a lighter mood by "the laughable Farce of *A Lady and a Gentleman in a Peculiarly Perplexing Predicament.*" Then all the spectators were free to wander about—to marvel at the stage 42 by 45 feet, at the scenery sixteen feet high and painted by Mr. Grain, "one of the best artists of the country," at the brilliant lighting made possible "by gas manufactured on board by H. S. Driggs who has patented the process which is perfectly safe," at the two ladies' dressing rooms behind the stage, and beneath it at the men's dressing rooms, the bedroom, the dining room for the whole company. Then they went home to talk about what they had seen.

New York's showboat was a quick success. Two days after the grand opening the *Herald* described her as "one of the most interesting and novel theatrical movements we have seen," and asked readers to imagine the city's Olympic Theater shipped on board one of the most elegant North River steamers. "An excellent company of performers, including two or three very pretty women," said the *Herald*, "have embarked their fortunes in this enterprise and really from the manner in which the performances went off last night, we are inclined to believe that their summer tour in which they propose to visit all the river towns, will be very profitable."

The *Temple of the Muses* company did not play *Our Flag, or Nailed to the Mast* again to a New York audience. But they played *Jack's the Lad, or the Pride of the Ocean* so well at the foot of Chambers Street in their second week that the *Herald* reported "this bijou of a theatre" to have attained a popularity unexampled in so short a time, and added significantly: "The old playgoers, the would-be *cognoscenti* who sneered at the undertaking and predicted for it certain failure now admit their mistake."

So many New Yorkers flocked to the river piers to hear and see the offerings of the *Temple of the Muses* that she was still playing to Manhattan audiences long after her advertised "few evenings before leaving New York" were over. One reason was that her managers had hit upon a melodrama so appropriate and so exciting that hundreds wished to see it. *The Floating Beacon, or the Wild Woman of the Wreck* had "all that the painter and the mechanist can bestow." It was as fine a melodramatic mixture of "Gothic" horror and

Shakespearean imitation as the period had produced and quite overshadowed the showboat's spirited rendering of similar pieces in her repertoire—*Black-Eyed Susan, Jackets of Blue, The Cherokee Chief*. New York audiences at the foot of Delancey Street, and later at the East River piers, easily saw why the play had run for a hundred and forty nights at the Surrey Theatre in London. Hardly had the curtain gone up before the audience were treated to the spectacle of a madwoman staggering about the deck of a rocking lightship during a thunderstorm. "Another and another dreadful flash succeeds, the breakers beat fearfully against these rocks as if to usher in new victims to the sanguinary assassins of the desolate beacon—the beacon of death, the abode of horror and despair!"

The shipwrecked hero climbs aboard: "I am exhausted; the rugged edges of these rocks have lacerated my brow. I bleed—I am strengthless—pity!" And when the crazed woman suggests, "You are young and prepossessing, doubtless you have hearts akin to your own in affection," he replies with aplomb, "Yes, I have friends who idolize my very name." In a little while she is telling the young man that she lives on the beacon as the slave of a demon, an abhorred monster. "Oh God! how often have I prayed for death that my blood, mine —could be shed upon the ebbing tide and bear to yon distant shore a crimson testimony of wrongs never to be effaced. A moment only is left me—here on the dark vessel's deck, amid the roaring tempest and the howling waters—hear me, heaven-sent stranger, relate a tale of maddening, heart-dissolving woe."

But the villain interrupts at this tense moment and the hero does not make an important discovery until several scenes later when the woman confesses that "to avert a dreadful fate" she had consented "to become the human monster's wife, curse her!"

"And wherefore should I curse her? No! No! though unparallelled adversity hath sunk her to the wretch's bitterest portion, her soul may still be unstained and pure as mountain ice! . . ."

"My child, my child. I am thy wretched mother!" She rushes into his arms.

Mother and child are soon thereafter enabled to thwart the villain's intent to "dye the yelling waves" with their blood by the fortunate and timely arrival of a company of marines. As the sea soldiers fire a cannon the *Beacon* founders and disappears into the waves and the rescuing boat comes into view with all the admirable characters saved and all the villains left to their watery graves. "Truly," as one reviewer of the play expressed it, "we hardly miss the presence of real water."

The production of a drama called *New York Will* apparently preceded the visit of the *Temple of the Muses* to the river towns, for after that, on May sixth, the showboat announced no more New York productions. I hope it reached the Great Lakes in safety and played profitably along the way. And I wonder where on its voyage up the Hudson it passed a steamboat towing a gaudy barge decorated with banners. For there was another showboat on the Hudson that summer, a boat launched with a cunning purpose—to make money by luring the upriver farmers to buy tickets for a performance in which the wrongs they were suffering from the manor lords were melodramatically reproduced.

The first cry of "Showboat!" had sounded over

Hudson water three years earlier when boys, racing to the landings from the high banks of the river, had hailed with delight the gay caravel of this steamer and its colorful tow. Early in 1842 Jersey City promoters had the idea of touring the river towns with a floating playhouse. Seeking a suitable craft on which to build a theater, they hit upon one of the big "safety barges," popular when frequent bursting of boilers had made travel on passenger packets hazardous. Hitched to laboring steamers, the *Lady Clinton,* the *Lady Van Rensselaer,* the *Susquehanna,* and many another be-cabined and be-saloned towboat had at that time furnished safe transportation untroubled by vibration, kitchen smells, or engine heat. As the speed of the racing steamers increased, however, most travelers were not satisfied to plow slowly but safely along behind second-rate vessels. Then the barges were made over into excursion boats or freighters, and one became Jersey City's floating house of drama.

Using the big hull as a foundation, the producers had reared upon it a theater that would hold an audience of a thousand. Then, with a hired steamboat to pull it from landing to landing, they made a summer jaunt upriver with a company damned in the records as "amateur." Apparently the trip was not very successful for, after a winter's mooring in the Morris Canal Basin in Jersey City behind the resort called "Thatched Cottage Garden," the barge made no voyage in the summer of 1843.

The eventful winter of 1844 made the showboat producers realize that an opportunity lay before them. All through the cold months troops of "calico Indians," masked farmers in calico dresses, had been in armed revolt against the manor lords in the river counties. They had so terrorized the valley that, after the arrest and imprisonment of their chief, Big Thunder (Dr. Smith Boughton in private life), the governor of the state had been obliged to call on many companies of militia to protect the city of Hudson from invasion. Boughton had been tried in March and the jury had disagreed. He was to be retried in September. Meanwhile all the upper Hudson valley was a seething channel of rage. Most townspeople and a few of the independent farmers were approving the stand of the Livingstons and Van Rensselaers. But thousands of farmers on the manors and thousands of others who sympathized with them were determined that Boughton should be acquitted and that the undemocratic custom of exacting annual payments in crops and labor from a farmer in return for the grant of an extended leasehold should be abolished.

The owners of the showboat remembered that in their three-year-old repertoire was a play entitled *The Rent Day*, chosen probably because it had been one of London's most popular Drury Lane melodramas in the previous decade. The author of the play, Douglas Jerrold, had been inspired to write it, so he said, by two of Sir David Wilkie's story-paintings, "Rent Day" and "Distraining for Rent," both of which portrayed the grievous condition of the English tenantry. But the Jersey City producers knew that in Martin (the honest farmer) and Rachel (his loyal spouse), the couple on whom the landlord's hired villains indulged their violent and dishonest practices, every tenant of the Livingstons and the Van Rensselaers would see the image of himself and his wife. They knew, too, that in nearly every speech made by Toby, Martin's poor scholarly brother, the farmers would hear their own bitterness put into melodramatic expression. Hatred of the manor lords had been smoldering into occasional flame for nearly a hundred years. The showboat was taking upriver a torch that might set the whole valley afire.

There is the typical showboat ring to the scene between villainous Silver Jack and virtuous Rachel. The producers knew, though, that to a Hudson valley audience the sneering sensualist would be the more contemptible because he was a rent collector for a rich landlord, Rachel the more admirable because she was a penniless farmer's wife:

JACK.   Hear reason and take the purse. I tell you I do not mean—

RACHEL. You mean the worst. He who would destroy a happy fireside is vile and infamous, but he who would insult its wretchedness is base indeed.

JACK.   Base! Look you! Zounds! To be whipped by a woman's tongue!

RACHEL. Let me pass. I must, will to my children.

JACK.   And they may want breakfast.

RACHEL. Villain, though you insult the wife, have pity on the mother. Let me go.

JACK.   Not now—I have gone too far.

The angry mutterings that were sure to greet this revelation of the infamous purposes of rent collectors were calculated to grow into snarls of rage as poor Toby spoke out a blast that could not more accurately have expressed the feelings of each of the thousands of tenants of the manors:

COLLECTOR CRUMBS. But has your brother no one to speak for him?

TOBY.   Yes, there are two . . . in the church-yard. His grandfather and his father lie there. Go to the graves of the old men and these are the words the dead will say to you: "We lived sixty years on Holly Farm. In all that time we never begged an hour of the 'Squire. We paid rent, tax, and tithe! We earned our bread with our own hands, and we owed no man penny when laid down here." . . . This is what the dead will say. I should like to know what the living has to answer. . . .

And a few moments later Toby speaks again—words almost identical with those of the burning editorials the down-rent newspapers were printing all over the state that summer:

TOBY.   If the landlord lose at gaming his tenants must suffer for 't. The 'Squire plays a low card—issue a distress warrant! He throws deuce-ace—turn a family into the fields! 'Tis only awkward to lose hundreds on a card; but very rascally to be behind-hand with one's rent! . . . When you write back to the 'Squire, you can tell him if he must feed the gaming table, not to let it be with money wrung, like blood from the wretched. Just tell him while he shuffles the cards to remember the aching hearts of his distressed tenants. And when he'd rattle the dice, let him

> stop and think of the knuckles of the
> tax-gatherer, knocking at the cottage
> doors of the poor.

Though *The Rent Day* lost some of its force at the end by showing the landlord himself to be a kindly fellow unaware of the cruel duplicity of his hireling collectors, the Van Rensselaers and the Livingstons could hardly have hailed with enthusiasm his generous release of his tenant from further rents with its obvious suggestion that they go and do likewise:

> This farm has, I hear, been in your family for sixty
> years. May it remain so while the country stands! To-
> morrow shall give you a freeholder's right to it.

The huzzas with which the rest of the company were directed to greet this announcement were obviously baits for echoing response from the audience, and more than a hint that a similar course of action on the part of the Hudson valley landlords would be greeted with even heartier response by the debt-ridden tenants.

Bravely with *The Rent Day* the big theater barge returned to Hudson water in the summer of 1845 to compete against the *Temple of the Muses* with *The Floating Beacon*. Pop Robertson's orchestra of Jersey City musicians performed prodigiously (Pop was a hardware merchant in the wintertime) and all the gay flags whipped in the wind as the barge moved upriver slowly and in state behind a puffing steamer. The playbills, announcing that tickets could be obtained for fifty cents, stated that all performances were for the benefit of the poor, but one of her biographers remarks skeptically that none of her patrons ever heard what charity profited. As a light bit, probably to cool the burning emotions aroused by *The Rent Day,* an amusing one-act burlesque of grand opera—*Bombastes Furioso*—was added to the program, and between the melodrama and this concluding number a trio of Jersey City singers rendered popular songs of the day. The thousand seats were often full and the audience was elite. While the tragedy of Boughton awaited its denouement in September, *The Rent Day* contributed its share toward arousing public opinion against manor rents. Whether or not the arrest of the barge's owner for exhibiting without a license was occasioned by the Livingston and Van Rensselaer interests or by the owners of the *Temple of the Muses* I do not know, but the record says that he vainly tried to defend himself with a federal government coasting license and had to pay a fine of fifty dollars. One hopes that the two showboats never by unhappy coincidence were scheduled for the same landing at the same date. It would have been a pity for any of the Hudson valley playgoers to miss either the magnificent spectacle of the floating beacon rocking on simulated waves just a few feet above real water or fail to hear the sounding speeches of the honest farmers damning the manor lords. Records do not tell what became of the *Temple of the Muses,* but they say the Jersey show barge ended its days of usefulness as a floating restaurant at Coney Island. There possibly she was visited by some of her former patrons who remembered the Hudson's biggest showboat summer.

24

Eight Sides to a Home

ORSON SQUIRE FOWLER had already reached the height of a strange career when he first interested himself in houses. It had begun when he and a classmate in the theological course at Amherst, Henry Ward Beecher, journeyed to Boston to hear an Austrian scholar lecture on a new science—phrenology. Eagerly the two college boys hastened back to Amherst to set themselves up as authorities on such protuberances as the heads of the college afforded. At two cents a cranium they offered to tell each client whether or not he was endowed with generous, niggardly, or proper amounts of Ideality, Eventuality, Amativeness, or Philoprogenitiveness. Trade proved so brisk that, having pretty well exhausted the Amherst supply of heads, the partners moved out into the surrounding towns. There Beecher's golden voice and platform manner lured many a skeptic's brain beneath the practiced hands of Fowler, whose flattering interpretation of his "bumps" resulted in a complete conversion. When, after a solo jaunt of this kind, Fowler counted the forty dollars he had made, he decided to let Henry Ward Beecher go on to the churchly glory that awaited him; there was more of immediate fame and, incidentally, immediate gold in the new science.

As soon as he had graduated, Fowler hurried to

New York and opened an office at 131 Nassau Street. Having instructed his younger brother Lorenzo in the art of reading the heads of clients who dropped in, he continued to lecture and, between engagements, began to write on phrenology. The result of this was a book entitled *Phrenology Proved, Illustrated, and Applied.* It took America by storm and sold in tens of thousands, going through no less than sixty-two editions. Then with the unerring taste of a born writer of nonfiction best sellers, Orson Fowler turned out two books on sex, *Love and Parentage* (forty editions of a thousand and more) and *Amativeness, or Evils and Remedies of Excessive and Perverted Sensuality* (forty editions and still going strong in 1844). These he followed with *Intemperance and Tight Lacing Considered in Relation to the Laws of Life, Fowler on Memory* (foreshadowing Addison Sims of Seattle), and *Fowler on Matrimony.* Sales were Gargantuan. America accepted the "religion of bumps" and proclaimed the Fowlers as its prophets. The office was moved to larger quarters at 308 Broadway. The brothers sent to their upstate New York home in Cohocton for their sister Charlotte and put her to work. Lorenzo Fowler married Lydia Folger of Nantucket and she immediately took over her share of duties. Charlotte married Samuel Robert Wells, a firm disciple, and the group established their own publishing house, Fowlers & Wells, thereby increasing the revenue from Orson's books.

The east bank of the Hudson was still the most highly valued locale for country houses in the 1840's, and Orson Fowler yearned to build there a residence which would be a monument to his spectacular rise from Cohocton farm boy to successful scientist, writer, publisher, lecturer. And so he began to study houses. While on a lecture tour through Wisconsin he had seen an imposing place at Janesville known thereabouts as "Goodrich's Folly." The stuff of which it was made was a mixture of cement, small stones, and sand, known to builders as gravel wall or grout. With this as recommended material, Fowler set about designing a distinctive form for his mansion. He worked out the idea for an octagonal dwelling and at once claimed it to be wholly original. Some architectural critics disputed this by pointing out the famous haunted Octagon in Washington (now the property of the American Institute of Architects), which was Dolly Madison's temporary White House after the burning of the Executive Mansion by the British in 1814. They were confounded, however, by the discovery that the so-called Octagon, designed about 1800 by Dr. William Thornton, was really a hexagon and not at all like the house Fowler contemplated.

Orson Fowler, with characteristic energy, began building his great model house and writing about the idea of it at the same time—in 1848. He finished the writing first and in 1849 his vast American public began buying his little volume called *A Home for All, or the Gravel Wall and Octagon Mode of Building*. It took a decade to build the house. From an oval knoll just north of Fishkill its five octagonal stories (including the basement which was more than half above ground level) towered into the Hudson valley skies. The twenty-foot square glass-roofed cupola, crowning the central stair well, was eighty feet above the ground, and its windows framed a changing panorama that included vast reaches of the gleaming river and the spires of sixteen towns. Below it nearly a hundred rooms bore witness to the builder's varied interests and his architectural theories.

The entrance was through the basement so that entry drafts would be dissipated in the passage to the stair which was lined by storage, milk, and wood rooms on the left and sauce storage, laundry, furnace, and kitchen rooms on the right. The first floor contained four large rooms: parlor, drawing room, dining room, and amusement room. These were arranged around the center stair well, and wide double doorways made it possible to combine two of them into one large room or all four into a great reception hall or lecture auditorium. Among the other rooms were such startling innovations as a "gymnastic room for females" and a "dancing room." The four upper stories were bordered on all sides by verandas and these were connected by outside stairways. A balustrade surrounding the cupola at some distance left room where "clothes might be hung to dry or guests and their host might promenade."

For ten years the people of the mid-Hudson region had watched the building of "Fowler's Folly." There were long periods when all labor ceased and the phrenologist toured the country to obtain more funds to invest in the octagonal monument to his theories. When the house was finally completed and he went there to live, his neighbors flocked to his opening lectures in the four-rooms-in-one lecture hall. Fowler's popularity in the neighborhood was immediately established when, blindfolded, he felt over the head of the "meanest man in Dutchess County" and announced, "This man is too stingy to be honest." Some of the oldest inhabitants of Fishkill still chuckle over that. And they also remember with glee the story of Fowler and Fishkill's most officious citizen, the one who married one of the Van Wyck girls and got to thinking he was just as blue-blooded as his wife. At one of his lectures Fowler called for a boy to come up on the stage and have his head read. The officious citizen looked around him, grabbed a little half-witted ragamuffin and lifted him to the platform. Fowler got the idea, so the story-tellers say, that the imbecilic-looking youngster was the son of the man who presented him, and thinking to please a proud father, wound up his reading with the statement, "The boy obviously has the blood of an aristocrat in his veins."

In the meantime *A Home for All* had been steadily accomplishing its work. Some modernist architects might do well to read it now and be a little embarrassed to find expressed almost a hundred years ago ideas that they pride themselves on today as new and revolutionary. A sphere, said Fowler, was more beautiful than any other form and it enclosed the most space in the least material. Since, for residences, the octagonal was the practical form nearest to the sphere, it should be generally adopted. Eight surfaces, he continued, allowed for more receptivity of sunlight, and the octagonal shape not only eliminated the dark and useless square corner but decreased the distances between objects in the house because residents might go more directly to them without going around right angles.

Besides the novel features already described as a part of his own home, Fowler urged upon the literarily inclined as a part of the top story of his model house a studio lighted from the central glass dome of the cupola. Such a room, he said, would be cool in summer, warm in winter, inaccessible to mosquitoes, and particularly suited to the needs of sensitive authors. "Writers will bear witness," he wrote, "that in the all-powerful exercise of the whole mind required for writing what is fit to read, the blood forsakes the extremities and skin and mounts rushing to the head, leaving all the outer walls a prey to cold, which in addition to severe mental exertion is too much for any constitution sufficiently susceptible to write well. Most awful havoc have my own night writings made of my constitution —having almost destroyed it. Most horribly, almost as if actually dying have I felt by the hundred times, on rising in the morning after having written most of the night and retired cold in the feet and skin but hot at the head."

One other requisite of a good house he embarrassedly took the liberty of alluding to—an indoor toilet. This he would place under the stairs, having the primitive plumbing pass through one of the four chimneys which were to be centered in each of four sides of the house. Apologetically he explained that this plan was not submitted to "squeamish maidens and fastidious beaux" who would continue in their refinement to avail themselves of "the one generally used . . . outside." "But," he asked rhetorically of matrons and the aged and feeble, "is not such a closet a real household luxury?"

With many of Fowler's great reading public the reception of one of his ideas was but a prelude to action. Therefore, "Fowler's Folly," completed in 1858, became an actual residence only in the final years of the fad for building octagonal houses. From 1850 to 1853 was the big period. Then in nearly every community of the northeastern states some ardent follower was rearing an eight-sided dwelling with rooms shaped like pieces of pie. Octagonal schoolhouses were erected because Fowler had said that they provided more sociability, better light, and acoustics superior to those of a square room where "right angles break the sound and create echoes." Octagonal churches sprang up because they facilitated "the congregation seeing one another and thereby the interchange of friendly and benevolent feelings." On the old Ridge Road, stagecoach pike from Albany to Buffalo, a coach company built a tremendous octagonal horse barn. The stalls were in a circle about a central well and hay from the loft, pitched into this well, fell into every stall at once. The barn was so big that there was no necessity for backing to turn around: the driver just drove around the wide circular path outside the stalls and eventually came out where he had gone in. The spiritualist summer colony at Lily Dale in western New York built a separate octagonal séance chamber, feeling that eight-angled walls would be easier for spirit visitors to penetrate than four. Just outside Hammondsport, in the Finger Lake wine region, Timothy Younglove erected (in the same year in which Fowler completed his own house) an octagonal house, octagonal barn, and octagonal smokehouse.

Fortunately not all Fowler's disciples were willing to accept the master builder's idea on grout as a material. Most of the grout octagonals, including Fowler's own, proved their mortality in the first fifty years of their existence. But throughout New York

State and New England today stand proud octagons of brick, wood, and stone. Along the main routes of the Hudson valley many proofs are observable of the trust Orson Fowler's neighbors placed in him. Two stand next door to each other at Stockport. The public library at Red Hook is an unusually fine example. There is another in Kingston. The octagonal gatehouse of Blithewood, famous old Hudson River estate now owned by Mrs. Andrew C. Zabriskie, is a relic of the Fowler influence. Along the Cherry Valley route westward at Madison, New York, one enthusiast combined two upstate fads in one by building his octagonal home of cobblestone. At Geneva, in 1852, a rich deaf-mute from New York City and his deaf-mute wife built an elegant octagonal on which they grafted wrought-iron railings and many characteristically Italian architectural features. A more typical Fowler octagonal is to be found at Akron, near the Tonawanda Indian Reservation. East of the Hudson every New England state has many octagonals but none finer than the great old decaying structure at Danbury, Connecticut, which was constructed with almost literal exactness according to the directions given in *A Home for All*.

The bottom of Orson Fowler's happy world seems to have dropped out suddenly and in a single piece. Just as careful scientists turned on phrenology and savagely discredited it, the grout walls of the cesspool in the big Hudson Valley octagon allowed a seepage into the well. Typhoid raged through the house and a large number of distinguished guests were made desperately ill. Those who escaped death fled in terror. Discouraged, Fowler sold the house. It became a boys' school, then a boardinghouse. It changed hands more than thirty times in rapid succession. In 1897 it was declared unsafe by Fishkill authorities and destroyed by dynamite.

Orson Fowler, still believing in phrenology and his housing theories and fighting for them a brave, losing battle, finally retired to a small farm near Sharon Station, Connecticut, where in 1887 he died. Few remember the nation's most famous phrenologist, and the strange, eight-sided dwellings that dot the northeastern states are now the only reminders of a name that was once a familiar byword in nearly every literate family of America.

25

The Fatal Hudson River Steamboat Race

THERE was an early hubbub along the Hudson wharves at Albany on July 28, 1852. Awakened sleepers in the houses on the lower slope of the hill city looked from their windows down to the water where the night mists were being swiftly burned away by hot sunlight. They saw two long slim steamers, side by side, glitter in white and gold. "Hurrah for Harry of the West! Take the *Henry Clay!*" men shouted along the docks, but their cries were answered by other runners: "Be in New York first. Take the *Armenia*. No decent American would board the *Henry Clay!*" Prices for the voyage had started at a half dollar but the competing runners cut them desperately, calling twenty-five cents a few minutes before sailing time.

Prim, maidenly Maria Hawthorne, sister of the distinguished novelist, much improved from taking the waters at Saratoga Spa, stepped in dignity up the gangplank of the *Henry Clay* on the arm of her uncle, old John Dike of Salem. She was returning home by way of New York so that she might see the scenic grandeur of the Hudson; even Europe was said to have nothing that surpassed it. Joseph Speed—genial Baltimore bachelor and boon companion of young Jerome Bonaparte in the days when Betsy Patterson, his shapely mother, was still trying to marry him off to someone suitable for the son of a king—tripped aboard more swiftly. He was glad to be on his way home after a visit with his York State relatives in Tompkins County.

It was seven o'clock and more than three hundred other passengers had come aboard when the *Henry Clay* moved out into the river, her white-coated black stewards in a knot at her bow, waving and cheering. Two hundred and six feet long, built less than two years before, she looked every inch the "new and swift steamer" she was advertised to be. She had cost $38,000 to construct and was designed to beat even the champion racer of the river, the great *Reindeer*. Thomas Collyer, proud builder and part owner of the big boat, was himself aboard. Collyer and his employees had built the *Armenia* too, in his East River shipyard at the foot of Twenty-first Street, New York, and had sold her to Captain Isaac Smith only a few years before.

Prostrated by food poisoning, Captain John Tallman of the *Henry Clay* lay ill in his cabin, confident that Mr. Collyer with all his river-boat experience would be able to command the crew expertly on the daylong trip. Collyer and his partners had recently made a contract with Captain Smith not to race their boats, and agreed that the *Henry Clay* was to sail in advance of her rival.

The *Armenia* did not sail until the *Henry Clay* had cast off but she was under way a moment afterward. Thick ribbons of smoke trailed out behind the two steamers and live sparks flew from the tall stacks. The horizontal beams above the steeple engines moved up and down with swift regularity and the big side wheels thrashed through the water leaving long white wakes. It was evident that the *Armenia* was striving desperately to catch up with her rival. The run to Hudson seemed short and the *Henry Clay* was well out ahead as she swung toward the landing. Sudden cries of consternation rose from her decks as the *Armenia*, failing to follow, steamed straight ahead down the Athens channel.

There was a great bustle on the Hudson wharf. Passengers who had bought tickets on the *Armenia* vociferously demanded their money back and more vociferously objected when the price of a passage on the *Henry Clay* rose immediately to a dollar, twice the advertised fare for the entire voyage from Albany to New York. The landing was desperately hurried. Baggage was thrown aboard and distinguished elderly Stephen Allen, once mayor of New York City, was rushed up the gangplank with less respect than his white hairs, wealth, and public achievement bespoke.

The *Armenia* was over a mile ahead when the *Henry Clay* once more hove into the channel. Lady passengers and some of the more timorous gentlemen felt relieved, assuming that the boat would not attempt to overcome so great a handicap. Too many lives had been lost already, they said, through accidents caused by the racing of steamers on the Hudson, and they spoke of the tragic fate of the *Swallow,* wrecked in her race with the *Rochester* and the *Express* on the rocks of Noah's Brig in the Athens channel one April night in 1845 with the loss of scores of passengers.

Their previous fears were doubled when the shaking of the boat, under the increasing pressure, and a loud humming noise, given off by the blowers, plainly showed that Mr. Collyer and his crew had no intention of giving up the contest. A continuous blast of intolerably hot air came from the boilers amidships, making passage between fore and after decks practically impossible. Frantically some of the ladies pleaded with their escorts to ask the captain to stop the race. The indignant gentlemen were told by the crew that the captain was ill in his cabin and could see no one. A lady fainted and the gentleman with her appealed to John Germaine, the chief engineer.

"Are you afraid?" asked that officer.

"No, but the ladies are."

"The lives of my fellow officers and of the men are as valuable as those of the ladies. There is nothing to be afraid of," said Mr. Germaine.

Slowly the *Henry Clay* began to overtake the *Armenia*. The mile dwindled to a half mile, a quarter. As the *Armenia* swung in to the Catskill landing, the triumphant yells of her agents and runners on the wharf drowned the noise of her engines but she was only three lengths ahead. Quickly she took on passengers and baggage and was away again but not before the *Henry Clay* had landed and the two crews had cursed each other with loud and hearty sincerity. The *Armenia* had gained three-quarters of a mile before her rival was once more moving downriver. Again the *Henry Clay* began the long pursuit. Soot and fragments of unburned anthracite drifted down on her decks; the shaking was more violent and the humming noise grew louder.

"If there is a single gentleman aboard," said a lady loudly, "he will go and compel the captain to stop racing."

Isaac MacDaniel of Rutland, Vermont, traveling with his wife and daughter, proposed to two gentlemen, one from Canada and one from Missouri, that they find the captain and threaten to throw him overboard if he did not order the racing stopped. Mr. Mac-Daniel appealed to James Jessup, clerk of the boat.

"There is no danger," said Mr. Jessup.

In the *Henry Clay's* barroom exhausted firemen, smutty with coal and sweating streams, lifted foam-crowned glasses to eager mouths pledging success to the officers who drank with them and excitedly urged them to go back to their fires and keep them blazing high.

Now the *Henry Clay* was gaining again. In deep channel she was faster, and the *Armenia* seemed sluggish as her swift enemy approached. The distance that separated the two became a matter of lengths and the *Armenia* moved over toward the west bank as the *Henry Clay* bore down on her. Pilot Jim Elmendorf nosed her in close to the *Armenia* as she moved alongside. An officer called for fenders and a man stood on the paddle box ready to throw them out along the starboard rails as the distance between the boats narrowed. Now the two prows, only a few feet apart, were even and the long white boats swept on like giant twins straining to the utmost as they passed Turkey Point, about five miles above Kingston. Then the *Henry Clay* shot out ahead a yard, two yards, and Jim Elmendorf in the pilothouse suddenly spun the wheel. There was a grinding roar and the *Armenia's* woodwork just forward of the larboard wheelhouse splintered as the *Henry Clay* cut across her bow.

Above the shrieks of the ladies sounded the cries of the *Henry Clay's* crew: "All passengers to larboard." There was a rush away from the interlocked prows.

The maneuver lifted her starboard guard above the larboard guard of the *Armenia* and there it rested for more than five minutes as the *Henry Clay* relentlessly drove her helpless opponent toward the western bank, now within a stone's throw. The officers of the *Armenia* had to choose between throwing off her steam and being run aground. There were quick sharp orders, and she drifted clear as the *Henry Clay* steamed down the center of the channel, her crew shouting derisively.

The *Henry Clay* was not headed again but she kept on trembling and humming. She had cleared Kingston before the *Armenia* landed and, since she still pressed on with the apparent intent of defeating her rival by as great a margin as possible, twenty indignant passengers trooped down the gangplank at Poughkeepsie protesting that they would not continue to endanger their lives in a racing steamer. At Newburgh the *Armenia* was just a small blurred white spot to the north and her runners were asking only sixpence for passage to New York while the exuberant agents for the winning boat, cheering "Harry of the West," charged a shilling and shouted, "Take the *Henry Clay* —the *Armenia* won't get here till night." A large number of passengers followed this advice, among them Andrew Jackson Downing, with his wife, his mother-in-law—Mrs. John Peter De Windt—two of Mrs. De Windt's children, Frank and Mary, and the romantically beautiful Mrs. Matilda Wadsworth of New Orleans, a widow at twenty-six. The long white-covered tables in the dining salon were crowded and there were people waiting at the door for places as the hot July afternoon began. Miss Hawthorne might now gaze at the blue mist-shrouded Highlands to her heart's content. The grim walls of Sing Sing Prison, rising sheer from the green waters, could not fail to remind aged Stephen Allen that it was his report on the conditions of the old New York City prison that had caused them to be built. And Mr. Speed knew that with every turning of the big side wheels he was nearer to his beloved Baltimore home, to his prized portrait of the Duke of Wellington, strange present for a Bonaparte to give, and to all the amusing associations of his youth.

Steadily the *Henry Clay* clove to the middle of the channel, still at her top speed. The Palisades lifted above her now, dwarfing her and dulling the high, gilded eagle perched on her foremast. She had passed the town of Yonkers, lying in sunlight and making the shadowed west bank look lonely and cool. Still the rain of anthracite dust drifted down on the gay awnings of her top deck, still yellow sparks darted upward in the black smoke from her stacks. The ebb tide was running against a strong south wind and the river was choppy, filled with curling white-capped waves. It was three o'clock, the midday dinner was over, the journey was almost ended. A few of the passengers were laughing at a frightened man, Harry Lawrence, who had stationed himself far forward on the bow and had piled his baggage up as a barricade between himself and the boilers.

When they later recalled the events of that after-noon, no one seemed to remember who first noticed the wisp of smoke drifting from the midship hatchway. Beneath the deck a fireman was desperately throwing buckets of water on the flaring canvas cover of the larboard boiler. Almost overcome with smoke, his clothes ablaze, he staggered from the boiler room and

made for the deck. As he reached it and jumped overboard, the whole midship section of the *Henry Clay*
burst into flames. Jim Elmendorf, standing with his
wife in the pilothouse, took one look at the leaping
yellow streaks and spun the wheel over. Without dimin-
ishing her speed the *Henry Clay* swung sharply and
started for the east bank. White-faced Jake Zimmer-
man in the engine room already filled with smoke, put
on full steam and fastened the control so that the engine would work at top speed until the boat was
beached, before he leaped for the deck. Screaming passengers started forward, those on the afterdecks dashing through the flames. The bartender, suddenly assuming the duties of a ship's officer, urged them back,
shouting orders for all passengers to go aft, possibly
with the idea of lifting the prow as the boat ran ashore.
Many returned. Helplessly they lined the rails as the
Henry Clay raced for the bank. A gardener, working
among the flower beds along the river edge of Assem-
blyman Russel Smith's Riverdale estate, looked up to
see a blazing steamboat bearing down on him.

It was only a few minutes before the *Henry Clay*
struck with terrific force, her bow sliding up the shelv-
ing bank twenty-five feet and nosing eight feet into
the earth of a high railroad embankment. The shock
knocked over one of the smokestacks and threw benches
and tables about. Many passengers on the promenade
deck were hurled to the deck below or into the water.
A few far forward, including Pilot Elmendorf and his
wife and the foresighted Harry Lawrence, were thrown
to safety on land. The jolt seemed to have stirred the
fires and the flames united into a solid sheet that began
slowly moving aft, blown by the south wind. Now the

fatal stupidity of the bartender's order was obvious. There was no going forward and the stern was over deep water. It was burn or drown for the passengers who could not swim. A white boat with a green line about its gunwale suddenly appeared, its occupant rowing about aimlessly and picking up no one of the dozens already struggling in the water. A gentleman named Dunning seized upon a large wooden sign, a milliner's advertisement which stood on the deck, and leaped overboard with it. A gallant Mr. Edwards standing upon the taffrail saw a panic-stricken young lady in great danger of being burned and exclaimed (according to the report of the New York *Herald* for July 31, 1852), "Will you go with me into the water and run the risk of being drowned or will you be burned to death?" The report concludes, "The female accepted the noble offer and both were saved."

The flames were working aft swiftly now and the frantic passengers began to drop into the deep water by scores. A large black boat with a red streak arrived from upriver, picked up seven, and made for shore though it could easily have held fifteen. Mr. Downing, a strong swimmer, was very calm. He gave minute directions to all his charges, then went up on the promenade deck and threw many wooden chairs into the water. On two of these his tiny wife was able to float to shore. His children also escaped but Mrs. De Windt was drowned. A Newburgh passenger, struggling in the water, saw that Mr. Downing was trying to keep Mrs. Wadsworth afloat and that the task was difficult. Neither of them was seen alive after that.

Mr. Collyer, already ashore, had begun breaking up a rail fence and shoving the pieces out into the water to struggling people. Captain Tallman, at last aroused from his sickbed, and already so exhausted that he could not speak, was in the water, helping passenger after passenger to shore. Mr. Thompson, of Perry Street in New York City, let down from the deck a wooden settee, jumped after it, and had just climbed upon it when someone grabbed him by the leg and pulled him off. At that moment he saw his wife, who could not swim, jump into the water. He succeeded in working along the side of the boat with her to the paddle wheel, which they grabbed. The weight caused the wheel to revolve, throwing them off and emptying flaming fragments on them. They finally floated to safety on fence boards.

The gardener, who had been the first to see the burning boat from shore, and Mr. Smith's coachman had just launched a small boat when they saw a sloop, occupied by four men who did not help with the rescue but were picking up floating valuables, robbing helpless, drowning victims. Bravely the two servants boarded the river pirates, threw them overboard, and used the sloop to save as many as it would hold. One gentleman, said to be from Newark, New Jersey, methodically saved his wife and each of his nine children. One at a time they jumped and were rushed ashore by the valiant father, who was hurried away "entirely senseless" by his grateful brood and their mother. A train puffed along the embankment and stopped, its men passengers scurrying from the coaches down to the river to help in the rescue work.

"A noble Newfoundland dog named Neptune [to quote again from the New York *Herald* of July 31] rushed into the water and seized a young child that was drowning by the dress near the shoulders and bore it safely to shore. He returned and approached a woman to assist in the same way, but she was so frightened that the dog had to be called off and he was thus deprived of the opportunity of extending that relief to the sufferers to which his noble nature prompted him."

All was over in about twenty minutes. The watch found in dead old Stephen Allen's pocket, along with a slip of paper reading "Keep good company or none," had stopped at 3:26. Along the shore for over a mile lay hats, shawls, dresses, an occasional body. The *Armenia* loitered out in the channel, its two small boats searching the waters for any sign of a living being, but the *Henry Clay* had raced on too far ahead of her. The train moved on bearing a distressing load of the burned and drowned. Another train came down from the north and stopped. In the hot sunlight on the river men worked, slowly dragging for corpses, while the *Henry Clay* burned to the water. Isaac MacDaniel, searching among the bodies on the shore for his dead wife, came upon James Jessup, the clerk who had so smugly reassured him a few hours before.

"Is there any danger here?" said Isaac.

By five o'clock nothing was left except a fragment of the bow, some ten or twelve feet high, which burned slowly "like a warning beacon to light up the shapeless wreck of charred timbers and iron below." William Lawrence, coroner of Westchester County, wrote in his tent beside the water that night: "The last scenes of the day were singularly impressive and solemn. The night was remarkably clear, the full moon dimly lighting up the river and the hills; at one side of a gloomy arch over the railroad was the wreck, the bow still slowly burning; half revealed in its lurid light lay the bodies of two men; above the arch a group of some twenty persons were busy with newly discovered corpses, trying to identify them. . . . The surface of the stream, placid and silent as the grave, was broken only by the oars of a few men who were still dredging for bodies."

They covered the dead that moonlit evening with green boughs. The coroner and his jury had to draw guns and threaten a dark craft filled with plunderers, "sacrilegious harpies who hover about." All night long cannon boomed out over the Hudson as the workers ashore tried to dislodge bodies and bring them to the surface of the river.

And in the morning the details of the disaster reached New York. Stephen Allen was dead. Andrew Jackson Downing was dead, and so were his mother-in-law and the lovely, tragic Mrs. Wadsworth. Miss Hawthorne had been lost, and genial Mr. Speed. The number of dead was reported as eighty and Captain Tallman was already regretting his early statement to a passenger, "There were only ten or fifteen persons drowned and they were common people." In the Astor House Gentlemen's Parlor an excited crowd of men, some of them with tear-stained faces, denounced Mr. Collyer, Captain Tallman and his crew, the officers and crew of the *Armenia*, for racing their steamers in complete disregard of the safety of passengers. Answering these accusations on the next day, the owners of the two boats made public announcement of their agreement that there would be no racing, and pilot Isaac Polhemus of the *Armenia* wrote a letter, which was immediately published, stating that the latter steamer had not attempted to beat the *Henry Clay* because racing had been forbidden by her captain and owner, Isaac P. Smith (who was not aboard on the day of the disaster). Charges of criminal murder against the owners and officers of the *Henry Clay* were set aside by Judge Edmonds in Westchester County but he held the accused to bail for manslaughter in the jurisdiction of the United States District Court.

In the meantime James Gordon Bennett, editor of the New York *Herald*, waged an editorial war against steamboat racing on the Hudson, a campaign made more bitter by complaining letters from passengers of the steamers *Frances Skiddy* and *Alida* which frequently entered into competitions, and by the boiler explosion of the racing *Reindeer* at Bristol Landing in September of the same year. Mr. Bennett wrote: "How long are human hetacombs [*sic*] to be thus offered upon the altar of an avaricious speculation which sacrifices all things to itself?"

The trial of the defendants in the *Henry Clay* case ended in their acquittal on November 2, 1852. A few months later the New York State legislature passed a rigid Steamboat Inspection Act which finally put an end to the racing of steamers on the Hudson.

26

Tin-Horn Rebellion

WHEN in 1844 slim Dr. Smith Boughton and his attractive wife moved from Rensselaer County into Columbia County there must have been at least a few neighbors in both places who wondered why. A talented young physician would hardly select the manor section of a Hudson River county as an environment promising material success. He must have known that in the hills and valleys encompassed by the forty-mile square of the Van Rensselaer grant and on the hundreds of thousands of acres of Livingston Manor the farmers lived on land first taken on perpetual lease by their ancestors. If they sold that land they were bound to pay a quarter of the price to the manor lord who had forced them into a kind of feudal servitude which included rendering menial service to the proprietor and sharing crops with him. He knew, too, that the Livingstons and Van Rensselaers refused to sell their lands and simply awaited payment of the hens and wheat and days of labor due them annually through no merit other than that of their having inherited the lands granted their forebears. To the complaints of the poverty-stricken farmers that the American Revolution had been fought to free men from just such tyranny, he had heard the manor lords reply, "The Livingstons and the Van Rensselaers were heroes of the

American Revolution," and continue to insist that the duly constituted officers of the law collect rents from any farmer in arrears.

By the time Dr. Boughton's strange removal from a prosperous community to a barren one was noted by the authorities of Columbia County things had begun to happen. Rumor brought word to the manor lords that the young physician's calls on his neighbors were not entirely to purvey medicines. Boughton was said to be a dangerous organizer who was telling the tenants that the titles to the vast land grant were not secure and that he was establishing a farmers' alliance to discredit these titles in the courts. For each acre they tilled the farmers were to pay annual dues of twenty-five cents into a fund to finance a legal struggle.

On a November day soon after this tale had reached them, a spy for the manor lords, riding through the township of Taghanick, heard a tootle and a boom coming from a near-by field. What he saw a moment afterward he tried later to describe. "Old Dan Tucker," played on a fife and a drum, had set a stirring beat for the march of hundreds of masked men in swinging calico dresses. Red, blue, yellow sheepskin masks, on which grotesque eyes, spread noses, contorted mouths had been painted in contrasting hues, covered heads and necks. Dresses "made like a woman's nightgown" hung below the men's knees, brilliant in solid colors, bold figures, garish stripes. Calico pantaloons, large and full, showed above boots that had weathered many plowings. From fancy belts hung silken tassels, rattlesnake skins, bright tin horns that gleamed and jingled in the marching. Each man carried a weapon in his hands: spear, tomahawk, pistol, club, pitchfork, or rifle.

A big crowd of spectators in everyday dress cheered the polychrome army as it stamped a final round of the field and halted before a raised platform. A figure that somehow showed itself slight and graceful beneath a straight-hanging dress walked out on the boards and the calico soldiers raised a shout. "Big Thunder!" they yelled, and the spectators pressed in close about them repeating the words.

"Down with the rent!" shouted Big Thunder and the grotesque figures below him brandished their weapons and gave back a shattering wave of sound. It died out with his next words: "The Livingstons and Van Rensselaers have taken from us and our fathers in manor rents many times what our land is worth. It is treason to pay rents to robbers who forfeit citizenship by calling themselves lords and refuse honest citizens the right to own their homes. Do not pay them. Be still and do nothing. The Natives you see here (Indians, we call ourselves) will take care of you. When the sheriffs come to take your farms, the Natives will come out from the rocky glens and caves in the mountains and drive them off. They will come at night and return at night and no one will know whence they came and where they went."

Again the men in calico waved their spears and guns and clubs, shouting "Down with the rent!" Someone began to sing and they all joined in, the drum and fife sounding faintly above the strong male chorus. The tune was "Old Dan Tucker" again but the words were not those of the old song:

> The moon was shining silver bright
> The sheriff came at dead of night

High on a hill an Indian true
And on his horn a blast he blew.

Get out of the way, Big Bill Snyder,
We'll tar your coat and feather your hide, sir.

Bill thought he heard the sound of a gun
He cried in fright, O my race is run
Better that I had ne'er been born
Than come within sound of that big horn.

Get out of my way, Big Bill Snyder,
We'll tar your coat and feather your hide, sir.

At appropriate moments in the song the singers reached for the tin horns that hung from their belts, put them to their lips, and blew mighty blasts. The watching spy sensed the rise of a dangerous mood and hastily retired without observing how the meeting ended.

Columbia County officers soon enough found out all they needed to know about the calico Indians. Disregarding upriver reports of officers dipped in hot tar while the tin horns blew, Sheriff Henry Miller and one deputy set out from Hudson a couple of weeks later to sell the farms of Steve Decker and Abe Vosburgh who had got behind in paying their annual tribute of chickens and wheat to the Van Rensselaers. When they were riding through Ancram they heard horns blowing and a few moments later met a long column of calico warriors accompanied by more than a thousand undisguised spectators. Hastily the officers dismounted and ran into the back room of Sweet's Tavern but the chiefs of the Indians followed them. Even with pistols and swords at their breasts, sheriff and deputy refused to turn back. They brushed the weapons aside, returned to their horses, and rode to the first farm scheduled for sale—the whole rout of calico Indians and spectators streaming behind them. As they were beginning their auction some of the crowd saw a slight man in dress and mask push his way up to a place beside the officers and there was a sudden cry of recognition: "Big Thunder!"

"Shall we take their papers and burn 'em?" asked the sonorous voice of the speaker of the previous meeting.

The left hands of the men in calico rose in a silent unanimous vote.

"Do the palefaces agree?" called Big Thunder.

A great shout answered and the frightened sheriffs, helpless before leveled guns, gave up their papers. Then Big Thunder led the procession back to Sweet's Tavern. At a safe distance from the steps a tar barrel was already blazing. As Big Thunder threw the papers into the flames the whole crowd yelled approval. A few moments later they jeered the released officers riding disconsolately back toward Hudson. All the upriver towns heard talk that the next big meeting of the Indians would be at Smoky Hollow (near Hollowville) on December eighteenth. Big Thunder, who had already called the land titles of the Van Rensselaers worthless, would this time attack the Livingstons! The people of Hudson were getting uneasy. Each new meeting was nearer and the farmers were boasting they would yet gather on the courthouse square in Hudson itself.

The down-renters began arriving at Bam's Tavern, Smoky Hollow, early in the cold morning of the eighteenth. Many brought their dresses with them and put them on in the upper rooms. Thousands of would-be spectators from all over the river country came in wagons, on horseback, afoot. They made a great circle around the silent inn, watching the first and second floor piazzas where they expected the Indians to appear. A gunshot and a war whoop—and the first masked warrior in calico sallied out on the upper level. Leaping, yelling, firing his pistol, he made for the stairway that led below. As he reached it, a second fantastically garbed figure rushed out. In long single file then the calico Indians followed. They had topped their masks with cowhorns and on the backs of their dresses the tails of raccoons and foxes flopped about. More than a hundred, gesturing wildly, uttering savage cries, shooting, had hurled themselves from the upper doors of the tavern into the weaving parade when some of the spectators saw that one of their own number, a young man, had sunk in agonized position to the ground. Those who bent over him found blood bubbling from a wound in his chest. A bullet fired by a careless parader had gone through his heart and he was dead. Excitedly they identified him as Bill Rifenburg, a boy from a near-by farm, while the Indians, unconscious of the tragedy, kept up their mad play. More than two hundred had dashed out now, and they were going through a complicated drill in the open field beside the tavern while the corpse lay within a few feet of them. Then the marching suddenly stopped as Big Thunder, standing on the second-floor piazza, began to speak.

The listeners did not hear an antirent diatribe. The chieftain spoke slowly, saying that the shooting of young Rifenburg was a regrettable accident, that he and his warriors had come to this meeting armed because they were afraid they would have to fight off the sheriff who had sworn in a posse to arrest him. Out of respect for the deceased, he said, the meeting was dismissed.

Quietly the crowd drifted away. The body of young Rifenburg was carried to his home. December sunlight slanted on the empty, trampled field and the panes of the old tavern. Inside, dresses removed, the leaders of the Columbia County down-rent party sat by the fireplace and talked, not knowing that the belated sheriff and his posse were even then on their way.

Hearing of the death of Rifenburg, Henry Miller had left Hudson with the district attorney and one officer. While passing through Stockport he had picked up three other deputies. Before the antirenters knew who they were, the six had walked boldly into Bam's Tavern and had searched the lower floor. Then the sheriff dashed up the stairs. By the fireplace in the big ballroom from which the Indians had recently made their spectacular exit into the parade, he saw a group sitting in earnest conversation. With his five companions behind him, Henry Miller walked quickly to a slight, young-looking man and said, "Dr. Boughton, you are under arrest." Then he turned and said to all in the room, "I command the assistance of all of you."

With their prisoner in their midst the six men walked from the room down to the first floor and out on the piazza. They heard the pounding of boots on the stairs behind them. Boughton stopped, pulling back desperately.

"Help!" he shouted.

Out of the door shot Mort Belding, known to his

comrades as Little Thunder, and hurled himself upon
the posse. Behind him came Big Sam Wheeler from
Taghanick and a half dozen others. There was a grunt-
ing, thumping struggle as the sheriff and the four deputies tried to pull the prisoner into their waiting carriage. Tin horns were blaring out of the tavern
windows and some of the antirenters who had started
for home were running back toward the sound.

Then from the entrance steps District Attorney
Theodore Miller began to speak. Somehow or other he
caught the attention of the crowd. Their forming about
him seemed automatic, as if they were incapable of
any other action. He said that they must not stand
in the way of the law and it would go hard with anybody who tried to keep the sheriff from doing his duty,
that the prisoner would receive a fair trial. For a half
hour he spoke to snarling, sullen men while Henry
Miller and his deputies fought off those who would not
listen. Inch by inch they dragged Dr. Boughton toward
the carriage.

At last he was in the back seat and held powerless.
Then the sheriff, who had been a blacksmith, grabbed
Mort Belding with one hand and hurled him in beside
his leader. A deputy whipped up the horses and they
trotted off on the road to Hudson. The carriage rattled
through a countryside echoing to the blasts of countless
horns. Behind it, at a discreet distance, trotted a growing band of mounted men in dresses and masks. The
news of the capture of the leaders said to be Big Thunder
and Little Thunder was spreading with unbelievable
speed and the Hudson valley farmers were rallying to
their aid. The story had flashed into Hudson ahead of
the sheriff's team and a crowd was waiting to cheer

him at the end of the long drive and to shake defiant fists at the sullen pursuit, halting in thwarted rage.

It was a vociferous, singing impromptu parade that escorted the posse and their prisoners to the jail. "They've got Big Thunder. They've got Little Thunder," the crowds chanted triumphantly. But when the jail doors had closed and everybody had gone home through the dusk to supper, Hudson was a frightened town. From the purpling hills around came the incessant blasts of tin horns. There were moving torches on the other side of the broad river and the evening breezes that ruffled its darkly gleaming surface carried a far blowing that seemed to come from the cluster of lights that marked the town of Athens. The men in calico were rounding up their forces. All night long the wakeful city heard sounds that meant more trouble.

In the morning came a message: if the prisoners were not released at once a thousand calico Indians would march into Hudson and burn it down. The mayor ordered the Hudson Light Guards to be ready to fight at the first peal from the Presbyterian steeple. Word came that a courier sent to the governor in Albany had been captured and was being held on a farm to the north. Frantic clangor of bells streaming upriver told the besieged town that its messenger had crossed the Hudson safely and galloped into Catskill. A night patrol, twenty watchers for each ward, was established. A hundred men were hastily sworn into state service and stationed before the jail with four pieces of artillery. Five hundred volunteer minute men were called for and most of the able-bodied males of Hudson responded. Long hours after sunset the up-rent men of

Catskill and Athens marched out of the darkness down by the river into the lighted town. News came that someone had finally got through to Albany and arms and troops were on the way.

The next few days were filled with strain and uncertainty. There was little gaiety at Christmas but the Hudson children liked it, for on that day, with drums beating and colors flying, the Albany Burgesses Corps in full uniform marched from the railroad station into town. Still the feeling of danger and suspense continued. In the country districts hundreds of farmers were reported riding from upriver and downriver to join the calico Indians in their attack. Before a big public meeting, on December twenty-sixth, the mayor of Hudson read a proclamation: "Deeply must all good citizens deplore the exigency which now demands, for the first time in our history, the gathering of a standing armed force in this city." Hudsonians gave the sentiment a cheer but it was not so loud as their anguished roar when they heard a moment later: "Remember, citizens, no policy of Insurance will cover losses by Fire when caused by Invasion or Insurrection or Civil Commotion." That brought immediate action. North and south went the appeals of terrified Hudson.

Meanwhile a special detail of the Albany Burgesses set out on a below-zero morning to capture White Chief, born Walter Hutchins, most dangerous of the leaders of the calico army still at large. They swooped down on Proper's Tavern south of Hudson, but White Chief had just left. They rode on to Blue Stores, but the quarry was gone and darkness had come. Soon after six the next morning they were in Minkville where

White Chief was said to live. He was not there. They caught sight of him near Gallatin but he rode into the woods and got away. After a night of shivering at Hot Grounds, the Burgesses returned, crestfallen and discouraged, to find that Hudson was fairly bursting with four more companies of Albany militia and the cheering word had come from Kingston that her Ulster Greys, the Rondout Guards, and the Hurley Rifles were ready to march at a moment's notice.

In New York City, Captain Krack's troop of German-American cavalry standing solemnly in uniform at the military funeral of a comrade, had been surprised by an order to move upriver at once. At two o'clock in the morning they rode aboard a chartered steamboat bound for Hudson. When they arrived they found that all the best houses of the city were filled with officer guests, the inns were packed with militia, mostly Albany Irish, and even the cabins and bunks of the ice-festooned, gilt-decorated steamboat *Fairfield* (wintering at Hudson) were filled with soldiers. The German troopers were obliged to make their transport their barracks.

The officers in command of the allied companies decided upon January third, the day after the cavalry arrived, for a procession to display the formidable military forces gathered to defend the town. All the people of Hudson lined the streets to cheer the soldiers and among them stood many a down-rent farmer wistfully comparing the gold braid, the plumes, the dashing cut of the rich uniforms with his hidden calico dress. Captain Krack's New York Cavalry led off, "noble looking and effective," their horses dancing skittishly as the Hudson brass band thumped and blared. Behind them,

marching with a precision that had made them famous
in the state, came the Albany Republican Artillery.
Modestly at the rear of the six visiting companies
stalked the hosts of the day, the Hudson Light Guards
in silver-buttoned blue coats and white pantaloons,
their snowy plumes floating like a hundred little clouds
above the tops of their tall bucket-shaped, white
leather hats. At the end of the glittering line straggled
the Citizen Volunteer Corps of Hudson, mechanics and
storekeepers in their Sunday clothes, their hunting rifles
on their shoulders.

The parade was a great success. The people of
Hudson looked upon it and were suddenly comforted.
No farmers in calico would dare to attack so brilliant
a military array. Almost hysterical in its relief, the
town was suddenly gay with dinners and receptions.
With hundreds of uniformed beaux the Hudson girls
began to have a better time than Hudson girls had ever
had. A military ball was announced for the evening of
Wednesday, January eighth, at the big white-pillared
Hudson House. The elaborate function was nearly
ruined, however, by a strange incident which took place
before that very hostelry early on the appointed day.
According to the report of Private Flannagan of Albany, sentry guarding the hotel entrance while his comrades slept within, a solitary horseman walked his
mount slowly up the dark street toward the Hudson
House just as the town clock was striking the third hour
after midnight. When he had come within twenty feet
of the hotel colonnade he wheeled his horse to face it.

"Who goes there?" said Private Flannagan duti-
fully. The lone rider drew a horse pistol and fired. The
ball missed the sentry's head by three inches, passed

through a heavy pillar, and lodged in a corner of the house. By the time Private Flannagan was ready to return the fire (from behind another pillar) the horseman was gone.

This inexplicable attack so stirred the military command in Hudson that for a time it was feared the ball might be abandoned. It was finally decided, however, that the attack had been an individual gesture and did not signify an immediate general invasion. And so the ball came off—a splendid affair attended by the beautiful and the brave. Beneath wall decorations of flags and crossed arms, all the available officers in their most resplendent uniforms led out the city's prettiest girls to dance to an orchestra full and complete and to partake of a collation bountiful and elegant.

Having danced, according to a newspaper account, "until the wee hours," New York's Captain Krack seems to have been inspired by all the admiration he received to immediate and valiant action. The next night, depending upon the day's snowfall to deaden the sound of his horses' hoofs, at the head of twenty of his troopers he made a sudden dash on Minkville.

There to his great delight he found, crouching in a garret, the fugitive White Chief, Walter Hutchins, prize for which the Albany Burgesses had striven so eagerly and vainly a few days before. A galloping courier brought the tidings into Hudson in the early morning, announcing that the gallant captain would lead his troopers through the streets of the town in military array, parading their prisoner in a wagon. All Hudson seemed to know the news in an instant and long before the riders were in sight the townspeople lined the path the procession was to take.

Then, as the crowd waited, its chattering was suddenly hushed by a strange wild crying that seemed to
be hanging over the hill down which the soldiers would
ride. It grew louder—and it was a man's voice let go
with terrific force in short staccato sounds. The parade
came over the brow of the hill and the nearest spectators
could see Captain Krack and his score of German-
American troopers in full uniform riding rigidly at
attention. In the center of their formation rolled a farm
wagon drawn by a team. The strange noise swelled
again and the waiting crowd could see its source at last.
On the platform of the wagon stood Walter Hutchins.
He was laughing. As the troopers advanced, their faces
set in self-conscious disregard, Walter danced about on
the wagon boards, pointing at their fancy boots, their
plumed hats, their shining sabers, and emitting great
bursts of hilarious sound. Mighty haw-haws ricocheted
from the walls of houses, rolled downhill and flattened
out in long echoes over the surface of the Hudson.

The crowd began to feel embarrassed. All this military show over one of their neighbors, a Columbia
County farmer with a tin horn and a calico dress,
seemed out of place. They could understand the use of
soldiers to run down and imprison the eloquent, educated, dangerous Dr. Boughton who had come from
Rensselaer County to stir up trouble. For more than ten
days bloodshed as a result of Big Thunder's rebellious
crimes had seemed inevitable and the prospect created
both terror and fortitude. Now all at once the idea
seemed a little ridiculous. Something had been over-
done. A parade of uniformed troopers to display a captive from whom some of the spectators frequently
bought eggs and butter was surely absurd. Suddenly the

troopers were no longer noble defenders; they were just a lot of stout New York Germans in outlandish costume. Their brave display wilted as they advanced. And as the wagon squeaked an accompaniment to the roars that shook the White Chief's sturdy frame, all the heart went out of a crisis. Tin horns blowing in the night called more for talk than for artillery.

Self-consciously a few days later the Albany Burgesses picked up their knapsacks and went home, parading through the streets of the capital city without having lost a man. Soon other Albany companies joined them, displaying a field piece taken without combat from the calico army. Captain Krack and his troopers steamed off downriver, bound for the Bierstuben of Manhattan. A newspaper reporter went to the jail to interview the terrifying Big Thunder, and found there quietly reading, "a young man of genteel appearance and prepossessing address, the reverse of everything, indicated by Thunder, big or little." He asked Dr. Boughton how he felt. "I do not feel well," replied the man charged with manslaughter, robbery, assault, riot, and conspiracy. "I have left a young wife and infant child at home. The thought of that is enough," and the scourge of the manors burst into tears.

Suddenly deserted by giddy uniforms, embarrassed custodians of a small, scholarly physician, Hudson people went a bit shamefacedly back to work, hoping that rent troubles were over. It was not until the short first trial of Boughton in March, when, to their dismayed surprise, no sufficient witnesses could be found to swear the prisoner was Big Thunder, chief of the calico Indians, that they realized the farmers were not nearly ready to call quits. With Boughton out on bail in July,

as a result of the first trial jury's disagreement, and
with the sheriffs of every river county having been
treated to horn concerts and coats of hot tar all
through the early summer, it seemed certain that when
the next court convened early in September the greatest struggle of all between the up-rent manor lords
and the down-rent farmers would begin.

During the whole of the long hot summer bitter
feeling grew. When Judge John W. Edmonds made his
opening address at the new trial on September 3, 1845,
the little Hudson courthouse was crowded with observers influential enough to obtain seats. Outside
milled a threatening crowd of thousands of down-rent
farmers. The speech was a powerful denunciation of the
lawbreakers who had taken part in violent outbreaks
against the manor lords. Nevertheless, said Judge Edmonds, he had noticed time and again that the intelligence, morals, and industry of men who owned their
own land were superior to those qualities in men who
held leases from the manor lords. He could hold out
little hope to the poor people. Violence would avail
them nothing. Nor could they look to the legislature
for aid since that body could not pass laws impairing
the obligations of contracts. Only public opinion and
a sense of justice might bring about amicable sentiment. The farmers outside jeered when, through the
open windows, they heard this conclusion. They and
their forebears had been waiting for more than a hundred years, they said, for public opinion and a sense of
justice to do something.

The eager spectators soon got the show they were
looking for. The prisoner was late for the first session
and Judge Edmonds rebuked him severely. Immacu-

lately dressed, his combed red whiskers framing his ardent, handsome face, John Van Buren, attorney general of the state, rose to question the first prospective juror. The ladies gasped at sight of "Prince John" who had danced with young Queen Victoria and set American tongues wagging about a romance, but the farmers growled, remembering his old father living downriver at fancy "Lindenwald," a poor tavernkeeper's son who had begun the road to the White House by attacking the manor lords. Lanky, sarcastic, white-haired Ambrose L. Jordan, attorney for the defense, set himself in John Van Buren's path and refused to budge. Jordan had little regard for either the judge or the handsome prosecutor and with all the ability at his command— he had once won for a male client a thousand-dollar award in a breach of promise suit—he obstructed the conviction of Smith Boughton. On the third morning Judge Edmonds opened court at eight-thirty in spite of Jordan's absence. As another defense attorney questioned a juror, Jordan walked in, sat down, and interrupted.

"One at a time, if you please," said elegant John Van Buren.

"We are one at a time," said Jordan.

"That is false."

"You're a liar."

Van Buren swung his forearm backward from the elbow, catching Jordan across the face. The old man came out of his chair fighting, his fists flailing at his shorter, younger opponent. "Order!" yelled Judge Edmonds. "Order! Stop them, stop them!" Officers grabbed the slugging men and forced them back into their chairs.

Judge Edmonds ordered the attorneys to jail for twenty-four hours for contempt of court. Contritely John Van Buren apologized and begged that a fine be substituted for imprisonment. The request was refused. The gaunt Ambrose Jordan said, ". . . As this affair has happened here in a court of justice I regret it. . . . I have, however, no whining apology to make nor any favors to ask except this, that the court will do me the favor to confine us both in the same room." The next twenty-four hours John Van Buren spent in the office of the sheriff writing letters, talking, sleeping, while Ambrose Jordan made himself as comfortable as possible in the janitor's room. Outside of a courtroom he never spoke to Judge Edmonds again. That social gentleman had planned a pleasant Sunday downriver at Lindenwald with the attorney general and his ex-president father, but feeling was running so high that he dared not accept the invitation though John Van Buren begged him to come.

It took two weeks to complete a jury. Desperately the defense tried to get at least one south-county downrenter accepted, but to no avail. As Van Buren was about to approve selection of a farmer who claimed no prejudice, Judge Edmonds informed him privately that the man was antirent and the prosecutor issued a panic-stricken challenge. As soon as the examination of witnesses began, the quality of the audience reached a new high. The Hudson reporter of the New York *Herald* wrote: "Our court house for the last few days has been crowded with the beauty of the city. Judge Edmonds who is renowned for his courtesy to the fair sex, has invited generally the ladies of this place to attend the trial of the Doctor who so terrified them last

winter and we have in addition to our own belles the
bright-eyed, rosy cheek'd and languishing Miss W. of
Jersey City, the charming and captivating Mrs. J. of
New York, the beautiful and fair complexioned Miss
McC. of Greenport. . . . Our court house has assumed
a rather recherché appearance and the sombre walls and
cold formality of a criminal court have turned into
a heaven of sunshine by the smiles and beauty of our
pretty women. Oh! for a pen dipped in the golden rays
of the setting sun to describe them!"

John Van Buren's hope of convicting the young
doctor rested largely on the evidence of Abram Carle
who admitted having been Chief Tuscarora of the
calico Indians. Carle claimed that he had lent Boughton his own mask and cap and his brother's calico dress
for his appearance as Big Thunder at the Copake meeting. He swore that he had helped Boughton disrobe in
Bam's Tavern after the burning of the sheriff's papers.
Upon this and other weaker identifications of Boughton
as Big Thunder, and on Sheriff Miller's testimony, John
Van Buren rested his case.

Ambrose Jordan at once called Abram Carle's
mother and his wife as witnesses. The mother said
Abram had been hit on the head by a ninepin ball
when he was a little boy and had never been quite right
since. He had even been so out of his head at times
as to insist proudly that his horse had an extra joint
in each leg, making him capable of great speed.
Abram's wife, between outbursts of weeping, substan-
tiated the story of her mother-in-law. During the midday dinner intermission, the two women avoided Van
Buren's irate cross-examination by jumping into their
wagon and beating their horses into a wild gallop that

took them thirty miles across the Connecticut border just ahead of pursuing Sheriff Miller.

Through the services of a friend who had joined the antirenters for the purpose of keeping him informed, Judge Edmonds always knew in advance the strategy of the defense. He was therefore not at all surprised when Ambrose Jordan introduced a one-armed tin peddler as an alibi witness. The peddler said he saw Boughton in civilian dress at Bam's Tavern while Big Thunder was outside talking to the sheriff. A tailor followed with a story substantiating this testimony.

"Why did you say you saw Boughton inside the tavern?" said a farmer to the tailor after he had testified. "You told me you was going to swear you saw him crossing the public square."

"So I did but the darned peddler got him into the house and I couldn't get him out."

Next to the military ball of the previous winter, the two days of summing up gave Hudson the greatest social thrills of its history. All the Van Buren family, with the ex-president at their head, and with "the bright-eyed, rosy cheek'd and languishing Miss M. . . . whom Rumor reports to be engaged to the Prince of Lindenwald" sat in their reserved seats and marveled as the eight hours of oratory poured from the frame of John's golden whiskers.

The spectators were not so happy on the next day. Counselor Jordan, in the full knowledge that he was fighting a losing battle against the influence of the Livingstons and Van Rensselaers, against a prejudiced court, against the letter of the law itself, turned upon them the great flood of disillusion and bitterness that many years of legal battling had damned up within him. They squirmed and giggled as the tall old man reminded them of their frantic terror in the preceding winter and ironically referred to Big Thunder (whoever he might be) as "that mighty monster whose hydra head and fantastic costume so frightened our sheriff." The fashionable audience, the great crowd of farmers outside, slim Dr. Boughton sitting with his pale young wife, the prosecuting attorney and the jury, even Jordan himself knew that he had made the speech of his life but that there was little chance of his client's being acquitted.

Judge Edmond's charge to the jury ended at eight in the evening and the jury retired. All that night the roads leading to Hudson were choked with wagons as the down-rent farmers rode to town with hope in their hearts. Early in the morning they stood in a great crowd about the courthouse—waiting. Judge Edmonds was awakened by a messenger from the jury saying they had disagreed and wished to be discharged. He hastened to the courthouse, summoned the jury, and told them they must agree. To prove that he meant what he said, he ordered breakfast served in the jury room. As the jury watched from their window, he rode off leading another horse bearing a sidesaddle. This evidence that he was to ride with a lady and would therefore be gone some hours had a sobering effect on the jurors. They realized that time was of no importance to the judge and that they might be confined indefinitely.

Edmonds later told the story: "I then took a ride of two or three hours accompanied by a lady who was a stranger . . . in those parts. In order to show her the beautiful scenery . . . I took her to many by-roads and thus it happened that, when I struck the main road on my return, I met one of the sheriff's officers who told me the jury had agreed." As a matter of fact, the sheriff's men had been frantically searching for him for more than an hour.

"Guilty," said the foreman of the jury, and Judge Edmonds, thanking them, adjourned court for a short period. In anticipation of such an outcome he had already arranged to call together five county judges, the mayor of Hudson, and four of the town's aldermen to advise with him on the sentence. He met with these gentlemen—with the exception of an antirent judge who refused to come—in a near-by office, and at once announced that he was in favor of life imprisonment. The mayor promptly supported him but none of the other advisers would agree to more than twenty years. When it seemed that the deadlock might be interminable, there was the sound of a bell.

"Come, judge," said one county judge to another, "there's the dinner bell. I'll go for life if you will."

It took Judge Edmonds more than fifteen minutes to get back to the courtroom. The down-renters now fully realized that once more they had lost in the century-old struggle. They closed about the judge as he advanced through them and shook their fists at him, damning him to hell. They shrieked and cursed but the magistrate steadily moved to the courthouse door. The crowd inside were all standing, many on benches and tables. As the judge took his seat there was sudden silence. Sheriff Miller spoke to Edmonds in a whisper. He said he dared not bring the prisoner in through the crowd. They would rescue him sure. The judge said simply in a voice loud enough for all to hear:

"Bring in the prisoner."

The sheriff marched the slim, spectacled prisoner from the jail through grim ranks of silent men into the courthouse.

"Have you anything to say why sentence of the law should not be pronounced upon you?"

"I have never done anything forbidden by the country's institutions as I understand them. I beg that my wife be allowed to stay with me in the jail until I am removed."

Then Judge Edmonds began the speech which was to end with the sentencing of Dr. Smith Boughton. He said that, though the charge was robbery, the crime of which the prisoner had been convicted was really high treason—armed rebellion against a lawful government. Until Dr. Boughton had come into the county the tenantry had been, outwardly at least, quiet, orderly, lawabiding. The doctor had suffered none of the evils against which he campaigned. A man of education, "possessed of a species of popular eloquence," he had come into the county as a volunteer agitator. He had been the first to introduce disguises for the purpose of evading the law.

"In imitation of your example, peaceable inhabitants have been driven from their homes at night. Houses have been torn down, farms laid waste, the laws forcibly resisted, and the officers of justice fired upon and wounded while in the discharge of their official duty."

The judge paused for a moment and then, almost

choking as the words came singly from his lips, he said:

"The sentence of the Court is that you be confined in the state prison in the county of Clinton at hard labor, for the term of your natural life."

The languishing Miss W. was in tears now. There was a clearing of throats and a blowing of noses throughout the room. Only the slender prisoner, white and fragile, seemed unmoved. Those who had most wished him to be convicted now quietly wept over him in an orgy of pathos. Slowly, with wet cheeks, they left the courtroom.

Outside the reaction was quiet too, but different. The quality townsfolk, going home with misted eyes, saw no expression on the faces of the Hudson valley farmers standing in the courthouse square. Only their eyes spoke tragedy. The manor lords had won again— against the best leader of all. Feudalism and crop-sharing still held the upriver counties. In the heart of a free land a man might not own a home without paying tribute.

They did not know that in this defeat they had won. They did not know that the "two hundred thousand honorable men" whom weeping Dr. Boughton claimed to represent as he entered Clinton Prison were the advance guard of hundreds of thousands more who would sweep sympathetic John Youngs into the governor's chair at the next year's election, obtain the pardon of Boughton and other imprisoned down-rent rioters, and effect the adoption of the state constitution of 1846 which at long last did away with feudalism in the Hudson valley.

27

"Like a Palace Built for Angels"

I THINK I had rather have missed the Hawk's Nest, the Prairies, the Mississippi, and even Niagara than this," said Harriet Martineau, noted English writer, after she had stood on a rock nearly half a mile high and looked out over eight miles of countryside to the waters of the Hudson. Like most distinguished foreign travelers of the early nineteenth century, she had been driven in a four-horse stage over the twelve upslanting miles from Catskill to stand at last in front of the Pine Orchard House on South Mountain and see the Hudson's "noblest wonder." And like nearly every other witness of that scene, foreign or native, she had been moved to extravagant expression.

James Fenimore Cooper in *The Pioneers* made Natty Bumpo describe the spot as it was before the hotel was built "where one of the ridges juts out a little from the rest, and where the rocks fall for the best part of a thousand feet so much up and down that a man standing on their edges is fool enough to think he can jump from top to bottom."

" 'What see you when you get there?' asked Edwards.

" 'Creation!' said Natty . . . sweeping one hand around him in a circle, 'all creation, lad. . . . The river was in sight for seventy miles under my feet, looking like a curled shaving, though it was eight long miles to its banks. . . .'

" 'It must have been worth the toil to meet with such a glorious view.'

" 'If being the best part of a mile in the air, and having men's farms and houses at your feet, with rivers looking like ribands, and mountains . . . seeming to be haystacks of green grass under you, gives any satisfaction to a man, I can recommend the spot.' "

The grove of evergreens which was cleared away to make room for the tremendous Greek revival tavern named "Pine Orchard," stood on a rock ledge 2,250 feet above the river's surface. The company that chose to erect the house there in 1823 built well, for the massive white façade with its thirteen tall white pillars crowned by gilded Corinthian capitals (once compared by an American writer with those of the Propylaea of the Athenian Acropolis) still looks out over the sheer rock wall into the vastness of the valley of the Hudson. The promoters planned well too, for the Catskill Mountain House—as, in spite of its first title, it was inevitably to be called—at once became to native Americans and visiting aliens a symbol of the lavish extent of the young nation. The formula for everyone who came from abroad to see the experimental republic was to spend some time in New York on arrival, then take a "floating palace" steamboat to Catskill Landing whence the stage would convey him to the Mountain House, and after a visit there to proceed upriver and westward to behold the state's other great natural phenomenon, Niagara Falls.

Pine Orchard House, standing only a few feet

from the verge of the precipice, is a long rectangular building with wings extending some distance to the rear on either side of the main portion. Entrance steps in the center lead up one flight to the big "piazza" on which during the last century thousands of American women have indulged in a great American pastime invented by Benjamin Franklin and scathingly commented upon by an English actress, Fanny Kemble—rocking.

The interior of the house is spacious and its visitors thought it almost as elegant as the American steamboats. The principal drawing room consisted of three large "saloons" opening into each other to form one. "The dining room," wrote Mrs. Ellett, a visitor, "is large enough for a feudal banqueting hall, its effect being increased by a range of pillars for the whole length down the centre; and these pillars are wreathed with evergreens while between the numerous windows stand hemlock or cedar trees during the season, quite in baronial taste."

By June of 1827 Pine Orchard had become so widely and favorably known that the aristocratic English travelers, Captain Basil Hall and his wife Margaret, felt it necessary to make the trip by chartered stage in order that the impressions of America which they had come abroad to obtain might be complete. Margaret Hall, as snobbish an English blue blood as ever found Americans boorish, was enthusiastic about the ride over the green mountains covered with pink honeysuckle. She was pleased, too, that the hostelry was kept by English Mr. Webb and that the food was cooked by English Mrs. Webb who spared her "the extraordinary rivers of butter and oceans of grease that belong to American cookery. Though she was annoyed that there were no three-pronged forks—"two-pronged being all that we are indulged with in this uncivilized country"—and with the swift gobbling of American eaters, the Webbs somewhat modified her unfavorable impressions: "Everything in short partaking in some degree of that refinement that becomes a second nature to English persons." Of the awe-inspiring view that she and her husband had come to see her one complimentary remark was that "The immense plain below us is as much cultivated as Yorkshire."

As more travelers of distinction came to the foot of the Catskills and looked up at the white spot on South Mountain before they set out to visit it, the practice of giving literary expression to the emotions aroused by the journey and the vision at its end became so general as to be almost a competitive game. From the river the Pine Orchard House was to the British actor, Tyrone Power, in 1833 "like a dove-cot raised against the dark hill-side"; to other travelers it has been "a small white cloud in the midst of the heavens" . . . "a drift of snow that had not melted in the spring" . . . "like the eagle's or the Lammergeyer's nest, or some feudal castle on its foe-defying height" . . . "a white pearl against a dark green evening gown." "It should be a monastery to lodge in so high," wrote Nathaniel Parker Willis; and added with the afterthought of an epicure, "But here you may choose between Hermitages, 'white' or 'red' Burgundies, Madeiras, French dishes, and French dances, as if you had descended upon Capua."

Even those artists of the Hudson River school, painters of the vast on vast canvases, whose brushes did not falter before Niagara, were nonplused by the "sublimity" of the scene from the Mountain House. Critic Tuckerman wrote in an essay on Thomas Cole: "The view indeed from the lofty plain called Pine Orchard, whither enervated citizens repair in summer, has been deemed too extensive for definite impression." Though it proved "too extensive" for Cole's painting, it did not halt his pen which scribbled a description beginning "The mists were resting on the vale of the Hudson like the drifted snow."

The literary formula for the writer contemporary of the art-school painters required first a statement similar to Tuckerman's. He must say that no words could picture such a scene. Then he could go on with his wordy description.

"Station yourself upon that projecting rock that hangs in such terrific altitude over the immense space beneath, but attempt not to give utterance to your feelings—language could not express them," wrote poet and essayist Park Benjamin. Then he continued, for two pages, elegantly to disregard his own admonition: "Observe that quiet stream attenuated to a brook. One bound would carry you to its opposite bank, were it what it seems, and by that bound you would leap the noble Hudson."

"Good Reader! expect me not to describe the indescribable," exclaimed Willis Gaylord Clark, and rushed on without warning to a passage reading: ". . . far beyond where that noble river, diminished to a brooklet, rolled its waters, there opened mountain after mountain, vale after vale, State after State . . . while *still beyond*, in undulating ridges, filled with all hues of light and shade, coquetting with the cloud,

rolled the rock-ribbed and ancient frame of this dim
diorama! . . . Listen to those voiceful currents of air
traversing the vast profound! What a mighty circumference do they sweep!"

And Bayard Taylor, more scholarly, restrained and
gifted than his already named contemporaries was on
his fourth visit so moved by the "grand aerial depth"
below him that he overbalanced his likening of a man
plowing a field far below to a "black bug on a bit of
striped calico" with this outburst: "There are, also,
brief moments when the sun or moon is reflected in the
Hudson; when rainbows bend slantingly beneath you,
striking bars of seven-hued flame across the landscape;
when, even, the thunders march below, and the fountains of the rain are under your feet."

As years went on and the great hotel took on the
nickname "Old Beach" from the Beach family who
owned it for generations, new writers and men of other
professions entered the unorganized literary competition with titles such as "Sunset from the Catskill
Mountain House," "Moon-rise at Pine Orchard,"
"Storm in the Catskills," "Dawn from South Mountain." The picturesque moments of day and night,
the varied and ever-changing phenomena of nature
were claimed and exploited in fancy language by thousands of creatively inclined travelers from west and
south, while, as Bayard Taylor noticed, "young gentlemen from afar sat on the verandah and wrote in
their notebooks." The layman authors found a key
precedent in an early description of a storm as seen
from above on the hotel veranda by Colonel William L. Stone, editor of the New York *Commercial
Advertiser:* "The thunder muttered and roared like an

earthquake below. The lightning, brighter than the sun above, played upon the upper surface of the clouds like the crinkling scintillations along the conductor of a powerful electrical machine." Wallace Bruce, author of a Hudson River guidebook, found sunrise from "the House" like an "Oriental dry-goods store with costly goods in the show windows raising opposition to the muslin and dimity filled window cases of the west."

Preacher Charles Rockwell, whose study was within sight of the Mountain House, was one of the few to take a different point of view and describe not the panorama but the hotel itself: "large and long, with its imposing colonnade in front, all of purest white . . . when it rests as a light, airy, unsubstantial castle or palace in the air, on a dark, wild background of clouds, as if itself a shadowy part of the moving panorama . . . as if it had floated down from above, or was soaring upwards from below." No longer able to contain himself even in such prose as this, he then burst into the verses of a poem entitled "The Catskill Mountain House" and written "in full view of what is described by them." He wrote that "the stately mansion resting on the mountain's brow" was

> Like a palace built for angels
> Pausing in its heavenward flight,
> With its walls of snowy whiteness,
> Shining in the sun's fair light.

and continued:

> Here the maiden, fair and lovely,
> Sinking to an early grave,
> Finds the healthful mountain breezes
> Have a power to cheer and save.

Rest then ever, noble mansion,
On the lofty mountain's height,
Shedding round thee joy and gladness,
Like the morning's cheering light.

Another preacher, the Reverend Dr. Murdoch, provided the most startling narrative contribution to the literature of the tavern. He said that in the summer of 1845 he had arrived on a day of dreary, dense mist and was listening to the complaint of a Yankee who had come all the way from Cape Cod to see the view, when he heard someone say that the house was going past on the outside. He rushed to the piazza "and there, sure enough, was the perfect image of the vast building, plainly impressed upon a *thicker* cloud than the general *envelope* that had covered us. It was a great mass of vapor, moving from north to south, directly in front, and only about two hundred feet from us, which reflected the light of the sun, now beginning to appear in the west, from its bosom, like a mirror, in which the noble Corinthian pillars . . . were expanding. . . . The visionary illusion was moving with the cloud, and ere long we saw one pillar disappear, then another. We, ourselves, who were expanded to Brobdingnags in size, saw the gulf into which we were to enter and be lost. I almost shivered when my turn came, but there was no eluding my fate; one side of my face was veiled, and in a few moments the whole had passed like a dream."

The Catskill Mountain House has not, so far as I know, inspired in recent years any such outpourings of the enchanted heart as a cloud of witnesses dedicated to it in the middle decades of the last century. Perhaps increasing ease of access has made the advertised "World-

famous View" less inspiring. The Catskill Mountain
Railroad shortened the stage trip considerably in 1882
by depositing passengers a few miles from the hotel, at
Lawrenceville. Ten years later, the "longest incline railway in the world," attaining a height of sixteen hundred feet over a distance of seven thousand, brought
passengers in an Otis elevator car to the plateau on
which the hotel stands.

Now motorcars and buses transport visitors to the
Catskill Mountain House. The ledge before the old
pillared veranda is crowded every summer with hundreds of guests who look out over a peaceful farming
countryside not much changed since the days when
nearly all of America's dignitaries and the great majority of the nation's honored guests made pilgrimages
to this high shrine. The enormous public rooms have
not changed and plaster busts of Daniel Webster and
Henry Clay and other gods of American democracy
stand in dignity in the early American parlors. The
Beaches do not run the old place now. Jacob, Eli, and
David Andron lease it. The "rivers of butter and oceans
of grease that belong to American cookery" have given
way to kosher cooking. Many of the patrons are comparatively new Americans who speak with traces of
the accents of Russia and Germany. Though they are
less literarily articulate than the guests of other days,
as they stand beneath the old white colonnade and look
out over seventy miles of Hudson water the same spell
is at work which has been felt by all who have ever
stood there.

28

Ghost Towns and Ghost Trades

DOWN on the level flats by the river's edge at Castle Point, Colonel John Stevens built a circular track. On it he placed a four-wheel platform truck that carried a vertical tubular boiler capped by a conical hood and a smokestack. Then let heaven help the guest at Stevens Castle who refused a ride on America's first steam railroad. At six miles an hour the colonel and his helpless visitors whizzed around and around the big circle by the water. That was in 1825.

Six years later a locomotive, eleven and a half feet long, was ignominiously taken for a steamboat ride up the Hudson. Built at the West Point Foundry in New York, the *De Witt Clinton*, without whistle, bell, or brake, was delivered in Albany during the last days of June. On the ninth of August a distinguished group of Albany businessmen rode in three Goold stagecoach cars behind the little engine to Schenectady and back.

Freeman Hunt, a citizen of New York, seated himself on May 10, 1836, in one of the "passage cars" of the new railroad from Troy to Saratoga. The car was eight feet wide, three times as long, divided into three compartments by removable panels. The seats were "cushioned and backed with crimson morocco trimmed with coach lace."

The exterior of the car Mr. Hunt had chosen was

even more elegant. Fawn color running into buff served as background for a half dozen or more picture panels with rose, pink, and gold borders and "deep lake" shading. To spaces within small moldings of vermilion and opaque black had been "transferred" a number of the most splendid reproductions of the ancient and modern masters—"Napoleon Crossing the Alps," "The Wounded Tiger," "General Washington" (a replica of Stuart's portrait), and Byron's lovely disheveled "Mazeppa" cruelly bound to the back of a snorting stallion. "The *tout ensemble*," wrote Mr. Hunt, "is more like a movable gallery of the fine arts than like a train of railroad cars."

The colorful chariot rolled over the waters of the Hudson on the big new bridge from Troy to Green Island, and in two hours of "flying as it were on the wings of the wind" behind the beautiful locomotive *Champlain* the train had covered the twenty-five miles to Ballston Spa. After a short period of rest, then, during which he partook of the wellings of a medicinal spring at the fashionable Hotel Sans Souci, owned by felicitously named Mr. Waters, Mr. Hunt returned by rail to Troy before dark, having traveled fifty miles since two-thirty in the afternoon.

A dozen years went by before the residents of the houses along the pathway of the palatial steamboats realized the significance of the recent developments in overland transportation. The Verplancks were one of the river's oldest and most firmly established families. They owned about two and a half miles of waterfront —white sand and green grass and tall trees—all in sight of the fine house they had built to replace the one the British ship-of-war *Vulture* had set afire with hot shot in 1776. In 1835 they had been offered $250,000 for Verplanck's Point. And so, thirteen years later, when the Hudson River Railroad promoters offered them $5,000 for a right of way on which to run their noisy dirty engines the Verplancks turned them down so coldly and disinterestedly that the amazed financiers doubted the offer had been heard. Before the end of another year the property had been condemned at an appraised value of $1,800 and the Verplancks forced to accept the decision. A new spirit had come to the banks of the Hudson, a spirit long evident on the water in the ruthless conflicts of the competing steamboat companies. The aristocrats were no match for the river pirates. Business was going to have its day on the Hudson. Verplanck was helpless before Vanderbilt.

Near mid-century, Nathaniel Parker Willis was writing from "Idlewild" near Newburgh: "It is a curious thing that the Western bank of the Hudson River for the first fifty miles from New York is as much a wilderness at the present moment as any river-bank of equal length in the far West. . . . From the first settlement of the country, the Eastern shore of the Hudson has been a garden of Dutch aristocracy. It was divided up into the estates of 'old families' from Manhattan to Albany . . . While the Eastern bank . . . has been two hundred years in settling and embellishing the Western bank will start new and overtake it in from five to twenty."

The curly-haired, pink-cheeked poet keenly observed the changing life. He spent much time along the Hudson, riding the mare Lady Jane, with smooth-haired terrier Flippertigibbet nipping at her heels, or his more spirited mount Black Prince, with black New-

foundland Don Quixote (named for his attack on a
water wheel) bounding behind. He knew that farmers
were selling their waterfront lands for $200 an acre
to the new-rich princes of American business—who
could pay well for scenery—and buying fertile lands
out of sight of the river for $5 an acre. He saw Ohio
pork come to the Newburgh end of the railroad "legs
down," and start for Manhattan with position reversed
after a visit to "a slaughterhouse as long as Westminster
Abbey and filled with a wilderness of busy butchers."
He saw lanky mountainmen bringing to the river landings bristling wagonloads of "mountain wheat"—
sapling hickories—to be sold for hop poles. He
watched the freight steamers, laden with fruit and vegetables of the west bank, leaving the Cornwall docks
at nine o'clock in the evening for New York City's
North River wharves, where they would arrive at three
in the morning. He knew that the new trades along
the river valley were making money and he saw the
villas of a new aristocracy of wealth rising in tasteless,
ornate grandeur. He encouraged the practice of calling
both the old and the new homes that looked out over
the river by poetic or whimsical titles—Belgrove, Placentia, High Cliff, Rose Hill, Wodenethe, Uplands,
Mount Hope, Blithewood, Presqu' Isle—and he carried
on a successful campaign to change the Yankee name
of beetling Butter Hill (the Dutch called it Klinken-
berg) to Storm King.

The expansion of one early river-shore business in
particular, Willis noted, was considerably annoying the
owners of estates. In a distant age lakes had been formed
as the melting waters of the retreating glaciers filled
the hollows that the ice had gouged in its advance

from the north. On the shores of these lakes in the Hudson region certain clays were left behind. One of Tarrytown's early Dutchmen named Van Loon found that he could dry the clays, add sand, and bake the mixture into bricks. As building increased all along the course of the river, and particularly in New York, the number of brickyards at the water's edge suddenly grew large. They gave a hearty welcome to the thousands of Irishmen whom hard times, the potato famine, and dreams of a land of plenty brought to the mouth of the Hudson.

"Brickyards are our eyesore in the scenery of the Highlands," wrote Willis. "They will be until the bank of blue clay along the edge of the river is entirely exhausted. . . . Among my wealthy neighbors there has lately been a 'strike' as to 'commuting' any longer upon the lower turnpike, all combining to ignore it. . . . It is a loose and lively Irish fringe to our quiet American neighborhood. . . . If not the cleanest and best behaved of our wayside populations, however, the Irish are a variety that comes in well for contrast and invigoration. . . . In the stout legs and arms, rosy cheeks and honest proportions of the women . . . there is a supply for the lacking bulk and bloom of our American race." Riding down the lower road, Nathaniel Willis found a "certain relief in a mile or two of jolly and careless faces."

In the days when the Irish were the "brickyarders," making bricks was a longer and harder job than it is now. After the pure blue clay had been dug from its bed and weathered into disintegration, it was mixed with sand and coal dust, molded, and then dried in the sun for weeks before baking in a kiln. There could be no sun-drying during cold winter months. Modern brickyards may continue working the year round, however, for bricks can be dried in a superheated chamber in less than a day. Such artificial processes have done away with seasonal occupation in the brickyards, and the depletion of the smaller clay deposits has lined the Hudson on both sides with the picturesque weathered ruins of many yards, their chimneys standing lonely beside tumbled, weed-grown walls and staring, empty windows.

But still the brick-laden barges in long procession descend the Hudson as they did a century ago. Behind puffing tugs, from nearly fifty active brickyards, the heavy vessels, stained with pink dust, bring their burdens to market. About three hundred million bricks come down the river each year from Ulster County landings alone. At Roseton, just above Newburgh, the yards of the Spanish sugar planter Juan Jova, who fled his native land to the Hudson's banks in the 1890's, are now a modern, thriving enterprise under the management of the refugee's three sons. North of Haverstraw the long drying sheds extend for almost two miles, ending in a decaying, mellow cluster at Grassy Point. During the day smoke rises in billowing clouds through the roofs of the kilns. At night the river beside the dark, low-lying silhouettes of the yards glows dully with the eerie light of the brickyard fires.

Brickmaking was not the only growing business that welcomed the Irish invasion of the Hudson valley. Along most of the wild west bank the florid, temperamental men and women of the far green island busied themselves in many ways at making the prophecy of the poet of Idlewild come true. Axes that had last sounded in Kilkenny, Cork, and Galway rang again throughout the summer months in Ulster County and Greene as hemlocks crashed to earth to be stripped of their astringent bark for the valley tanneries. In the very region where the German tarmakers had cut the pitch pines in 1710, Irish and Yankee barkpeelers more than a hundred years later were advancing through the forests leaving behind the white decaying corpses of tall trees. Tanning had begun to grow as an industry in the first quarter of the nineteenth century, but it was not until after the Irish had added their quota of laborers that it reached its peak. Then up the river came dark-stained freighters, their olive-skinned crews singing Spanish songs to the music of guitars when they were not unloading thousands of salt-rubbed cowhides from the Argentine and Brazil upon the docks at Saugerties, Rondout, and Catskill.

On plank roads down the steep sides of the mountains—from Pine Hill, Shandaken, Phoenicia, and Samsonville, from Prattsville, Tannersville, and Palenville—to the river landings Irish teamsters drove wagons heavy with sides of sole leather. Slowly the returning horses dragged the raw South American hides up to the tanneries, stopping beside the road at Terry's and Garrison's and Slosson's where a man with wages in his pocket could overcome a thirst. So heavy was the traffic on those narrow roads that often fifty halted teams separated the teamster from the tannery that hired him. High quilted clouds of yellow smoke hung above each tannery, strikingly indicating its position.

Gradually the hemlocks disappeared from around Sundown and Red Hill and Olivebridge, from the slopes to the north of them near Big Hollow and the

Black Head Mountains, from the woods back of Surprise, Climax, Result, and Limestreet. Only the old walls of the tanneries tell the story now.

In the winter months neither the brickyarders nor the barkpeelers could ply their trades, but the Hudson gave many of them work as soon as prolonged cold froze it over. Eagerly the valley people awaited the glad news that the river was closed. Skaters were the first to appear on the ice, then the fast trotters and pacers, their hoofs beating swift tattoos on the hard courses, the drivers in the smartly painted sleighs shouting and snapping their whips. The iceboats, "wings on skates," careened with incredible speed and skill through the whole tangle.

And when the ice had reached a thickness of ten inches, suddenly the river's cold dry surface would be shot through with quickly cut dark canals, and thousands of men would be working beside them. All day and all night they would cut ice furiously, afraid that a drop in temperature would make it too thick or a thaw would thin it. As the cutters sawed large ice cakes from the edges of the canals and pushed them into the channels, other workers poled the pieces toward shore where they were tumbled in pairs on moving belts that bore them upward, iridescent and glittering into the vast darkness of tall storehouses. Covered with sawdust, the ice awaited the hot summer when it would be loaded on scows bound for simmering New York. Even the domestic servants in the big houses could hardly finish the supper dishes for wanting to join the workers out on the gleaming floor where they could earn a little extra during the winter evenings while torches flared and the black canals were alive with bobbing translucent ice cakes.

There are now few of the dank weathered icehouses, once so frequent along the shore as to seem only a stone's throw apart for many miles. Farmers have been growing mushrooms in these and the crops have been good. The pollution of the water by sewage from upriver towns and the general use of artificial ice have ended the river's annual winter harvesting.

The quarrying of bluestone along the ledges at the foot of the Catskills was a colorful business. When stoneboats left Jockey Hill and Stony Hollow over the old plank road for Rondout Landing, it took a big redheaded son of Galway to "walk a man-size slab." In those days Manhattan's curbings were all of bluestone, a York State stuff that would not crack as Yankee granite does every time there is a hard frost or the boys build a decent election bonfire. Bluestone will come back with its pastel mist color and its fine weathering —mark the words of all the men of the west-bank upriver counties. It is a good paving, a strong curbing, a fine building stone for houses, and a workable medium for sculpture.

But of all the Hudson's booming mid-century trades, none brought such wild days to the banks of the river as the cement works. The construction of the hundred-mile Delaware & Hudson Canal, begun in 1825, lured hundreds of Yankee, Dutch, Irish ditchdiggers to the country south of Kingston. It also uncovered a vast deposit of cement which, though slow to set, was hard and durable. The little farm town of Rosendale near the mines began a sudden growth comparable only to that of the mining towns of the Far

West. Almost overnight it became a brawling, roistering town of three thousand hard-drinking, hard-fight-
ing "cement burners." At the end of a day they poured
out of the caves in the mountain and charged down
into the garish town where nearly every door swung
into a barroom. After long hours of digging in semidarkness, the workers plunged into a night of consuming Ulster County applejack and betting on Johnnie
Daly's fighting cocks against the cocks of the world.

Down from the green hills of Vermont poured
the lanky, Yankee, hard-rock men—Shalligees, the
river Irish called them—scorning the easy digging in
cement but willing to make money at it, bragging of
the strength that granite puts into a man. There was a
famous night when the Irish Vermonter, Jack Dillon,
built "like the stump of an oak, short but tough," was
confronted on the Rosendale Bridge by a gang of his
own countrymen from downriver.

"Anything on your mind?" says one of them.

"Not a thing," says Jack, and let him have it between the eyes.

The width of the bridge allowed only two men to
reach Jack at a time, so he used his left hand to lick one
of them while his right beat down the other. It took
Jack most of the night because all the Irish in town
heard about the fight and lined up in a long two-col-
umn queue behind the bridge to await their turn.
Standing like a latter-day Horatius, Jack systematically
finished off the community. Then everybody stopped
at Sam Haley's place where Sam was keeping open all
night in honor of the occasion.

Although the ambition of each of the Irish workers was "to settle down in a little rum hole of me own,"

most of them lived in big tenement houses, one of which bore a title they all deserved, "The Mad House." Sam Haley got the bulk of their earnings. The valley farmers, sitting high on their wagon seats and shouting at their fine teams, came jingling into town in late afternoons with loads of green apples. Later they staggered out of Sam Haley's to ride home in the moonlight, their feet on the seat and the horses guiding themselves. Sam had a miraculous faculty, the Rosendale folks used to say: he could pour you a drink of his applejack and then tell you how far—to the very bend in the road—you would be conscious on your way home. Sam used to tell the story of an Irishman who took a temperance pledge and came racing down Pistol Hill an hour later demanding a drink because an empty whisky barrel with arms and legs had chased him home from mass.

There is Rosendale cement in Brooklyn Bridge, in Croton Aqueduct, in the base of the Statue of Liberty. It lasts almost as well as the stones it binds together. The workers dug a lot of it out of the west-bank hills, leaving a labyrinth of cold, dank caves. Some Ulster County people say you can walk all the way from Rosendale to Kingston through the middle of the earth if you know the way. Others say it is so cold in one of the caverns that the underground lake which has formed there stays frozen the year round, and midsummer skating parties could be held if the guests could find their way to it.

Sociability ruined the Rosendale cement business, the Ulsterites say. While a mason waited for it to harden he would get to talking and he would finish his story before he started working again. Fast-drying Portland cement drove Rosendale out of the market at the turn of this century. Some builders prefer a cement stronger than Portland even if it is not so quick to dry. So now work is beginning again. Orders have come in for the repair of Brooklyn Bridge. A few of the old-timers are back in the ghost town, Rosendale. The long row of saloons has become a series of shops and there is no roaring of bully-boys as there was in the wild Irish days. The giant round silos are full again and the scows are moving downriver carrying Rosendale cement to builders who prefer quality to speed.

29

They Loved the *Mary Powell*

T HE Hudson valley loved the *Mary Powell*. People who are more than thirty years old still love her, for her slim white image moves, swift and quiet, on waters called back to mind from long oblivion. "She was a lovely boat," they say. "Her bell had a silver tongue. Her whistle was a golden sound."

Absalom Anderson planned her in 1861 and she was built by Michael Allison in Jersey City. From the hour she came off the ways she was the river queen. Not even the *Alida*, the *Chauncey Vibbard*, the *Jenny Lind*, the *Onteora* could be compared with her. She was the fastest on the river—and the smoothest.

In vain the captains tried to take her trade away. The *Armenia* tootled proudly on her new 34-whistle calliope, arousing strange echoes among the jealous Highlands with "The Belle of the Mohawk Vale," "Way Down Upon the Swanee River," and "Jordan's a Hard Road to Travel." Wheezing apoplectically, the *Glen Cove* and the *General Sedgwick* raised their voices in song, slowing down as the steam that was meant for pressure released itself into staccato melodies blown on the whistle organs.

Commodore Hancox, the *James B. Schuyler's* skipper, who had been known to try to keep a boat from passing by taking pot shots with his rifle at her pilot-

338

house, thought up a new scheme to enhance his boat's reputation for speed. He had a good band aboard and whenever a rival drew alongside he marched them to the deck nearest her and ordered them to play *fortissimo*. As the passengers on the other steamer heard the entrancing music they rushed toward it, weighing down one side of their vessel so greatly that the paddle wheel on the other side was lifted completely out of water and spun aimlessly. With her band playing a triumphant paean, the *James B. Schuyler* would forge into the lead and stay there until her opponent's passengers had redistributed themselves. (The commodore caught a Tartar once, though, for hardly had his trombones begun to woo the *Dean Richmond* to lopsided helplessness than her skipper ordered all safety valves lifted. Then calmly he went his noisy way, knowing his patrons could not hear the *James B. Schuyler's* band.)

But not all the tricks the shrewd captains played, not all the speed the fast boats mustered, could ever make a difference to the *Mary Powell*. Serenely she skimmed past the swiftest, not stirring a ripple on a cup of coffee in her dining room. She had clean lines— three hundred feet of them in one long symmetry. The rococo dreams of the poets of the jigsaw were not for her. The other boats with their drippings of cheap ornament were fancy girls beside the river queen. Absalom Anderson sold her once, and her new masters decked her out in lavish wooden laces. His proud heart broke until he got her back and stripped her clean again for speed. He knew that the less a steamboat carried the better she looked, the faster she went. Some say he hired a black boy just to keep the flies from lighting on her rail and slowing her with their weight. They claim

THE OTHER BOATS WERE F.

LS BESIDE THE RIVER QUEEN

he mixed whale's grease into her paint to give her easy sliding through the water. And once in a river barroom I heard some poet say, "He hitched her to a porpoise four-in-hand."

She steamed away from Kingston in the morning. By noon she moored below New York's high towers. At three she took the tide again. At nine her silver bell was sounding over the dark waters of Rondout Creek and the sweet Negro voice of deckhand Seymour Darling was calling, as it called for thirty-four years, "Last Stop, Home Port, Kingston Landing!"

Absalom Anderson kept the *Mary Powell* so clean that the Dutch housewives of Hurley could find no speck on her—and he kept her respectable too. He never ran her on Sunday and he never sold liquor aboard her. Like the captain whom Fanny Kemble commended in 1832 for personally escorting a drunken passenger to a raft of logs "floating along shore about twenty miles below West Point where he was bound," Absalom Anderson had scant patience with the intoxicated. He always sifted such sinners from his embarking patrons and returned them to the dock. He ran a family boat and everyone could feel safe on her, even the young, unchaperoned females often entrusted to his strict charge.

The *Mary Powell* never had a major accident. She never lost a passenger. She carried fathers from hot labor in the city to cool riverside homes where their families waited. She was a honeymoon boat, she was a children's boat. She carried young boys to West Point and she returned them officers in the United States Army. Once, in a coffin wrapped with a flag, she brought the long body of George Custer to West Point.

The Indians of the western plains at last had won his yellow hair.

"You could depend upon the *Mary Powell,*" the river families say. "She was always on time." They laugh and say the Military Academy used to time its formations by the sound of her bell because it was always nearer right than the West Point clocks. Even on the day the cyclone hit her, twisting her broadside against the rushing wind and tumbling her stacks overboard, pilot Guernsey Betts brought her into Rondout on schedule. On ordinary days she had minutes to spare. She never wasted effort at a landing. Sometimes Guernsey Betts did not bother to make fast her landing lines —just held her up against the dock while the gangway was run ashore and the passengers came aboard. He knew how to take advantage of every tide, every whorl and eddy on her course. Once he had given the boys in the engine room the jingle she would be off like a race horse. She could slip into top speed while other boats were casting off. The only time she ever gave him trouble, he used to say, was when he would try to pass the mouth of Rondout Creek on one of his few trips to Albany. She was so accustomed to turn in there that she would bear to the left no matter how firm he held the wheel—as if she had some sort of curvature.

Only once in all her years of service was the *Mary Powell* beaten on the river. That was in the June of 1885 when the Herreshoffs brought their new ninety-foot yacht *Stiletto* down from Bristol, Rhode Island, to race with the queen of the Hudson. Although the *Mary Powell* was almost twenty-five years old and carried passengers and all regular equipment, she was only five minutes behind at Sing Sing where the *Stiletto* stopped racing.

When Absalom Anderson died, his son, Captain A. E. Anderson, carried on the tradition. Gracefully the *Mary Powell* grew old and he aged with her. Before her nearly sixty years were over she was known and loved not only in America, but in all countries of the world whose citizens had visited the banks of the Hudson. The skipper of a Nile steamboat once recognized Captain Anderson on a vacation tour and insisted that he accept the honors and privileges of his rank while on the Egyptian craft. Captain Anderson the second died before she made her last journey. She ended her career peacefully, faithfully, on the Day Line run.

At Sunflower Dock on the Rondout, just out of sight of Hudson water, in the days of the Great War, junk dealer John Fisher dismantled the *Mary Powell*. Down came her tall stacks of Day Line brown—always black when Absalom Anderson owned her. From above the wheelhouse came the silver bell to adorn the Day Line Park at Indian Point. The *Robert Fulton* now speaks with the deep voice of her whistle. And in the Senate House Museum at Kingston stands the pilot wheel that Guernsey Betts's hands knew so well. But the *Mary Powell* lives in more than these relics of her past. She is a complete and lovely image in thousands of memories. "She had a silver tongue," they say. "She had a golden throat."

30

In a Mountain's Shadow

THE winding drive was lined with round stones painted white. I drove through the gateway cut in the high hedge and followed it. When I stopped my car I could hear the pleasant drone of a lawn mower. Suddenly it ceased, then became a series of staccato notes. I looked down toward the sunlit river. A short man in limp tweed knickerbockers and jacket was pushing the mower about the legs of a huge iron dog that stood in alert attitude facing the Hudson. The man saw me and came toward me slowly, taking off his glasses to wipe his brow.

"I've been expecting you," he said in a mellow voice with a clipped accent that sounded rather English. "You needn't have written. We are always here and glad to see people if they ever drop in."

He sounded wistful and I tried to be hearty as I waved an arm in the direction of the lawn.

"I'm glad to see you're keeping up Andrew Downing's work so well."

He smiled and put his glasses back on his nose.

"I'm not so sure that he planted this place," he said. "But he landscaped a lot of them around here. Won't you come into the house and meet my sister? We can sit on the veranda and sip a bit of sherry while we talk."

I left the car and walked with him to the wide-spread frame house. It loomed ahead of us in the misty air of a summer midafternoon on the Hudson. There was a round stained-glass window just below the center of the largest gable. It was framed on two sides by slanting vergeboards cut into fantastic scroll-saw patterns. A forest of other gables made the roof a heaving sea of shingles. Big rectangular windows below them caught the blaze of the sun. On the off-river side I saw that the drive led to a porte-cochere two stories high— the second story a kind of outdoor gallery whose spindle railings swelled at regular intervals into round wooden balls. An equally elaborate though differently carved veranda of great length looked out over the water from the other side.

My host looked at me quizzically. "My grandfather tore down the family's Dutch house to build something more elegant," he said. There was a quick satiric gleam in his eye and I liked him.

His sister stood in the dark doorway. She was a tall, white-haired woman, dressed in blue and white checked calico. Her face had a stonelike quality that made me think, as I approached her, of a paragraph in Edith Wharton's memoirs which I had read the day before. She had written of her aunt's house near Rhinebeck, "an expensive but dour specimen of Hudson River gothic." There was, she said, "a queer resemblance between the granitic exterior of Aunt Elizabeth and her grimly comfortable home, between her battlemented caps and the turrets of Rhinecliff."

"We're glad to see you," said my hostess, though there was no evidence of the truth of that in her keen blue eyes. "I will bring the sherry to the veranda."

A half hour later, after we three had said the usual uninteresting things that most people say when they are feeling their way toward a subject that is inevitable, my host, looking vaguely out over the valley, said:

"This Amontillado isn't all it should be. The last of our cellar wines went about ten years ago, the year my brother-in-law died. My sister's two children were playing down there and one of them tripped and fell on the last bottle."

"That was a real tragedy," said the sister, so sharply that I wondered if she meant to be ironic. "You would be surprised how even a little incident can upset the lives of people who live as quietly as we do."

"Where are the children now?" I said.

"They are away in school," said their mother, "and at last they're beginning to improve."

"Improve?"

"For the first few years we got very bad reports of them. It's the same way, though, with most children brought up on these big old places. They aren't sociable. There's never been much running about between the families of the estates. The children associate only with adults. They get accustomed to being alone and they become self-sufficient. They can entertain themselves. Then when they go to school the other children call them snobs because they are not co-operative and because they don't seek companionship. I guess they are snobs in a way. They inherit it."

"That brings me to one of the questions I wanted to ask you," I said. "What do Hudson River people of the old families, people like you and your brother, think of themselves?"

"Well, if you really want to know," she said a

little defiantly, "they are pleased with themselves. They are proud of their families and their traditions. They dislike progress for fear they'll get too far away from what they once were. They have always taken it for granted that they could do what they please and so they're independent and they're difficult when they're crossed. They've never had much to do with the towns-people along the river. People have some sort of com-munity life over on the west bank. They have bridge clubs, church socials and so on. The old families on this side wouldn't think of attending such affairs. When they want to see anybody they invite him for a visit."

"Hasn't there been any intermarriage between people of the big houses and of the towns?" I said.

Her face set in grim lines.

"No," she said shortly.

"You know perfectly well there has," said her brother, smiling wickedly.

"Not enough to count," she said.

"One of our next-door neighbors is an exception to prove the rule." He sipped at his sherry with a look of satisfaction. "And one of our own ancestors, the one whose portrait you'll see in the hall—she did worse than that."

"How could she?" I said as I was undoubtedly ex-pected to.

"She married a man from across the river." He giggled, apparently surprised at his daring to reveal this blasphemy before his sister. "I think it's a good idea, too. Constant intermarriage of members of the same little group of river families hasn't improved us much. That's my idea, at least. Now one of the Chanlers, I can't remember whether it was Bob or Louis, laid our situation to something else. He said once a man had lived in the shadow of a mountain he'd never be sane again."

"Do you believe that?" I said.

"Of course he doesn't," said his sister sharply.

"Well, I don't know," he said in measured words. "Of course my family has been on the river here as long as any in these parts and—"

"What about your friend next door?" I said, recalling a name that is old in the Hudson valley.

"My family built the dock his ancestors landed on," he said and grinned. "But if I were questioned as to whether he or I were a little cracked I wouldn't know quite what to say. We've both lived on these adjoining estates most of our lives—all of them, I guess, except for our college days and trips to Europe. One by one we've seen the estates around us drop away to become hospitals, schools, monasteries, and I don't know what. One by one we've seen young people grow up in the big houses and go away and not come back. Young people don't like this quiet life. Only a few of the names are left—Verplanck, Livingston, Delafield, Bigelow, and one or two others.

"Now that my neighbor's married a young town wife we don't see much of him any more. I think he thought she'd take him around and give him a good time with her friends, but she rather likes being exclusive in his old house and not seeing a lot of the people she grew up with. I don't know whether the shadow of the mountain has anything to do with it or not but he should have known there's always been and always will be a line between folks like us and townfolks. They

keep it as much as we do. It's something you can't de-
fine but it's always there."

"Do you feel it too?" I said.

"Not as strong as some," he said, proudly, "but it's
there all the same."

The sun was dipping toward the far line of green
hills across the Hudson. High in the locust tree on the
slope below the veranda a cicada was singing. A tiny
tug steamed upriver and two long flat barges lay in
single file behind her. A train whistle sounded far away.

"I must be going," I said, feeling mellow and
sleepy from sunshine and sherry.

"You must see the portraits," said the white-haired
woman, taking charge with authority.

"And a couple of the old diaries," said my host.

An hour later I had spoken my grateful farewells
and was walking the stone-bordered drive to my car.
The limp brown tweeds were beside me. I climbed in,
turned about, and was ready to be gone.

"Good-bye," I said.

My host stepped closer.

"You know, there's a CCC camp near here. The
boys work on the roads and clean up the parks and so
on."

"Yes, I've seen them."

"I go over there evenings sometimes," he said, "and
sit around with some of them, especially the ones that
are not from the valley. I get along with them pretty
well."

He turned and began walking over the grass toward his lawn mower. As I started on he turned halfway about and waved his forearm in a cramped half-
sweep.

31

The Silverbacks Are Running

In April a day comes to the banks of the Hudson when the sun shines, small white clouds ride on soft air blowing steadily upriver and the silver-backed shad are running. Then from the shadow of Manhattan's towering uptown apartments to the shacks on the pebbled shores above Kingston men in weathered clothes turn weathered faces to the water. Small boats loaded with slim oak poles put out from the foot of Seventy-fourth Street and soon the poles stand upright in the current as the fishermen's sledges drive them with echoing strokes into the river bottom. The crews of other boats are at work to the north of them and from the Jersey side comes the sound of strong hammers. The poles rising like reeds five or six feet above the surface make a forest inexplicable to most New Yorkers. But men who follow the river know that with the next flood tide the drying nets, hanging like strips of yellow mist on horizontal wooden rods beside the sunlit river, will be stretched from pole to pole beneath the surface to entangle the firstcomers of the shad run, the silverbacks.

The poles are usually in shallow water too far out of the main traffic-filled channel to catch many fish, yet they give the city fishermen their only chance of capturing some of the countless shad that go up the river

351

to spawn every April. Long before any white man ever
came to this continent the people of the Hudson valley
knew that spring would bring them all the fish they
could eat. Even in these times between two and three
million pounds of shad are taken from the Hudson each
year.

The fishermen to the north—at Nyack, Grassy
Point, and Cold Spring, at Marlborough, Milton, Came-
lot, and Poughkeepsie—look on the pole-set nets with
contempt. The only way to catch shad, they say, is to
go out in a boat and chuck a gill net overboard at the
beginning of a tide. At the end of the tide, if the net
has been weighted so that it fishes about twenty-five
feet below the surface, you'll have some shad.

The few times I have fished for shad I have been
lucky enough to be with Johnnie Allwater. Johnnie
comes from the river town of Highland, as his father
did before him. He's always been a pretty independent
fellow and he left home when a boy to see something
of the world. But he has never liked being far away
from fishing. In the old days Johnnie used to follow the
shad run right up the coast—the St. John's River in
Florida, a little later the Albemarle in North Carolina, and then there would be a run on the Delaware.
Coming north with the spring was pretty nice and a
good living could be made especially when Johnnie was
lucky with the roe. Some seasons his shad would be all
bucks and the whole kit and kaboodle not worth as
much as a smaller catch the next year when the roe
would be running strong. Now that Johnnie is over
sixty and has a boy in high school he stays closer home,
though he is as strong as ever and doesn't look a day
over forty-five.

The first time I went out with Johnnie was on the earliest of the really warm mornings of May. I had wandered in warm sunlight down to the river flats between the Mid-Hudson Bridge and the railroad bridge at Poughkeepsie. I sat on a rock for a while and listened to a quarrel between two men who were trying to decide whether to buy a pint of cheap whisky with the proceeds of the last shad they had caught or set their short net for another drift in the hope of making enough to buy a quart apiece. Soon one of them started for town. He was back in an incredibly short time with a bottle from which considerably more than half the contents was already missing. That led to another wrathful controversy which went on until they had piled the net into their boat, embarked rather unsteadily, and were singing lustily on the glittering water.

"They git that way and stay that way for two months every year," said a voice beside me and I looked up into the sharp, tanned face and clear blue eyes of Johnnie Allwater. "Catch just enough to keep 'em practically unconscious the whole spring. They git a real good time of it fishin' and drinkin' and drinkin' an' fishin'."

"I'd like to go out just to see how it's done," I said. "The fishing part, I mean. I've never fished a river with a net."

"I'll take you for a short drift if you want," said Johnnie. "Best time is at night. I'm just down here mendin' net—wasn't plannin' to go out and we won't catch much fish but I'll take ye."

"I'd be glad to pay," I said, but with the quick generosity I later found characteristic of him Johnnie waved aside the idea. In a half hour the outboard motor

on his flat-bottomed boat was pushing us steadily upriver. Johnnie had acquired a crew, a young man named
Henry who was "taking the day off from high school
to row for somebody." We had not far to go. A few
yards above the railroad bridge Johnnie stopped the
engine and Henry took the oars.

"We'll start here on the ebb," said Johnnie, "and
we'll get a drift downriver to Marlborough." He stood
in the square-built stern and lifted the end of his net
from the box in front of him. Tied at regular intervals
along one edge of the net were long cords with rectangular white blocks of wood at the ends. Tied close
to the other edge were metal rings.

"White buoys are best for a night drift," said
Johnnie. "Fancy-colored ones are better in the daytime
but I don't do much day fishin'." He threw the first
length of net into the river and I heard the plop of a
ring and the skittering splash of a wooden block.

"These new rings weigh five ounces," said Johnnie,
turning in deliberate rhythmic motion to the net.
"Carry the net down a little further, hold it a little
straighter." (Plop, splash.) "These buoys are tied to the
top semline on cords about twenty feet long. When
they're restin' at the surface they're eighteen feet apart.
Limit you can set is two thousand feet." (Plop, splash.)
"The Coast Guard watches to see you don't set no
more. I'm only settin' two shot this time."

"How much is a shot?" I said.

" 'Bout eight pounds. Fellows around here set
about three shot most o' the time."

"That big farmer that was below us last night,"
said Henry, rowing slowly with as steady a beat as a

metronome, "he's got more darned shot than anyone on the river."

"He ain't got more fish," said Johnnie.

It seemed a long time, and was probably about fifteen minutes, before Johnnie stopped his rhythmic dance—bending over the box, straightening, letting the net fly out over the water with a quick upward lift, throwing the buoy and its long line out away from the boat. As the last one dropped into the water Johnnie seated himself with a sigh.

"Now we can take it easy," he said. "Got time to whitewash a ton o' coal if we want to."

For a half hour, then, Henry rowed us along the line of white buoys to make sure that the net was not tangled anywhere. By that time it had begun to drift with the ebb tide and was already under the railroad bridge. We stretched ourselves on the wide seats in the sun and waited. I was dozing comfortably twenty minutes later when I heard Johnnie speak in the low, tense tone that fishermen use when their unseen prey begin to make their presence known.

"She's fishin'," said Johnnie. I looked in the direction his forefinger indicated and saw a white buoy slowly disappear below the water. It bobbed up again and again went down.

"There's another," said Henry, pointing to our far left.

"She's a-fishin', she's a-fishin'," said Johnnie, and I thought how many times he must have said that before in his life and yet how great his present delight was.

"Dark tide is better," said Johnnie. "Sometimes a bright sun like this drives 'em too deep for the net."

A ferryboat bore down on us bound from High-land to Poughkeepsie.

"Won't she ruin your net?" I said in alarm.

"Not her," said Johnnie, waving an arm at the man at the boat's wheel. "She don't draw enough water but the pilot won't go over the net anyway. Nice fel-low—always goes out of his way."

As he spoke the ferry veered off downriver for some distance and then turned toward the Poughkeepsie dock.

"Don't the big boats bother you sometimes?" I said.

"Once in a while. When they do, they sure raise hell. Cost you more'n fifty dollars to get your net fixed after one of them has cut it up. Don't happen often, though. Sometimes a sturgeon will go through your net. The river used to be full of 'em but they don't run any more—just one or two in a year. A shad net won't hold 'em, though."

"How many shad do you get on a drift?" I said.

"Depends," said Johnnie. "Last year was a good year and we got four or five hundred. I got an order for thirty-five hundred shad at forty-five cents for roe and twenty-five for buck. Nine days later I delivered 'em. The fellow says, 'I'll take fifteen hundred more.' Know how long it took me to catch that little reorder? Two whole weeks."

The ferryboat was at the Poughkeepsie dock and a few boys were daring the cold waters of early May, swimming around it and shouting. An old man rowed about near the dock in a seemingly aimless way.

"Old feller's dredgin' for coins," said Johnnie. "A few years ago a fisherman that lived up on the high bank there took to comin' down to the dock after dark and folks that lived near enough could hear him throwin' things into the water. They thought he'd gone crazy at first, an' then one night some kids spied on him and managed to figger out by the light of the little flare he was usin' that he was dredgin' the bottom around where the day boat's been comin' in for about a hundred years. You know how the boys swim around and holler for passengers to fling 'em coins to dive for?"

"Yes," I said.

"Come to find out, he'd picked up between two and three thousand dollars in the first two weeks he'd been at it before anybody got wise to what he was doin' —that is, countin' in the price he got for two or three old coins that collectors paid him hundreds of dollars for. Now everybody on the river's got a little dredge of his own. I've picked up some extry dollars that way myself. There's somethin' about the waters around here that turns nickels black. I save all I get to play in slot machines at a sort of club run by a friend o' mine down near Germantown. I took a whole bag o' nickels down there an' he says to me, 'What you doin' now? Makin' any money?' 'Yeh,' I says, 'I'm makin' money but I can't seem to make it come out the right color,' and I throws that bag o' black nickels on the bar. You ought to seen his face!"

A swift cabin cruiser painted a brilliant red slid by us and Johnnie waved his hand at the man on its high bridge—then shook his head.

"Carp boat. Nice Jewish fella runs it. He's on the river too early this year. Carp ain't runnin' yet. When we catch a carp in our nets we string it overboard to keep it alive till he shows up. He's got a big tank o' ice water on that boat—uses his engine to make the ice somehow—and he buys the live carp from us and slings 'em into that tank. When he gets a tankful he takes 'em downriver to the Jewish butchers in New York. You know there's somethin' in the Jewish religion about how their butchers have to get the fish alive or it ain't no good. The Jewish ladies stuff carp and make somethin' they call 'gefilta fish' out of it."

"It's time to eat," said Henry. "My mother always puts up twice as much as I can eat, all except pie, and you're welcome to help yourself."

"I got more'n plenty too," said Johnnie.

"I'm glad," I said, and the three of us began devouring sandwiches, coffee, and pie. The hot stillness of early afternoon was settling by the time we had finished. The food, the heat, the silence of the river had their way with each of us and we lay in our separate torpors for an hour or so. Finally Henry sat up and looked around.

"Tide's changing," he announced. "The net's goin' back."

"Row up to the near end," said Johnnie, "and we'll pull 'em in."

A few moments later the first yards of net were in the boat and Johnnie was carefully bringing over the side the first shad of our catch. Its gills were entangled in the net and Johnnie had a hard time extricating it.

"It's a roe," Johnnie said excitedly. "That's a good sign. Damned if this one ain't as pretty as one o' them early silverbacks."

"How can you tell a roe?" I said.

Johnnie held up a sturdy, beautifully curved fish

about two feet long. Its scales were lavender and silver and they gleamed in the sunlight.

"There's a bulge below the belly," Johnnie said, "just behind the dorsal fin. A roe ain't got the red of a buck neither." He began pulling the net in slowly, pausing now and then to speak sharply to Henry about keeping the boat at the proper angle. Shad after shad came over the side and went into the fish box in front of me. I looked down on a treasure that shone with purple, silver, red, lavender, white. When the last bobbing buoy had been gathered we counted the catch.

"Forty-five roe and thirty buck," said Johnnie. "Not bad for goin' out late on a daytime ebb. I'm gettin' forty cents a fish for roe and twenty for buck. What I ought to do is get a partner with a good truck and peddle 'em through the town. You can get a dollar apiece for good roe if you do it that way. Sellin' to butchers you don't make so much."

As Henry rowed us back to the little line of shacks and short gray piers at the river's edge a group of young boys passed us, two of them rowing in hearty unison for the west bank.

"Scapping for herring," said Johnnie.

"Want to know how?" said Henry, with a twinkle in his eyes.

"Why, yes," I said, "I guess I do."

"You have to have one live herring to start with. You put a safety pin through his lip and close it. Tie just four or five feet of line to it and tie the other end to a pole. Set your net in shallow water about eight feet down. Then when you see a school of herring playin' along the surface you drop your bait herring right amongst 'em and make him act crazy. If they're goin' round one way, make him go round the other. Make him act like he ain't got sense at all. Pretty soon all the others'll begin wonderin' what he's actin' that way for and they'll begin followin' him. Keep him actin' crazy but ease him along until he's got 'em all right over your net. Pull up then—and you've got a mess of herring."

A crowd meets every boat when it puts in at one of the little piers—butchers, other fishermen, folks who like to sit in the sun and listen to fishermen. Johnnie and Henry and I stepped out proudly and busied ourselves getting our catch into Johnnie's little icehouse.

"Here," said Johnnie, suddenly holding out two of the largest roe, "take these home to your missus."

"I'd like to," I said, "if you'll let me pay for 'em."

"Can't do that," said Johnnie shortly. "Tell her to cut 'em in the back o' the neck to bleed 'em. Then wipe 'em off with a cloth. Fry 'em in olive oil until they're about the same color as my net there. I dyed that net with oak-bark tea so they couldn't see it so good. When they're about that color take 'em off and eat 'em."

"I'll tell her," I said.

"If she bakes 'em instead, tell her to empty the belly and fill it up with vinegar and sew it up. The vinegar melts the bones."

"I'll remember," I said.

"You better come back soon and take a night drift with me," said Johnnie. "It's mighty pretty and peaceful on the river at night."

"Nothin' prettier than shad scales in the moonlight," said Henry. "They shine like the blue lamps you see in theaters sometimes. And it's nice to watch the lights of the houses on the banks go out and then come on again early in the morning. Once in a while a big boat goes by with lights in her cabins. Don't forget to come back."

"I won't forget," I said, and I have not forgotten.

32

"The Dutch Companee Is the
Best Companee"

A STRONG voice from the depths of the next room said to come in and I entered. After I had accustomed my eyes to the light of the big oval room I saw behind the flat-topped desk the gleam of his glasses and then I saw his big, strongly built face, his serious blue eyes. His hand came up to meet mine in a hearty gesture.

He said to sit down and suggested that a book about a river was a new sort of venture for me.

"Yes," I said. "And I'm pretty excited about it."

He waved his hand toward the room's light walls on which Currier and Ives prints of the Hudson River Series were a regiment of colorful squares and smilingly said I could see his interest in the Hudson. He hoped I had noticed, too, that an effort was being made to keep to the Dutch influence in most of the government building in the valley—the new postoffice at Rhinebeck, for example. A people that stuck through the years to its own language and customs in a foreign land, he said, deserved to be remembered.

"My grandfather used to sing me a song when I was very young," I said. "He told me his great grandfather, Isaac, used to sing it to him. Isaac was born in the Hudson valley in seventeen hundred and fifty, fought in the Revolution, settled on the upstate military tract around eighteen hundred, died at the age of a hundred and two. When old Isaac—Fawdy they called him—was nearly eighty, his great grandson (my grandfather) was born. Fawdy used to put the little boy astride his boot and sing the old Dutch nursery rhyme 'Trip-a-trop-a-tronjes.' When that little boy was an old man he sang it to me."

The man behind the desk said that the Dutch were a remarkable people. That up to about the time of his birth, even a little after, there were isolated communities a little back from the river where some Dutch was still spoken. They had been living in America for nearly two hundred and fifty years, surrounded by English speaking neighbors and with practically no contact with their mother country.

"We're a stubborn lot," I said, and we smiled at each other.

He asked me if he could help me in my work.

"Well," I said, "knowing your interest in boats I wanted to tell you what I have done about them in my work and ask for some suggestions." I was in the middle of one of the Hudson's whaling yarns—the one about the wreck of the Poughkeepsie whaler, *Lawrence*—when I was aware that someone else was in the room. A young man was standing before the desk and smiling at me apologetically. I stopped talking.

"About that sauce," he said to the man behind the desk, "the chef says he wants to veto that idea of yours. He wants to make it with apple."

The blue eyes assumed a contemplative look. Their owner took off his glasses and pondered a moment. Then he nodded and said he thought that would do very well.

The young man went away.

I went on telling the story but not as well as before because I was wondering whether the conversation I had heard was really about a sauce to be made with apple.

After we had talked Hudson River boats for sometime the man behind the desk asked about other subjects I had worked on.

"Some of the aestheticism along the river," I said, "about the castles they built so that the Hudson would look like the Rhine, and the ruins they built to give the river an antique look."

He smiled and said that the Roosevelt property had one of those, built by the Clews family when they had a place at Hyde Park.

I began to tell him of the ruins on Cruger's Island and the strange story of the eighty-year sojourn of John Lloyd Stephens's Mayan statues among them. While I was talking a young woman came into the room, smiled at me, put a letter down on the desk. As her employer signed it she said to him in a low voice, "They're waiting."

"I'll make it quick," I said and I did, but he did not end the interview.

After I had told the story he said I ought to have a chapter called "Vaulting Ambition." Here is a family, he said, who must have a replica of the Petit Trianon built in marble on the banks of the Hudson at the cost of millions. Now their descendants will not live in the place. If it were sold it wouldn't bring a quarter of its cost. Here is a man who builds a Florentine castle high above the river and puts two millions into it. After seven years of building it is left unfinished to decay. There is the great place Colonel Paine built, "Wiltwyck" they called it. It cost millions, too. It was bought by an institution, for a song. Many of the descendants of the old Hudson River rich folks who built the elaborate old houses and got the east bank called "Millionaires' Row" wouldn't be found dead in their ancestral villas now. And had I ever heard how some of the valley was settled by refugees from the Wyoming valley massacre?

"No," I said and as I said it I saw the smiling, attractive secretary again approaching with a letter. Again, as the pen scratched a signature I heard her voice. I could not hear what she said but I felt the firmness of her tone.

Her boss looked at me quizzically. There was a humorous twitch about the corner of his mouth.

I rose and he held out his hand, saying he would like to help me in my researches, and just to write to his wife and tell her what I wanted. Then she would talk it over with him and let me know. I knew, he said, what the Hudson River must mean to him, and of course he was wishing me luck with the book.

"Thanks ever so much," I said. "Good-bye, Mr. President."

33

Come All Ye Gallant Shanty-Boys

O<small>N</small> a clear summer morning I drove from Albany north through Mechanicsville. Great piles of spruce and poplar cut into four-foot lengths and stripped of bark lie there beside the water awaiting their turn to be fed into the vats of a pulp-paper company. The smell of wood and chemicals is strong. North of these wooden towers the stream is narrower and seems more intimate. Roomy farmhouses stand on the banks and near them in the water are small piers to which rowboats had been moored. One sign read "Night-crawlers for sale"; another simply "Minnows." I drove through Schuylerville and the bustling city of Glens Falls, whose citizens are generally well-to-do, and turned west and lost sight of the Hudson for a while as it meandered off into the Big Bend. Then I took the old dirt road over the mountain and came down steeply into Corinth—pronounced by natives with the accent on the second syllable.

I had returned to the Hudson at the middle of the bend. There were occasional floating logs in the river now. In a few moments I had passed Luzerne and was rolling along the west side of the Hudson to Warrensburg. It is a stretch of loveliness, a series of river vistas that are unforgettable—though comparatively few lovers of Hudson River scenery know them.

After Warrensburg where the Schroon tumbles, splashing over gray rocks, into the Hudson, I began climbing a dark road lined with the characteristic blue-green foliage of the Adirondack woods. I passed North Creek and then Minerva. There by the post office I asked a man where "Yankee John" Galusha could be found, and a few moments later I was knocking at the door of a comfortable white frame farmhouse beside a dirt road.

Yankee John opened the door himself. "I know what ye come for," he said, his watery eyes blinking a bit in the light and his drooping mustaches moving up and down as he spoke. "You ain't the first," he added as he moved his long, spare figure aside and motioned me to enter, "but come right in and set down and have some victuals with us. Then we can talk and maybe have a song or two."

My protest was waved aside. In a moment I was seated at Yankee John's table with his wife and his son and daughter, vigorously and silently consuming great portions of beef stew, potatoes, beets, and finally apple pie and coffee, as is the Adirondack way.

When Yankee John and I pushed our chairs back I was in a warm, slightly somnolent yet talkative mood and I could see he felt the same way.

"The Hudson," he said, going straight to the point of our interview, "was the first river to carry single trees to the mill. There was a lot of rafting in the old days but somebody up this way thought of just branding the logs to tell who they belonged to and then whopping 'em into the stream. After that the mills ate up a lot o' logs in a hurry."

"How did they brand 'em?" I asked.

"With irons. They still do. International's brand is a cross with a circle round it. Thompson is an anchor with a circle. Hinckley, Bradley, Underwood, Blow Brothers—they all had brands in the old days. It was a lot harder then than it is now. You've seen the peeled logs down below?"

"Yes," I said.

"They used to leave the bark on so a fellow in cork soles could catch aholt. I've seen men come ashore on the logs after breaking the dam. And I've seen 'em twirl 'em while they ride 'em. And when the spring freshets come down and they tripped the spruce dam I've seen some good jacks lose their lives tryin' to keep the logs from wingin' up on the banks or gettin' stuck in a jam. Fellow named Russ Carpenter says once, 'This is my last run, I been on the river twenty-five years and this is my last spring. I'm goin' to show the boys how to take the jam boats out.' He started out and they see his boat smash on the rocks. A jack named Repetoy jumped his boat to save him and they was both drowned. The water took Carpenter's body almost to Luzerne and buried it. A fisher boy saw a handkerchief stickin' out of the sand by the river and tried to pick it up but couldn't get it loose. He dug down a little—an' there was Carpenter."

"Did the jacks make up a song about that?" I asked, broaching at last the real reason for my visit.

Yankee John looked at me craftily.

"No," he said; "can't say that they did." He was silent a moment and then he said cheerily, "I could sing you about 'The shantyman leads a drearisome life,' though:

Transported I am
From the haunts of man
On the banks of the Hudson Stream
Where the wolves and the owls with their terrible howls
Disturb our nightly dream.

You know that one?"

"They sing that," I said, "in every bunk house between here and Portland, Oregon—changing the name of the river, of course. And don't try the 'Lumberjack's Alphabet' or 'Flat River' on me."

"I guess you've talked to shantymen before," he said, "but maybe you'd like to hear me sing 'The Jam on Gerrion's Rock.'"

"They call it Gerry's rock in Michigan," I said coldly. "I want to hear some York State Hudson River songs."

"There's one about Joe Thomas," said Yankee John. "That happened around here and it's just about like Russ Carpenter's experience except Joe didn't get killed and buried. It goes like this." The mustache quivered a bit and a high, husky tenor came from beneath it:

"He said he's been a boatman for sixteen years or more
 He'd run the Hudson River where the thundering torrents pour
 He dread nor feared no danger while in his own canoe
 He'd run the Hudson River and the Indian River, too.

It was on a Sunday morning just at the hour of ten
 Joe Thomas and his boat crew their business did begin
 He slammed his boat against the jam and split her bow in two
 And soon she filled with water and washed away his crew.

The current was swift and nimble from the jam she swept
  away
And spite of all that Joe could do for the cellar she made
  away
I guess she done some business that kept him busy there
For she turned a handsome somersault and her bow stood
  in the air.

He'd bothered Norton all the spring to let him run the
  boat
I guess he got his fill of her when from him she did float
For his boat lays on the bottom and her rigging's cast away
Joe's breaking jams along the shore for a dollar'n a half a
  day.

Watch her, catch her, jump her, juberjew
Give her the wind and let her go if Joe can shove her
  through.
You ought to heard 'em howlin' as they went floatin' by
With face the color of snow, my boys, and a tear in every
  eye."

"That's better," I said after the little silence that
we both offered as tribute to the song, "although it
sounds pretty much like something they sing on the
shores of Lake Ontario where I come from. They call
it 'The Bigler.' "

"It happened right here," said Yankee John de-
fensively. "There was another one we used to sing
called 'Banchee River.' You know, the one that ends up:

'This young man's name was Jimmie Judge I mean to let
  you know
I mean to sound his praises wherever I may go
His hair it hung in ringlets, his eyes were like the sloe
And he was admired by old and young wherever he did go.'

That's a sad song."

"I like those about things that happened around here better," I said.

"Well, there's the 'Cold River Line,' " said Yankee John. "That's all about workin' this here country. Cold River's up north o' Newcomb where the Hudson starts:

Come sit yourself down and listen for a time
We'll review our vacation on the Cold River Line.
We'll talk of our skidways of spruce and of pine
Talk over old times on the Cold River Line.

He was a good teamster, was young Johnny Carroll
In descending a hill where the road was quite narrow
Broke over the hill and laid on the switch
And wound up his bobbin in a fourteen-foot ditch.

He started for the landing, was getting on fine
Till he met a road-monkey half froze and half blind
Says to him Johnny 'The hill it is fine'
And he dumped all his logs down by the roadside.

Says Johnny to himself 'Now don't that beat hell'
As he looked by the roadside where the logs they had fell
He thought it all over and looked at the time
And he wished he'd never seen the Cold River Line.

Now it's farewell to our foreman, farewell for a time,
Farewell for the tall spruce all along that long line
Farewell to the hemlock, farewell to the pine,
But we did not fare well on the Cold River Line.

Now it's farewell to our cooks, we'll not leave 'em behind
For God truly knows they have served well their time
I hope that they'll never, no never in time
Go cooking again on the Cold River Line.

Now to finish my story, to finish my song
I'm going out to Newcomb, I won't stay there long
I'm going to Glens Falls and have a good time
And spend all my money from the Cold River Line."

"That's the kind I wanted," I said gleefully, "I
liked that. And I'd sort of like to get some good lumber
stories to go with it. Couldn't you tell me a couple—
you know—stories that happened around here?"

Yankee John thought a moment. Then he said:

"There's a fellow near here tells 'em pretty good
—name o' Jack Loveland. We might go over there and
see if he's home." He stood up, reached for his hat, and
started for the door. Suddenly he stopped.

"There's another one," he said. "Happened over at
Blue Mountain Lake near Eagle's Nest and Towahloon-
dah after we'd cut the sides of Big and Little Pisgah
mountains. All that stuff come down the Hudson. It's
the same tune as some o' the lakers used to sing called
'Red Iron Ore' but I tell 'em we was cuttin' trees and
singin' it here long before they heard o' iron dust near
the big lakes."

"How does that one go?"

Come all ye good fellows wherever you be
Come set down a while and listen to me
The truth I will tell you without a mistake
'Bout the rackets we have round Blue Mountain Lake
Derry down, down, down, derry down.

There's the Sullivan brothers and Big Jimmy Lou
Oh and Mose Gilbert and Dandy Pat too
A lot of good fellows as ever was seen
They all work for Griffin on Township Nineteen
Derry down, down, down, derry down.

Bill Mitchell you know he kept our shantee
As mean a damn man as ye ever did see
He'd lay round the shanty from morning 'til night
If a man said a word he was ready to fight
Derry down, down, down, derry down.

One morn before daylight Jim Lou he got mad
Knocked hell out of Mitchell and the boys was all glad
His wife she stood there and the truth I will tell
She was tickled to death to see Mitchell catch hell
Derry down, down, down, derry down.

You can talk of your fashions and styles to be seen
But there's none can compare with the cook of Nineteen
She's short, thick, and stout without any mistake
And the boys call her Nellie, the belle of Long Lake
Derry down, down, down, derry down.

And now my good fellows adieu to you all
For Christmas is comin' I'm goin' to Glens Falls
And when I get there I'll go on a spree
For you know when I've money the devil's in me
Derry down, down, down, derry down."

It was a half hour's ride over narrow dirt roads to
Jack Loveland's. The shadows in the woods were long,
mists were lying along the ground, and the air was
chilling when we came into the clearing and saw his
little cluster of farm buildings. Jack came to the door
and, though he was very short, I was struck by his simi-
larity to Yankee John. He had the same thin, wiry
quality, the same slow speech, the same sort of mustache. We sat by the fire and Jack lighted his pipe. I
said we hoped he would tell us some stories of the Hudson River lumbering days.

"Seems to me there must be a lot of 'em by now," Jack drawled. "Some fellow I saw in Newcomb said there was a sawmill in Albany more'n two hundred years ago. He said they'd been snakin' logs out o' this section here for a hundred and twenty-five years. A pile of stories could happen in all that time."

"Well, in my day," said Yankee John, "if a man's first name wasn't Fight he might just as well move out. I went through the thickest and hottest of it all an' I never got peeled yet."

"There was some tough boys, all right," said Jack. "There was Les Bullard who couldn't sleep unless his feet was downstream with the river and would put up an awful scrap if anybody moved his bunk to crossways of the current. And there was John Joe who weighed more than three hundred pounds and was a mighty mean fighter besides. We had fights, all right, but we had a pretty good time too. There was always fiddlin' and carryin' on in the camps. Did you ever hear about the doughnut tree?"

Yankee John threw back his head and laughed. I said "No."

"They had a cook at one camp who was so bad the boys used to say she could cook for fifty but it'd take a hundred to eat it. Her doughnuts was a lot harder'n rocks. Well, one day Will Bolles who was runnin' the camp heard a Finch and Pruyn inspector was comin' in. That was a signal to tell the chore boy to get everythin' cleaned up spick and span and he done it. Will looked over the camp a little later and the garbage was all covered up with snow and there wasn't a sign of anything being wasted. Then he opened the back door of the kitchen and there was a tall pine decorated up

like a Christmas tree with a sugar doughnut hangin'
from every limb, enough lard and dough and sugar
wasted to feed an army. The boys had hung 'em there
for a sort o' complaint. Will yelled for the chore boy
and had to help him take them doughnuts down an'
bury 'em before the inspector got there. After that Will
fired the cook."

"That ain't the kind of story he means," said
Yankee John Galusha sophisticatedly. "Now I'll show
you. There was a strange jack come into the woods once
an' he begun braggin' to me about how he chopped this
many logs in a day and they was that thick. I let him
go on for a while and then I says, 'Well, sir, when I
chop wood in the wintertime I go back the next mornin'
to start choppin' and the chips is still fallin' out of the
air from the day before.' "

I laughed. "That's one kind I want, all right," I
said. "Tall tales."

"I don't know no tall tales," said Jack Loveland,
fondling the bowl of his pipe. "All I know is things
that have happened to me man and boy in the last fifty
years of workin' here beside the Hudson. I've done
some fiddlin' at parties, I've drove the river, and I've
done some guidin'. All I know is true stories."

"Tell us 'bout the time you guided the doctor,"
said Yankee John.

"Wasn't much to that," said Jack, peering solemnly
at us out of the side of his face and sucking on his pipe.
"We'd been out huntin' and the doc had run out o'
bullets, he was a bad shot—so I give him all of mine.
We was near camp so I started back to git supper when
I come upon an all-fired big black bear. I didn't have
no bullets but it was pretty cold that day, so cold it

made your eyes water and the tears that was rollin'
down my face was freezin' into little hard balls of ice
before they hit the ground. Jest for fun I grabbed one
of 'em, loaded my gun with it and let that bear have it
right between the eyes. He just grunted and walked off
and I didn't think no more about it.

"Next mornin' the doctor got up early and in a
little while I heard him hollerin' so I went out to him
and there he was tryin' to drag that bear into camp and
it was dead as a doornail. We dragged it in and the doc
said he'd found it dead like that and he couldn't find
what killed it. Finally he cut it up and looked inside
and then he sat down and begun shakin' his head and
sort o' mutterin' to himself. So I says 'What's the matter, doc?' 'Well,' he says, 'Jack, I've give this here bear
a complete autopsy and if I was diagnosin' the cause of
his death I'd have to report he died o' water on the
brain.' "

"I like true stories like that one," I said, "better
than the parcel of lies in tall tales. Do you know any
more?"

"There was that snake and the bullfrog," prompted
Yankee John. "That's sort of interestin'."

"That happened right in the Hudson over near
Bad Luck Mountain," said Jack. "I was drivin' logs
downstream with Grover Lynch, the fellow that married Polly Bissel and made Jack Casey kill himself. We
seen a rock out in the river that was about twelve feet
wide and on the edge of it set a big bullfrog. We had
one o' them small fish scales with us and we grabbed
that frog and weighed him and he weighed twelve
pounds. We set him back down and walked away and
just then I seen a big black snake crawl up on that rock

and I says 'I'll bet you twelve dollars that snake swallows that frog' and he says 'You're on.' That snake inched up on that frog and he was twelve feet long because he was just as long as the rock and we measured it afterwards.

"Well, sir, just as that snake got a good holt on that frog's behind the frog sees the end of the snake's tail, makes one jump for it and ketches it in his mouth. So there we set with the snake takin' in more of the frog every minute and the frog gettin' about a foot of snake down his gullet in the same time. It got to be mighty excitin' to see which one was goin' to get the other swallered first. Just as the twelfth minute was up they both give one last big gulp—and they'd each swallowed the other at the same moment. We saw 'em both disappear right before our eyes. We never could settle our bet. I claimed it but Grover says it was ridiculous to suppose that the frog had swallowed the snake if the snake had swallowed the frog. So we sort o' broke up after that."

"It was a weird experience," I said.

"Not weird," said Jack, stroking the bowl of his pipe contemplatively, "not weird exactly—but puzzlin'."

34

Witches Make Star Tracks

Back of the brickworks and cement factories at the water's level, back of the line of the towns and the great estates that look out over the river, the sides of the Hudson valley rise at intervals into steep wooded hills, rock-strewn and desolate. On the edges of these slopes, which are green and beautiful to passengers on the river boats, live a border people, independent, primitive, and in many cases physically handicapped. They make a poor living these days, from fishing and hunting and basketmaking, but they do not yearn for the things they miss. Occasionally, not often, a traveler may come upon a high pile of baskets making a grotesque moving pattern against the brown earth of a country road and, if he stops, he may see beneath and behind it a wiry little man with quick, sharp eyes and bronzed, wrinkled skin. On the west side of the river the basket merchant may be known, near Nyack, as a Jackson White, and near Kingston as an Eagle's Nester or one of the "B'ys from the Traps." On the east side he may be, near Hudson, a Pondshiner or a Bushwhacker; north of Albany, a Van Guilder. There are a number of differences between these small sociological islands set in the waters of New York State's civilization and there are many similarities. The most obvious variation is that on the west bank Negro blood is mixed with that of the Indians, the English, and the Dutch in some of the groups, while on the east side there is little evidence of negroid quality though the other three strains are usually present.

I had been riding in the late afternoon in the border country where the west side of the valley suddenly tilts upward. I had passed through Ohioville and Plutarch and it was dusk. For a long time the road had been steep and winding, and I realized that there were breath-taking views off toward the river but mists of early autumn and early twilight had made them indistinct. I had eaten no lunch and welcomed the sight of a gas station and a soft-drink sign beside the slanting highway. As I drove up beside the pump a tall dark woman, loose-jointed and gawky, came out and walked toward it. Her eyes were dark, her cheekbones high, her mouth twisted and sunken.

"Can I get a bite to eat here?"

"I guess you kin. It's about the only place in the Traps." She spoke slowly and with a nasal quality that reminded me of the voices of American Indians I know.

Inside the two-room cabin a guttering oil lamp stood on a small showcase that gave off fitful glitter. Beside the little iron stove on a wooden box in the center of the room sat a bespectacled elderly man. A big white mustache seemed the focal point of his appearance, for his face, the hair of his head, his dusty clothes, were dully gray in the soft light.

"Nice place you have here," I said, munching on a chocolate bar.

The man grunted.

"It's all I got left, jest one acre, and they're a-tryin'

to git *that*. Uncle Charlie owned most of this here mountain once. A lawyer come along an' says, 'Charlie, jest you sign these here papers an' you get this bran'-new five-dollar bill.' So Uncle Charlie signed an' lost all his propputy. Danged if I don't think that wife o' his didn't witch him into it."

"Sure she did," said the monotonous nasal voice of the tall woman. "She was a witch, all right. Uncle Charlie always said so. I seen her witchcraft once. It looked like a piece o' red chalk but I wouldn't touch the stuff. You had to burn it to make it any good."

"Where do you suppose she got it?" I said.

"Off'n that old Nan Peters, the one that used to witch my pa's horse," said the old man. "Every night my pa used to comb out his horse's mane. It was long and silky-like. Next morning it'd be all snarled up. He knew Nan Peters done it, so one day he boiled the water of that horse and after that he didn't have no more trouble."

"You know witches can't die till they sell out—I mean until they sell their witchcraft," said the tall woman. "Uncle Charlie's wife bought it off her to let her die."

"Nan witched Mary," said the man. "Mary was my brother's wife. My mother had an awful time curin' her because she was sick and the witchcraft was in her. She tried puttin' Bibles under her pillow at night and it didn't work. Then she tried havin' her sleep on a piece o' steel—that works sometimes. Finally, she took some water and put nine needles into it and then boiled it. She went into the kitchen to boil it and she waited and she waited till she heard a thump on the floor and then she went back into the bedroom where Mary was and shore enough she was all cured and the witchcraft had just plain dropped out of her.

"Sometimes it don't pay to try to get the witchcraft out'n folks, though. Gert Haps told me that she knew a woman that went out into a field to work and then after a while nobody seen her and a fella looked and there she was layin' on her back with her mouth open. Somethin' was buzzin' around her—sort o' like a bee. This fella took a big cornhusk and put it over her open mouth and at that this buzzin' thing tried to get back into her but it couldn't and in a little while she was a-dead. The witch couldn't get back in her and she died."

"I'm due in Poughkeepsie for supper in a few minutes," I said, "and I want to get out of here before dark. I'll be glad when I'm over the bridge, because I've heard witches can't cross running water."

The old man laughed.

"You don't want to take no chances," he said. "They was a city fella come up here once. He was a nice fella and we used to call him mayor of the Traps just for fun. His real name was Charlie Bill. When my brother's wife Mary had the witchcraft in her she come upon Charlie Bill an' she says, 'I can make yuh folly me 'round, Charlie Bill.' He laughed an' he said she couldn't make him do no such a thing. But she had her witchcraft and she put it to work and in a little while sure enough she was a-makin' him folly her around everywhere she went."

People around Kingston say no good can come out of Eagle's Nest. They look at the towering mountain just a few miles back from their river town and shake their heads. "Folks do what they damned please up there," they say. "They're mostly black sheep and they never save anything and they drink all they can get. It's the worst place in seven counties."

Once the dark pines grew so tall on Eagle's Nest that they shut out the daylight for miles around, the old people say. Eagles made their nests in the topmost branches that were close to the stars. The pines are not so tall now but they still tower above the low homes of the folks who do as they damned please. On a little cleared plateau at the top of an almost impassable road a spreading frame house shelters some of them.

Jacob Flodder was standing in front of that house when I arrived. Jacob is over six feet tall and, though he bears one of the most distinguished Dutch names of the Kingston region, looks like an Indian chief. He greeted me with dignity and we talked—a little constrainedly at first. He said he liked living in a high place where the view was beautiful. His folks had lived around here for a long time. His father had been part Indian and part Negro and he supposed the Indian side of the family had lived around here pretty nearly always. He wasn't quite sure what tribe they were but thought they were Mohican. His mother was all white and belonged to a Dutch family that kept records but they had all been destroyed when the house before this was burned.

"Jake," called a soft voice from the house.

"That's my wife," said Jacob Flodder. "She's part Indian too. Her name was Stella Yellow Bird before I married her."

We went into the house and I saw that the Indian strain in Stella Yellow Bird had been almost overwhelmed by the negroid. A number of chocolate-colored children were clustered about her. The whole family seemed completely at ease with a stranger. Stella pointed to a young, blond white man in overalls who sat in a rocking chair beside her stove and said, "That's Mike Casey," and Mike said, "How are yuh?"

I said I had wanted to find out what sort of people live on Eagle's Nest and had been told to come to see Flodder.

"He's a terrible wicked man," said Stella Yellow Bird and she and Mike and all the brown children laughed very loud but Jacob did not change his expression. He said a lot of the people around there were either Haasbroucks, Scullys, or Cantines.

"My folks were Irish," said Mike Casey. "They come to these parts either to work the bluestone quarry or dig the old canal. They liked it up here on the mountain so they give up that kind o' work for lumberin' and fishin' and huntin'. Been here ever since. I like it too, but it gets kind o' lonesome."

"He gets scared sometimes," said Stella Yellow Bird and again she and the children shouted with laughter.

"What of?" I said.

"It ain't nothin' much," said Mike shamefacedly, "except once in a while I come home at night and there's my rockin' chair a-rockin' jest like somebody's in it."

"That ain't so bad," said Jacob seriously, "as feelin' that somebody's lookin' at you through the window at night and goin' to the door and hearin' somebody run right past you but not seein' nobody."

"The worst was that time a few years ago," said Mike.

"That was because you went around a tree one side when four others went the other," said Stella Yellow Bird. "That's always bad luck."

"I don't rightly remember about that," said Mike. "Some folks say it was jest witches that done it, but this thing happened when I was drivin' my team home from town one dark night. We'd jest got to the Hollow Gate when a ball of fire jest about the size of a good-sized load of hay come straight down from the sky and hit the ground and begun rollin' towards us. If the horses hadn't of reared back when it rolled in front of 'em it would have cut 'em plumb in two. It didn't make no sound—just rolled on and went right into the side of the mountain. Nearly scared me and my horses to death. I told some folks around here about it and they said it was a witch sign that a war was a-comin' but I don't know if there was any war after that."

"The minister said not to take no stock in witch signs," said Stella Yellow Bird, "like it's good luck if you find a horseshoe with five nails in it or bad luck to kill a black cat or find a five-leaf clover."

"I don't need somebody to tell me a lot of things to think about God," said Jacob Flodder almost irrelevantly. "There's too much talkin' and too little doin' as I figure it. It ain't anythin' to get all excited about and sing out and holler. The less said about it the better jest so's everybody does the best he kin."

"The minister used to be a rich lawyer in the city," said Stella Yellow Bird, "and he give everything away to live like Christ."

"Talkin' about signs," said Jacob imperturbably,

"what about that story he tells about the big rock in the quarry that nobody could lift and there was a one-armed bluestone worker over there and after all the strongest men had tried he walks up to the stone and says 'Help me, Lord' and bends down and picks it up with one hand as easy as if it was a hickory nut. Ain't that a sign?"

"It's a good sign," said Stella Yellow Bird. "That's different."

The "Hill" is one of the wild Taghanick Mountains. Once it was a refuge for the near-by farmers whenever the manor lords prevailed on the Columbia County sheriffs to try to collect their rents. It has hidden more permanent residents too. Trails worn deep to cabin doorsteps still make a curving pattern in its woods, but the cabins now are roofless and desolate. The Pondshiners who lived in them for generations have "come out of the Hill" and are living at its foot close to the towns that dot the rolling valley south of Hudson. The vast families of the Propers, the Simmonses, the Hotalings now pick their berries and weave their baskets hardly more than a whoop and a holler away from the market that buys them.

The Hill is more than forty miles north of the Traps, more than twenty miles north of Eagle's Nest, and it is on the other side of the Hudson—yet near its base, more than anywhere else along the steep sides that wall the river valley, the atmosphere is murky with fear of the supernatural. Just back of the river estates where the massive houses are safe behind their iron gates, the owners comfortable and secure in their heavy, glassed-in motors, the Pondshiners live in terror. "I call them the Frightened People," said an intelligent school-teacher who lives and works in one of the near-by towns. "The woods they live in frighten them and the people who live outside the woods frighten them more. They are always looking behind them to see if they are being followed or to find a way of escape."

It is not so hard to visit a Pondshiner now as it was when the whole lot of them were on the Hill. Flo Higgins and her husband live just a few yards off an asphalted state road. They are young people, in their middle thirties, and their house is a board cabin. Flo has bobbed hair and wears glasses. Standing on her doorstep in a shapeless, figured calico dress, she seemed genuinely glad to see me.

"Come right in. That school teacher told me you're goin' to do somethin' about the witchin' goin' on around here and I tell you it's about time."

"I don't know what I can do," I said. "Can't you have a witch arrested for something or other?"

" 'Twouldn't do no good," said Flo. "You have to kill a witch to get rid of her and none o' them state troopers has got anything but lead bullets. It takes a silver bullet to kill a witch."

"But why do you want the witch killed?" I said.

She looked at me as if completely out of patience. Then resignedly she began:

"It all started six years ago. She come here one day and asked for a rootabaga and I said we didn't have no rootabaga and she said, 'I only want one roota-baga, just one little rootabaga.' Well, I give her one and then it was awful. To get witched yourself, you know, you gotta have dealin's with a witch. She turned herself into six cats and sometimes they're black and

sometimes they're gray and most often you can't see
'em at all. The first night they come they knocked
the lamp chimneys off and blew out the lights and
threw shoes at us in the dark. Next time they lifted
my big iron stove and bounced it on the floor—you can
see the cracks in it now. Sometimes now they turn our
milk as black as ink and I have to throw it out—and
sometimes they throw manure all over our food while
we're eatin' dinner."

"Have you tried to make her stop?" I said.

"I told her to stop an' she looked at me and she
said she was goin' to witch me to death. 'Jesus Holy,'
she says, 'I'm goin' to witch you to death, Flo Higgins.' Then them six cats went downcellar and began
poundin' and yellin' and rollin' balls of fire along the
cellar floor. They're always throwin' fire. Why, I never
see such capers in my life."

"Isn't there anything you can do?" I said.

"Seems like we tried everything there is. We put
the Bible around but it didn't do no good. We got some
water from that fortuneteller in Hudson but it only
made things ten times worse. One time we got some
rest from 'em by mixin' some nutmeg and some pepper
in a pan o' water and then puttin' the names of all
the witches we know on a slip of paper and throwin'
the paper in the water and boilin' the whole thing
three times a day."

"How can you tell somebody isn't just playing
tricks on you?" I asked. "How can you be sure they're
witches?"

"I seen their tracks," said Flo simply. "One time
they spilled flour all over the floor and we looked at

the flour and there was witch tracks in it—you know—
like when you draw a star—witches make star tracks."

Seward Higgins, wiry, sun-tanned, blue-eyed,
walked slowly into the room, his dusty felt hat on his
head.

"It's witches, all right," he said, "an' somethin'
ought to be done about it. They threw a pitchfork
at me one night when I was out in the barn milkin'.
They throw bottles at me now when I'm walkin'
around outside the house at night. They been at it
for six years—they just keep on doin' that stuff and
they don't never seem to die. Why, the one that's after
Flo is over ninety now and I know another one that's
over a hundred. But you don't have to believe us about
'em—just ask anybody that lives round here. Ask Martha Hargers that lives down the road a piece. And be
sure to ask Sammy Slingerland what she done to him.
Then you do somethin' to make 'em stop."

"I'll go see Martha," I said, and I walked out of
the house and down the steps. I looked back just as I
reached the line of the woods. They were both standing
looking at me with eager eyes.

"Maybe you'll fix her," called Flo, and Seward
yelled "Be sure you do," as I went out of their sight.

Martha Hargers was standing beside her stove
when she called to me to come in. Her face was flushed
and her eyes were bright. She is a middle-sized woman
about forty-five. Her husband was working with some
beeswax frames in a corner of the kitchen. I had discovered by now that the Pondshiners were not hesitant
in talking about witches and so I stated my business
at once.

"I say it's the devil's contest," said Martha. "I wish that old witch would dry up and blow away. She's a real devil's serpent. Why, when that fortunetelling fellow came to Hudson—the one they call L. Heren— he looked in a crystal and said, 'That old witch is doin' you harm and spreading evil spirits all over your place.' And he's a good fortuneteller and had his picture in the Hudson paper. Ain't that right, Peter?"

Peter nodded his head over the beeswax and it struck me that most of the Pondshiner men look alike and act alike.

"You can't be too careful around here," he said. "One late afternoon I was walkin' along by this house with my brother. We come to the big stone at the corner and standin' there beside it was a man without no head. It was a beautiful sight and had on beautiful pants and shirt—all white.

" 'Don't tech that thing,' I says to my brother, real quick. 'It may be witched and you don't know what will happen to you if you do.'

"Then all at once it rose into the air and you could hear the flapping of wings but there was such a burst of blinding light we couldn't see much. It went off and left us and we been worrying ever since whether it was an angel or a witch. I bet that thing was an angel."

"And I bet it was a devil," said Martha. "Witches can take most any shape. Look what she done to Sammy Slingerland. You ought to get Sammy to tell you about it. It was terrible. Jest you set down and wait until this soup's ready and I'll give you some and then you can go see Sammy."

Sammy Slingerland's gray frame house stands on the crest of a ridge. The hills on the river side of it are lower and patched with orchards and fields of grain. It is just off the fox farm road and to pay a call on Sammy a visitor must pass hundreds of wire cages in which little black foxes with silver-tipped tails loll about awaiting their deaths. On clear days—and nights —the sound of their barking is crisp and wild even as far away as Sammy's front yard.

Sammy was in that front yard when I saw him first. He is a wiry, short man, somewhat beyond middle age. When he takes his hat off, which is seldom, thick white hair falls over his forehead. His eyes are a weak, watery blue, his nose is large, his mouth small. He began to talk as soon as he saw me and I was again impressed with the fact that the Pondshiners assume that a stranger is always on an official mission.

"You kin tell me what to do," said Sammy. "I can't git no further than across the road but what Liza calls me back and I have to go help her. Can't do no work that way. Her daughter or somebody ought to come and stay with her. I got a stand o' timber down there a ways if I could only git to it."

"Is Liza your wife?" I said.

"No, sirree," said Sammy. "She's my uncle's wife and she's my second cousin and she's been livin' here for forty-four years. I ain't the marryin' kind." He inserted a thumb under the worn suspender over his shoulder and snapped it vigorously.

"Martha Hargers said you'd had a pretty hard experience with the old witch," I said, "but I wouldn't let her tell it to me; I wanted to get it right from headquarters."

"Well, you come to the right place," said Sammy, "and I hope you fox her good for what she done to me. I ain't what I used to be since I had my accident. Why, I was the best for miles around here to cradle oats. Many's the time I've cut a good cradler out of his swath."

"How do you do that?" I said.

"You start out behind him mowin' fast," said Sammy, "and you cut in a big curve round him and take over his swatch ahead of him. One time old Jim Soper hired me an' he says, 'I don't want no loafin',' an' I says, 'You jest start out an' I'll keep up.' I didn't cut him out of his swath. I jest kept so close behind that it worried him. My cradle never touched his—but it kept comin' mighty close. Finally, he got so excited he cut into a bunch o' hard weeds an' broke two ribs in his cradle. 'Well,' his wife says when she see us comin' up to the woodshed to fix it, 'did ye ketch a skunk?' That's old-time talk fer breakin' your cradle on somethin'. 'No,' I says, 'but I ketched up with one.'" Sammy began to laugh excitedly but abrupt stillness came on him when a high-pitched voice from the house interrupted:

"Sammy," it said, and again with a kind of hysterical emphasis, "Sa-a-mmy!"

"There she goes again," said Sammy resignedly. "I'll be back in a minute."

He went into the house and I settled down under a tree and watched the white clouds pile above each other over the distant lavender peaks of the Catskills.

"Did Martha Hargers tell you why that old witch was after me?" said Sammy, hurrying from the house a few minutes later.

"No, she didn't," I said.

"Well, you heard about all that witchin' goin' on up at Flo Higgins's place?"

I nodded.

"Some of the folks round here wanted me to try to stop it because I know somethin' about such things. So I went up there one night and I took a sharp stick and I drew three circles in the ground around Flo Higgins's house. When I finished one I says, 'God the Father'; when I'd gone around again I says, 'God the Son'; and the third time I says, 'God the Holy Ghost.' Then I figured no witch could get into that house 'cause they couldn't cross them lines and no witch could get outside them lines either and so if they was in there they'd starve to death. But she fooled me somehow and it made her mad at me and that's how I come to have my accident. I sure hope you fix her for that."

"Tell me about it," I said.

"I went down to town to the caucus and when I got there I seen her sister talkin' to the old witch but I never would 'a' knowed who it was because she'd turned small and was only about three feet high and her face was her face only it was black—black as a crow. She saw me an' she says, 'Sammy, I hear yuh tried to stop the witchin' up at Flo Higgins's the other night,' an' I says, 'I only done what God told me to do.' 'Well,' she says, 'ye didn't come it, did ye?' and she starts cacklin' the way witches do when they laugh. I says, 'I done the best I could,' and then I went over to the store. When I come out she was big again, bigger than she is, and she was walkin' along Hog Ridge with a can o' kerosene in one hand and a basket over her other arm. I starts walkin' along the road and she sees me

and stops and just then a motorcycle come along goin'
pretty fast. All of a sudden my mind went blank. If
I'd been in my right senses I'd 'a' got out of the way of
that motorcycle, wouldn't I?"

"Yes, you would," I said.

"She'd witched me right outa my mind and
witched me so I couldn't move a finger. I jest had to
stand there and let that motorcycle hit me." Sammy
took off his hat and pointed to the inside of the crown.

"Ye see that bloodstain? That's where I hit."

"Were you badly hurt?"

"Yes, sir. I was unconscious and some folks in a
car come along and took me to the hospital. When I
come to I says to the nurse, 'I got to get out o' here.
I got to go take care of Liza.' She says, 'No, you can't,'
and goes away. So I gets up and gets dressed and walks
down to the office and when they see me they sent
for somebody to come take me home. I thought that
as soon as the old witch had got me hurt she'd leave me
alone. So I didn't pay much attention to the boy that
come to drive me. He's one of the neighbors' boys, lives
down near the foot o' this hill. Now I look back at it
I remember he looked at me sort o' funny.

"Well, just a few nights later I goes to bed in my
room like I always do with the doors and windows shut
tight. Along about two o'clock in the morning I wakes
up sudden and I know, the way you do sometimes,
there's somethin' close to me that shouldn't be there.
The moon's on the other side o' the house by then
and the room's so dark I can't see nothin' much. Jest
then I hear clip, clip, clip along the floor and I looks
down from the bed and can jest make out an animal a
bit bigger'n a gray squirrel runnin' towards the bed. It

gives a jump an' lands on the covers over my feet an' starts for my head. I yells at it, and jest before it gits to my face I throws the cover back over it and jumps out o' bed. I can see it tryin' to get out from under the bedclothes, it's rollin' around and snarlin'. I see its tail come out first and I satchels onto it and pulls the animal off the bed. I swing it round my head three times with all my strength and then I hit the wall with it. Three times I hit the wall with it as hard as I can. Then I drops it on the floor. I can't see it 'cause the room's so dark but I can hear it moanin' and groanin' somethin' awful. I reach for my lamp and there ain't no wick in it. I grabs the burner off, takes a new wick off the shelf, spreads it with my thumb and starts to poke it through the burner. It won't go through. I pulls it out, spreads the top o' the wick again, and pokes it into the burner again. It won't go through. All the time the thing on the floor is groanin' an' carryin' on. The third time I try, the wick goes through and I git a match and light the lamp. The minute the flame comes up the groanin' stops and there's nothin' there where it was comin' from. I looks under the bed and the dresser and there ain't nothin'. I goes into the kitchen and gits the Flit gun and I begin squirtin' the poison around thinkin' it might get rid of the witchin'. Then I goes back to bed and I says to myself, 'If I killed that witched thing, whoever it was that changed himself into that shape will be goin' to hell and I'll hear his token. So I listens all the rest o' the night but I don't hear no token."

"What's a token?" I asked.

"It's the sound that tells you when somebody you know has passed on. Sometimes it's a rap at the door and you go and there ain't nobody there. Sometimes it's a quick drummin' sound in the middle of the night—like the beatin' of a big bird's wings; sometimes it's the sound of a screech owl comin' from some place where there ain't no bird. It's a way folks have of tellin' you that they're dead."

"And you didn't hear one that night?" I said.

"No, not all night, and so I says in the morning, 'I'll find out who that was last night jest by layin' low. Whoever it was he's got a couple of busted ribs where I whanged him against the wall.' So I jest kept my mouth shut for a couple o' weeks and never said nothin' about anybody tryin' to witch me. Then one day I seen that boy what had drove me home from the hospital comin' through that field across the road with a gun over his shoulder. When he clumb that rail fence right there I seen him takin' it mighty easy, so I says to him, 'How you gettin' on?' and he says, 'Not so good. I busted a couple o' ribs awhile ago.'

" 'Is that so?' I says. 'How'd you do that?' 'Fell off'n a stepladder,' he says. Then I laughed to myself because I knew the old witch had witched him into plaguin' me. I knew he didn't fall off no step-ladder."

The footpath to the old witch's dwelling runs through sumac and berrybushes, over brooks, and through tangles of vine, to a clearing. Her cabin of thick boards weathered dark gray has but two windows, one on either side of the heavy door. Solid wooden blinds are hinged beside them.

I rapped on the door several times before I heard any response. Then her sharp voice sounded, as if from a far depth:

"What do ye want?"

"Just to come in and talk awhile," I said.

She opened the barred door and stood peering into the sunlit clearing beyond me. In her wrinkled wizened face her blue eyes seemed to catch a gleam from the light outside, and burned with a fierceness that contrasted shockingly with her dead-white hair that hung in ragged short cascades about her neck.

"Come in," she said. "I ain't had time to clean up much. I was jest gettin' to it."

"That's all right," I said. Aside from an unmade bed, the interior of the cabin was neat and clean. "I've been trying to find out something about the witching going on around here and some folks said you'd know about it."

"I know what they've been sayin'," she said, and as she hobbled across the room I saw that her back was bent. "They say I've been doin' the witchin'. Some men come up here after midnight one time and waked me up and said I'd got to stop it. It's all that boy down at Flo Higgins's. He got some books about witchin' at the library in Hudson and he's been studyin' how to do it. Then everybody blames me. Why, one well-fixed feller who got him a telephone in his house cut the wires the other day 'cause he said I was sendin' witch lice into his house over 'em."

"So you don't know how to do any witching?" I said.

"I won't tell nothin'." She was silent for a moment.

"They're a bunch of hard drinkers and card players," she then went on, "and they're likely to get into trouble. I heard tell the other day, and that's all, I just heard tell, some of 'em were playin' cards one night over in Stove Pipe Alley and they put a lighted candle on the table and says we'll stop playin' when that candle burns down and goes out. So they played all night and when the sun was jest about to come up the candle hadn't burned down at all and all of a sudden all them kings and queens and jacks come alive and treated 'em all shameful and such carryin's-on you never did see. They better watch out if they know what's good for 'em."

35

Flow On

For nearly three centuries the people of moderate means in the Hudson valley sought to own land along the river and failed. The manor lords refused them the independence of freeholders for two hundred years. The powerful new-rich of the nineteenth century, with their ambition to emulate the luxurious life of the old families, fought their less fortunate countrymen off the shore line until after the turn of the century. Then slowly and in an unexpected way the people began to win the river.

The Jesuit "Blackrobe," Father Isaac Jogues, who was rescued in 1643 by the Lutheran Dutchmen of Fort Orange from the maiming fury of the Mohawks, made his last journey up the Hudson in the spring of 1646. He knew that in returning to the Indians he was going to his death but he had suffered tortures so exquisite that martyrdom held no fears. If his sainthood had already begun, perhaps he was able to console himself by looking into the future for more than two hundred and ninety years, to see in the soft spring air of 1939 hundreds of the golden crosses of his faith glistening in the Hudson valley skies.

For the Jesuits have come back to the Hudson, and with them thousands of followers of other Roman Catholic orders. The first New York mission of Father

Jogues's successors established itself on the river at West Park in 1876. In those days, and in the years immediately following, land along the water was valued at a thousand dollars an acre, and the brothers of the black robe were unable to obtain the property they wanted. Just before the twentieth century began, however, with the rise in popularity of Newport and other fashionable centers, caprice took the owners of Millionaires' Row away from the river and their homes were closed. Prices dropped and when they were lowest the Jesuits bought "Edgewood," elaborate estate of John R. Stuyvesant, three miles north of Poughkeepsie. Now it is St. Andrew's-on-the-Hudson, an imposing building into which many of the bricks and much of the carved black walnut woodwork of the old Stuyvesant villa are incorporated.

This, with variations, is the story of the estates of the wealthy on the Hudson. Once their builders had left them, the houses were too big and impracticable for private residences of people with tastes that had outgrown a love of the "grand manner." Moreover, the townships in which stood the great estates assessed their values at such high sums that taxes were prohibitive from the owners' point of view. But the big places offered many advantages to tax-free organizations seeking sites for institutions.

At Riverdale, on the former estate of America's great actor Edwin Forrest, stands Mount St. Vincent, Roman Catholic college for girls. "Fonthill," the castle Forrest modeled after the Duke of Devonshire's "Lismore" to give the Hudson a flavor of European antiquity, is now a museum. Near it lies a monastery of the Passionist Fathers who lead lives of prayer, away from worldly distractions, speaking only when conducting services.

Farther up the river at Garrison stands Glenclyffe, a monastery of Friars Minor Capuchins who live in silence but do not, as some local folk believe, dig at their graves each day or sleep in caskets. Near them at Graymoor the Friars of the Atonement publish a magazine, the *Lamp*, conduct an Ave Maria hour over a big radio station of the New York area, and act as hosts at St. Christopher's Inn where any wayfarer is welcome to a room and meals with no questions asked.

From beautiful safe Maryknoll, near Ossining, the Foreign Mission Sisters of St. Dominic go to far and dangerous lands. At Newburgh the residents of the Oblate House of Philosophy sit deep in religious contemplation. At West Park the Sisters of the White Cross conduct an orphan asylum not far from the retreat of the Christian Brothers of Ireland. At New Hamburg are the Augustinian Fathers; at Nyack, the Sisters of Our Lady of Christian Doctrine; at Beacon, Ursuline nuns. Barrytown has its St. Joseph's Normal Institute directed by the Christian Brothers, Peekskill its St. Joseph's Convent, where more than four hundred live in the community of the Missionary Sisters of the Third Order of St. Francis. And eight miles south of Kingston, on the former Robert Livingston Pell estate, rises the imposing mass of Mount St. Alphonsus from whose portals young Redemptorist Brothers go to the Indians on the wild banks of Brazilian rivers, as Father Jogues once went to the Mohawks.

The Roman Catholic Church owns more land on the shores of the Hudson than any other religious organization and houses tens of thousands of its votaries upon the old estates. Other denominations, however, have also taken advantage of the opportunities the valley offers. In the incredibly expensive statue-strewn Victorian villa once owned by Oliver H. Payne, "Wiltwyck," is housed a convalescent home of an Episcopal mission. "Father Divine" and his cult own the Crum Elbow estate that once belonged to Howland Spencer. The Episcopal monastery of Fathers of the Holy Cross is at West Park. There are along the river dozens of fresh-air camps for city children established by different churches. There are many orphan asylums including a large one for colored children and several homes for the wayward.

Further inroads on the old estates have been made by secular institutions. At Poughkeepsie is the big state-owned Hudson River Hospital for the insane. Near Beacon a number of the mid-nineteenth century estates, including "Wodenethe" and "Tioronda" (both associated with Andrew Jackson Downing), have been acquired by Craig House Sanitarium. At Irvington a very large convalescent home for children with heart ailments looks over the river. There are dozens of other hospitals, dozens of private schools as well—many of them occupying the fancily decorated, widespread family houses of Victorian days.

It is useless to continue with these categories. The lands on the Hudson in the last fifty years have been absorbed to an amazing degree by institutions. Some reaches of the stream seem to be completely occupied by them. Out of eighty country seats—each a named estate such as "Rose Hill," "Placentia," "Mount Gulian"—the able Poughkeepsie historian, Miss Helen Reynolds, found that thirty-three are no longer operated as estates and that of this number nineteen are occupied by medical, educational, or religious institutions. In other words, the number of people living on the Hudson now in groups as small as a family is continually growing smaller. Outside of the towns they live by hundreds in monasteries, hospitals, and schools.

Thus in a strange way the people have won the river. It is not the way they had planned. They had dreamed that a man might possess his own plot beside the water, tie his boat outside the front door, fish from his own pier, swim from his own short front of beach, grow his crops on fertile land beside the water. All these things men do in the northern reaches beyond Albany. But in the river counties between Albany and New York, during the past twenty-five years farm lands have decreased approximately a million acres. At the same time the number of people in the rural areas— partly because of the establishment of big groups in institutional buildings, partly because city people have been buying country homes within commuting distance of their businesses—has been growing steadily.

Aside from the inhabitants of institutions and aside from the commuters, the people are finding other ways of possessing the river—some of them old ways rediscovered. The shad are running as they used to, in countless throngs, and the men in the low, weathered shacks beside the water are happy. Some of the old river businesses that sank into the doldrums during the first years of the twentieth century—cement, bluestone, brick—have been revived. The trim white ships of the Hudson River Day Line still carry their millions of passengers every season and the big *Alexander Hamilton* looks cool and uncrowded even when she has five thousand passengers aboard—as she often does. She and the other ships of the Day Line carry thousands of children up the river to Catskill camps at the beginning of every summer and nearly all of them come back on the *Alexander Hamilton* on one day shortly before Labor Day—three thousand singing, dancing, sun-tanned children delivered safely to the parents waiting to receive them on the New York docks.

Other vessels than those of the loved Day Line are trafficking on the river. Hardly a summer day passes that the riverboats do not whistle salutes to seagoing weather-stained craft plowing the long reaches between New York and Albany. They carry to the upriver port cargoes from Buenos Aires, Rosario, La Plata in the Argentine, from Yokohama and Osaka in Japan, from Surabaya in Java and Viipuri in Finland, from Matanzas in Cuba, from Bombay in India, and Hudiksvall, and Härnösand in Sweden, from Leningrad in Russia, from Bergen in Norway, from Gdynia in Poland. And they take away from Albany on the long homeward voyages Hudson valley corn and lumber and the things men make beside the river.

New businesses that belong peculiarly and uniquely to the Hudson's banks have sprung up and helped the valley people along. Spring winds in old Rhinebeck, that smelled of tar when the Palatines settled it, are heavy now with the fragrance of acres of violets that will grow in Rhinebeck hothouses and nowhere else— not even if Rhinebeck soil is exported with the plants. Rhinebeck is the largest violet market in America.

High above the river near Highland sits an Italian winery so perfect in its construction that it seems to have been transported in one piece from the plains

outside Rome. There, with the grapes of the Hudson
River fruit belt to work with, Italian-American vint-
ners make wines that deserve good American names of
their own because they have distinction that should
not be disguised by foreign labels. The so-called Rhine
wine of the place is better than many that come from
the old home of the Palatines. Few grapes of the world
are better suited to the making of champagnes than
those named for their Hudson island origin—Iona.
These and others indigenous to the Hudson shore have
begun to break down an old-time prejudice against
American wines of unique taste.

To the north of Albany the melon fields lie green-
gold along the narrowing stream. People who live there
say that the Hudson valley melons have a recognizable flavor and taste better than other melons. Growers
send truckloads and boatloads of them down the river.
And so the business failures of the past have been forgotten in the valley and the people look to the generous
river with hope.

Their hope is not an idle one. The valley people
have loved the big stream long and they have showed
their love. Though the dream they once had of a river
lined with little smiling farms of independent freeholders has gone, they have replaced it with another
dream and they are working to make it come true.
Through a small organization, the Hudson River Conservation Society, the people have influenced their own
representatives in the legislature at Albany to create the
Hudson Valley Survey Commission. The purpose of
that commission has been to put into words the people's own conception of the Hudson of the future, and

to recommend legislation that will make that conception a reality.

The Hudson of the people's dream is a river of clean waters. In it their children may swim as safely as did the Algonkin boys and girls before the days of the white explorers. More than a score of municipalities along the banks, with an aggregate population of 250,-000, still follow the unhealthful but convenient practice of dumping their sewage untreated into the river. Many bathing beaches along the Hudson have been condemned because of pollution and others are threatened. Towns that have built sewage treatment plants to destroy pollution have been prevented from developing their shore fronts for their citizens by less foresighted neighbor towns which have refused to make the sacrifices necessary to restore the river to purity. Among the larger groups which through their officers or through referendum have refused projects to establish sewage treatment plants are the citizens of Cohoes, Poughkeepsie, Hudson, Newburgh, Rensselaer. They argue against the tax burden such projects would put upon them and they say the tides will bring pollution up the river from New York no matter what precautions the upriver towns take. While they have been arguing, New York City has spent $40,000,000 for sewage treatment plants and is offering to spend $106,000,000 more.

The people of the big valley know that cleaning Hudson water will take time—but they know, too, that it will be done. The recalcitrant towns love the river and are aware of what its waters, if purified, could do for them and their children. There will be beaches on the Hudson and the people will sit on them in the sun and they will swim in the water.

There will be boating for everybody, the people say. Up and down the navigable length of the river there will be basins—"marinas," the Survey Commission calls them in its report. In a marina a man can moor his boat, whether it be a canoe with an outboard motor or a yacht, and he can buy supplies, and from it as a home port he can take his family on proud journeys along Henry Hudson's River of Mountains.

The time will come—the people have dreamed it—when the river running down from its high source among the ancient rocks will ripple beside green parks and winding level roads all of its way to the tall gray city at its mouth. Its banks will not be scarred by quarries as they now are at Mount Taurus nor will they be made hideous by the signboards of outdoor advertising. Someday, they say, the whole course of the stream will be as beautiful as that part of their vision of the river which has already materialized, the Henry Hudson Parkway which provides breath-taking beauty of approach to the sky-piercing towers of New York.

The people of the Hudson valley have seen these things and many others in the Hudson valley of the future. They hope that nothing will prevent their making this dream come true. They look forward now over the space of only a little while to a new time on the Hudson. After three centuries of struggle and waiting, the people say, they will rejoice at last in a valley of happy reality served by a free and mighty river.

Acknowledgment

MANY people have been exceedingly kind to me in the three years I have been at work in libraries and in the towns and countryside along the river. I do not even know the names of some whose aid has been invaluable but I want everybody who helped me to know that I am grateful. All the people of the valley have been generous and thoughtful when I have asked for guidance—and I have asked for it from many of them—from the President of the United States, who arranged somehow to talk to me about his loved Hudson in the course of a busy day at the White House, from Lloyd Goodrich of the Whitney Museum of New York, who was kind enough to read and correct my chapter on the Hudson River School of Art, from a little boy, who walked for miles with me to show me a local landmark, and from countless other valley people.

I want particularly to thank a number of people who have interrupted the usual course of their lives to talk with me or my representatives about the Hudson River: Lieutenant Paul A. Smith, of the United States Coast and Geodetic Survey; Mr. and Mrs. Fred Richards, of Glens Falls; Mr. and Mrs. Chandler Chapman, of Barrytown; the Reverend Delber W. Clark, of Coxsackie; Mr. and Mrs. Noel Armstrong, of Newburgh; Mrs. V. A. de Prosse, of Kinderhook; President McCracken, Miss Cornelia Raymond, Mr. and Mrs. Nikander Strelsky, of Vassar College at Poughkeepsie; Miss Helen Reynolds, Mr. James Reynolds, Mrs. Elsie Davis, Mr. Silas Hinckley and family, of Poughkeepsie; Mrs. Paul Lund, of Sherman (Conn.); Mrs. Seward Green and Mr. and Mrs. Albert Akin, of Pawling; Mr. Poultney

Bigelow, of Malden; Mr. and Mrs. Bayard Verplanck, Mr. and Mrs. George W. Seaman, Mr. Louis Whittemore, Mrs. Grace Whittemore Newlin, of Beacon; Mr. and Mrs. Hugh McElhenny, of Stuyvesant; Mr. Dwight Akers, of Washingtonville; Captain George W. Murdock, Mr. Richard Gruver, and Mr. H. P. Eighmey, of Kingston; Mr. James Fleming, of Rosendale; Captain John E. Frazier, of New Hamburg; Mr. Aldo Bolognesi and family, Mr. John Allwater, of Highland; Mr. and Mrs. Michael Breen, of Tahawus; Mr. Joel E. Spingarn, of Amenia; Mr. William Norton, of Hartford; Mr. Robert R. Livingston, Miss Angelica Livingston, Mrs. Johnston Redmond, of Tivoli; Miss Mayme Thompson, of Ancram; Mr. Albert Fisher, of North Glens Falls; President and Mrs. Franklin D. Roosevelt, of Hyde Park; Mr. "Yankee John" Galusha, Miss Eloise Cronin, Mr. Jack Loveland, of Minerva; Mr. Will Hill, of Fort Edward; Mr. Bernhard Knollenberg, of Yale University Library; Mr. Alexander J. Wall and Miss Dorothy C. Barck, of the New York Historical Society; President Alfred V. S. Olcott, of the Hudson River Day Line; Mr. Pirie MacDonald, Mr. Edward Reid, Mr. Croswell Bowen, Mrs. Mary Trask, Miss Lucy Tompkins, Mrs. Cyril McDermott, Mr. Thomas Healy, Mr. Clarence Lewis, of New York City.

Bibliography

Books

ADAMS, JAMES TRUSLOW, *The Epic of America*. Boston: Little, Brown & Company, 1931.

ALEXANDER, HOLMES, *The American Talleyrand*. Harper & Brothers, 1935.

ARMSTRONG, MARGARET, *Five Generations, Life and Letters*

of an American Family, 1750–1900. New York: Harper
& Brothers, 1930.

AUSTIN, MARY, *Philip Freneau, the poet of the Revolution.*
Edited by H. K. Vreeland. New York: A. Wessels Co.,
1901.

BACON, EDGAR MAYHEW, *The Hudson River from Ocean
to Source.* New York: A. P. Putnam's Sons, 1907.

BECKER, JOHN P., *The Sexegenary.* Albany, N. Y.: W. C.
Little & O. Steele, 1833.

BLACK, JENNIE PRINCE, *I Remember.* Thomas Claydon
Printing Co., Inc., 1938.

BOYD, THOMAS, *Poor John Fitch.* New York: G. P. Putnam's Sons, 1935.

BRADBURY, MRS. ANNA R., *History of the City of Hudson.*
Hudson, N. Y.: Record Printing & Publishing Co.,
1908.

BRADLEY, A. G., *Colonial Americans in Exile.* New York:
E. P. Dutton & Company, Inc., 1932.

BRANCH, E. DOUGLAS, *The Sentimental Years.* New York:
D. Appleton-Century Company, Inc., 1934.

BRINTON, DANIEL G., *Library of Aboriginal American Literature No. V.* Philadelphia: D. G. Brinton, 1885.

BROOKS, ELBRIDGE S., *The Story of New York.* Boston: D.
Lothrop Co., 1888.

BRUCE, WALLACE, *The Hudson.* New York: Bryant Literary
Union, 1894.

—— *The Hudson River by Daylight.* New York: J.
Featherston, 1872.

BUTLER, FRANCES ANNE, *Journal.* (2 vols.) London: John
Murray, 1835.

Captain Talbot—Life and Surprising Adventures, etc. London: Barnard & Sultzer for Tegg & Castleman, 1803.

CHEYNEY, EDWARD P., *The Anti-Rent Agitation in the
State of New York. 1839–1846.* Philadelphia: 1887.

—— *Two Kinds of Leasehold Tenure.*

Collections of the New York Historical Society for the Year 1809—Vol. I. New York: I. Rily, 1811.

COLVIN, ANDREW, *History of Albany & Schenectady Counties*. Albany.

CRÈVECŒUR, HECTOR ST. JOHN DE (Introduction by Dwight L. Akers), *An 18th Century Journey through Orange County*. Middletown, N. Y.: Times Herald Press, 1937.

DENTON, *Description of New York, Formerly New Netherlands, 1670*. New York: William Gowans, 1845.

Diary of Philip Hone—1828–1851. Edited with an introduction by Allan Nevins. New York: Dodd, Mead & Company, Inc., 1936.

DONALDSON, ALFRED L., *A History of the Adirondacks*. New York: D. Appleton-Century Company, Inc., 1921.

DONLON, HUGH P., *The Story of Auriesville, "Land of Crosses."* Worcester, Mass.: Harrigan Press, 1932.

DOWNING, A. J., *The Architecture of Country Houses*. New York: D. Appleton & Company, 1850.

——— *The Fruits and Fruit Trees of America*. New York: Wiley & Putnam, 1847.

——— *Rural Essays*. New York: Leavitt & Allen, 1854.

——— *A Treatise on the Theory and Practise of Landscape Gardening Adapted to North America*. New York: Orange Judd & Company, 1859.

DUNLAP, WILLIAM, *A History of New York for Schools*. (2 vols.). Collins, Reese & Co., 1837.

DURAND, JOHN, *The Life and Times of A. B. Durand*. New York: Charles Scribner's Sons, 1894.

Dutchess County Historical Society—Vol. 4. 1918.

Dutchess County. Sponsored by the Women's City and Country Club of Dutchess County, New York. Philadelphia: The William Penn Association of Philadelphia, 1937.

EDMONDS, JOHN WORTH, *Reports of Select Cases*. New York: 1868–1883.

BIBLIOGRAPHY 411

ELLIS, FRANKLIN, *History of Columbia County*. Philadelphia: Everts & Ensign, 1878.

FISKE, JOHN, *The Dutch and Quaker Colonies in America*. (2 vols.). Boston: Houghton, Mifflin Company, 1899.

FLICK, ALEXANDER, *Loyalism in New York During the American Revolution*, Columbia Studies in History, Economics & Public Law; Vol. 14. New York: 1901–1902.

FRANCIS, JOHN W., *Old New York, or Reminiscences of the Past 60 Years*. New York: Charles Roe, 1858.

GEBHARD, ELIZABETH L., *The Parsonage Between Two Manors*. Hudson, N. Y.: Bryan Printing Co., 1909.

GILDER, RODMAN, *The Battery*. Boston: Houghton Mifflin Company, 1936.

GOODWIN, MAUD WILDER, *Dutch and English on the Hudson*. New Haven, Conn.: Yale University Press, 1921.

GOTTSCHALK, LOUIS, *Lafayette Comes to America*. Chicago: University of Chicago Press, 1935.

GOULD, J., *History of Delaware County*. Roxbury, N. Y.: Keeny & Gould, 1856.

GRANT, MRS., *Memoirs of An American Lady*. New York: D. Appleton & Company, 1808.

HALL, CAPTAIN BASIL, *Travels in North America in the Years 1827–1828*. (2 vols.). Philadelphia: Carey Lea and Carey, 1829.

HALL, MRS. BASIL, *The Aristocratic Journey*. Edited by Una Pope Hennessy. New York: G. P. Putnam's Sons, 1931.

HALL, EDWARD HAGAMAN, *Philipse Manor Hall*. The American Scenic and Historic Preservation Society of New York, 1925.

HALSEY, FRANCIS W., *A Tour of Four Great Rivers: Hudson, Mohawk, Susquehanna and Delaware in 1769*. New York: Charles Scribner's Sons, 1906.

HARRIMAN, MRS. J. BORDEN, *From Pinafores to Politics*. New York: Henry Holt and Company, 1923.

HASWELL, CHARLES H., *Reminiscences of New York by an Octogenarian.* New York: Harper & Brothers, 1896.

HEDRICK, ULYSSES PRENTISS, *A History of Agriculture in the State of New York.* New York State Agricultural Society, 1933.

HELLMAN, GEORGE S., *Washington Irving Esquire.* New York: Alfred A. Knopf, Inc., 1925.

HERRINGTON, W. S., *Pioneer Life Among the Loyalists in Upper Canada.* Toronto, Canada: MacMillan Company of Canada, Ltd., 1915.

HISLOP, CODMAN, *Albany.* Albany, N. Y.: The Argus Press, 1936.

―――― *Albany: Dutch, English, and American.* Albany, N.Y.: The Argus Press, 1936.

History of the State of New York. Edited by Alexander C. Flick (10 vols.). Published under the auspices of the New York State Historical Association.

HOWELL and TENNEY, *History of the County of Albany from 1609 to 1886.* W. W. Munsell, 1886.

HUDLESTON, F. J., *Gentleman Johnny Burgoyne.* Indianapolis, Ind.: Bobbs-Merrill Company, 1927.

HULKERT, F. RANDOLPH, *Wandering Strains from the Lyre of the North.* New York: Casper C. Childs, Printer, No. 80 Vesey St.

HULL, REVEREND WILLIAM, *The Palatine Parish by Quassaick.* Gettysburg, Penn.: J. E. Wikle, 1880.

HUMPHREYS, MARY GAY, *Catharine Schuyler,* New York: Charles Scribner's Sons, 1901.

HUNGERFORD, EDWARD, *Men and Iron.* New York: Thomas Y. Crowell Company, 1938.

―――― *Pathway of Empire.* New York: Robert M. McBride & Company, 1935.

INNES, J. H., *New Amsterdam and Its People.* New York: Charles Scribner's Sons, 1902.

IRVING, WASHINGTON, *A Humourous History of New York from the Beginning of the World to the End of the Dutch Dynasty by Diedrich Knickerbocker.* London: 1820.

ISHAM, SAMUEL, *The History of American Painting.* New York: The Macmillan Company, 1915.

JOHNSON, CLIFTON, *The Picturesque Hudson.* New York: The Macmillan Company, 1909.

JOHNSON, P. DEMAREST, *Claudius, the Cowboy of the Ramapo Valley.* Middletown: 1889.

KALM, PETER, *Travels in North America.* Translated by John Reinhold Forster (3 vols.). London: 1770–1771.

KEMBLE, FRANCES ANN, *Journal of a Residence in America.* London: 1835.

———— *Records of Later Life* (3 vols.). London: Richard Bentley & Son, 1878.

————*Further Records 1848–1883.* New York: Henry Holt and Company, 1891.

KIMBALL, FRANCIS P., *New York, The Canal State.* Albany, N. Y.: The Argus Press, 1937.

KNITTLE, WALTER ALLEN, *Early Eighteenth Century Palatine Emigration.* Philadelphia: Dorrance & Company, Inc., 1937.

LA FOLLETTE, SUZANNE, *Art in America.* New York: Harper & Brothers, 1929.

LEE, JOHN WILTSEE, *Stories of the Hudson.* New York: G. P. Putnam's Sons, 1871.

Letters About the Hudson River and its Vicinity, written in 1835 and 1836 by a Citizen of New York. New York: Freeman Hunt & Co., 1836.

Life and Surprising Adventures of Captain Talbot, The, Containing a Curious Account of the Varied Changes and Gradations of this Extraordinary Character.

LOSSING, BENSON J., *The Hudson, from the Wilderness to the Sea.* London: Virtue & Co., 1868.

McALLISTER, WARD, *Society as I Have Found It.* New York: Cassell Publishing Co., 1890.

McMASTER, JOHN BACH, *A History of the People of the United States* (7 vols.). New York: D. Appleton & Company, 1904.

────── *With the Fathers, Studies in the History of the United States,* New York: D. Appleton & Company, 1896.

MACY, WILLIAM F., *The Story of Old Nantucket.* Nantucket, Mass.: The Inquirer and Mirror Press, 1915.

MARQUISE DE LA TOUR DU PIN, *Journal d'une Femme de Cinquante Ans.* Berger-Levrault, Editeurs (2 vols.). Nancy-Paris-Strasbourg: 1924.

MARRYAT, CAPTAIN, *A Diary in America, with Remarks on its Institutions* (2 vols.). Philadelphia, Penn.: Cary & Hart, 1839.

MARTINEAU, HARRIET, *Retrospect of Western Travel,* Vol. 1. New York: Harper & Brothers, 1838.

MATHER, J. H. and BROCKETT, L. P., *A Geographical History of the State of New York.* Utica, N. Y.: H. H. Hawley & Co., 1848.

MAURY, SARAH MYLTON, *An Englishwoman in America—1848.* London: T. Richardson & Son, 1848.

MAYHAM, ALBERT CHAMPLIN, *The Anti-Rent War on Blenheim Hill.* Jefferson, N. Y.: F. L. Frazee, 1906.

MILLER, JOHN, *New York Considered and Improved, 1695.* Cleveland, Ohio: Burrows Brothers Co., 1903.

MILLER, STEPHEN B., *Historical Sketches of Hudson.* Hudson, N. Y.: Bryan & Webb, Printers, 1862.

Minutes of the Court of Albany, Rensselaerwyck and Schenectady. Translated and edited by A. J. F. Van Saer (2 vols.). Albany, N. Y.: University of the State of New York, 1926.

Minutes of the Court of Fort Orange and Beverwyck. Translated and edited by A. J. F. Van Saer. Albany, N. Y.: University of the State of New York, 1920.

Moss, Frank, *The American Metropolis from Knickerbocker Days to the Present Time—New York City Life.* New York: Peter Fenelon Collier, Publishers, 1897.

Munsell's Collections on the History of Albany. Albany, N. Y.: The author, 1865.

Narratives of New Netherland 1609–1664. Edited by J. Franklin Jameson. New York: Charles Scribner's Sons, 1909.

New York Colonial Documents XIV. Edited by O'Callahan.

Nichols, Thomas Low, *Forty Years of American Life, 1821–1861.* New York: Stackpole Sons, 1937.

Nissenson, S. G., *The Patroon's Domain.* New York: Columbia University Press, 1937.

Noble, Louis L., *The Course of Empire, Voyage of Life and other Pictures of Thomas Cole.* New York: Cornish Lamport & Co., 1853.

Notes on a Tour Through the Western Part of the State of New York. Reprinted from *The Ariel.* Philadelphia: 1829–30.

Odell, George C. D., *Annals of the New York Stage.* New York: 1927–38.

Partridge, Bellamy, *The Roosevelt Family in America.* New York: Hillman-Curl, Inc., 1936.

Power, Tyrone, *Impressions of America.* Philadelphia: Carey, Lea & Blanchard, 1836.

Powys, Llewllyn, *Henry Hudson.* New York: Harper & Brothers, 1928.

Preston, John Hyde, *A Gentleman Rebel.* New York: Farrar & Rinehart, Inc., 1930.

——— *Revolution 1776.* New York: Harcourt, Brace and Company, 1933.

Redway, F. R. G. S., *Jacques Wordlaw—The Making of the Empire State.* New York: Silver, Burdett & Company, 1904.

REES, JAMES, *The Life of Edwin Forrest with Reminiscences and Personal Recollections*. Philadelphia: T. B. Peterson & Brothers, 1874.

RIEDESEL, MRS. GENERAL, *Memoirs*. Translated by William L. Stone. Albany, N. Y.: John Munsell, 1867.

ROCKWELL, REVEREND CHARLES, *The Catskill Mountains and the Region Around*. New York: Taintor Bros. & Co., 1867.

ROSENBERG, C. G., *Jenny Lind in America*. New York: Stringer and Townsend, 1851.

RUTTENBER, E. M., *Obstructions to the Navigation of Hudson's River*. Albany, N. Y.: J. Munsell, 1860.

—— *History of the Town of Newburgh, 1825–1907*.

RYERSON, EGERTON, *The Loyalists of America and their Times* (2 vols.). Toronto, Canada: Wm. Briggs, James Campbell & Son and Willing and Williamson, 1880.

SABINE, LORENZO, *The American Loyalists*. Boston: Charles C. Little & James Brown, 1847.

SIEBERT, WILBUR H., *Flight of American Loyalists to the British Isles*. Columbus, Ohio: F. S. Heer Printing Co., 1911.

SIMMS, JEPTHA R., *History of Schoharie County, etc.* Albany, N. Y.: Munsell & Tanner, 1845.

SINGLETON, ESTHER, *Dutch New York*. New York: Dodd, Mead & Company, Inc., 1909.

—— *Social New York Under the Georges, 1714–1776*. New York: D. Appleton & Company, 1902.

SKINNER, CHARLES M., *American Myths & Legends* (2 vols.). Philadelphia: J. B. Lippincott Company, 1903.

SMITH, ARTHUR D. HOWDEN, *Commodore Vanderbilt*. New York: Robert M. McBride & Company, 1927.

—— *John Jacob Astor*. Philadelphia and London: J. B. Lippincott Company, 1929.

SMITH, HELEN EVERTSON, *Colonial Days and Ways*. New York: The Century Co., 1900.

SMITH, THOMAS E. V., *The City of New York in the Year of Washington's Inauguration, 1789.* New York: Anson D. F. Randolph & Co., 1889.

SPAULDING, E. WILDER, *His Excellency George Clinton.* New York: The Macmillan Company, 1938.

STONE, HENRY DICKINSON, *Personal Recollections of the Drama, 1873.* Albany, N. Y.: C. Van Benthuysen, 1873.

SUTCLIFFE, ALICE CRARY, *Robert Fulton and the "Clermont."* New York: The Century Co., 1909.

Taintors Guide Books: Hudson River Route. New York: Taintor Bros & Co., 1889.

TERRY, ROBERT M., *The "Hudsonian," Old Times and New.* Hudson, N. Y.: E. C. Rawley, 1895.

TOMLINSON, E. T., *Mystery of Ramapo Pass.* Boston: Houghton Mifflin Company, 1922.

TROLLOPE, MRS., *Domestic Manners of the Americans.* New York: Dodd, Mead & Company, Inc., 1901.

TUCKERMAN, HENRY T., *Book of the Artists.* New York: G. P. Putnam & Sons, 1867.

—— *Life of Silas Talbot.* New York: J. C. Riker, 1850.

TURNBULL, ARCHIBALD DOUGLAS, *John Stevens.* New York: D. Appleton-Century Company, Inc., 1928.

United Empire Loyalists' Association .of Canada Annual Transactions. 1904–1913. Brampton, the Conservator Book Dept., 1914.

VALENTINE'S, DAVID THOMAS, *Manual of Old New York.* New York: F. P. Harper, 1900.

VAN TYNE, CLAUDE HALSTEAD, *The Loyalists in the American Revolution.* New York: The Macmillan Company, 1902.

VERPLANCK, WILLIAM E., and COLLYER, MOSES W., *The Sloops of the Hudson.* New York: G. P. Putnam's Sons, 1908.

Vertoogh van Nieu Nederland. Translated by Henry C. Murphy. New York: 1854.

Voyages of Captain Jacob Dunham. New York: The Author, 1851.

WECTER, DIXON, *The Saga of American Society.* New York: Charles Scribner's Sons, 1937.

WEISE, ARTHUR JAMES, *Troy's 100 years—1789–1889.* Troy, N. Y.: William H. Young, 1891.

WHARTON, EDITH, *A Backward Glance.* New York and London: D. Appleton-Century Company, Inc., 1934.

WHEELER, EVERETT PEPPERELL, *Daniel Webster, the Expounder of the Constitution.* New York: G. P. Putnam's Sons, 1905.

WHITLOCK, BRAND, *LaFayette* (2 vols.). New York: D. Appleton-Century Company, Inc., 1929.

William Thompson Howell Memorial—The Hudson Highlands. (2 vols.). 1933.

WILLIS, NATHANIEL P., *Out-doors at Idlewild.* New York: C. Scribner, 1855.

———— *Rural Letters.* New York: Baker & Scribner, 1849.

WILSON, WARREN H., *Quaker Hill.* Privately printed, 1930.

WILSTACH, PAUL, *Hudson River Landings.* Indianapolis, Ind.: Bobbs-Merrill Company, 1933.

WINFIELD, CHARLES H., *History of the County of Hudson, New Jersey.* New York: Kennard & Hay Stationery Manufacturing & Printing Co., 1874.

WOLLEY, A. N. CHARLES, *A Two Years' Journal in New York.* Cleveland, Ohio: The Burrows Bros. Co., 1902. Reprinted from the original edition of 1701.

WOODWARD, W. E., *New American History.* New York: Farrar & Rinehart, Inc., 1936.

WORTH, GORHAM A., *Random Recollections of Albany from 1800 to 1808.* Third edition. Albany, N. Y.: J. Munsell, 1866.

Pamphlets and Manuscripts

AKERS, DWIGHT, *Outposts of History in Orange County.*
Washingtonville, N. Y.: Harrison Press.

BARKER, VIRGIL, *A Critical Introduction to American Painting.* Whitney Museum of American Painting.

Bulletin of the Geological Society of America. Vol. 47.
December 31, 1936.

CARR, WILLIAM H., and KOKE, RICHARD J., *Twin Forts of
the Popolopen.* Bear Mountain Trailside Museums.

CRÈVECŒUR, HECTOR ST. JOHN DE, *An 18th Century
Journey through Orange County.* Middletown, N. Y.:
Times Herald.

Dutchess County Manuscripts. New York Historical Society.

Geology, Fauna and Flora of the Lower Hudson Valley.
Prepared by the American Museum of Natural History
of the New York Botanical Gardens and by them presented to the members of the Eighth International Congress of Applied Chemistry. September 8, 1912.

GOODRICH, LLOYD, *A Century of American Landscape Painting.* Whitney Museum of American Art.

HOPKINS, A. S., *The Trails to Marcy.* Albany, N. Y.: State
of New York Conservation Department, 1935.

INGERSOLL, ERNEST, *Illustrated Guide to the Hudson River
and Catskill Mountains.* Chicago: Rand McNally &
Company, 1908.

Livingston Manuscripts, The New York Public Library.

McKNIGHT, JAMES, *A Discourse Exposing Robert Owen's
System as Practised by the Franklin Community at
Haverstraw.* New York: John Gray & Co., Franklin
Square, 1926.

Minutes of the Council of the City of New York for 1766.
New York State Library in Albany.

New York Zoological Society Bulletin. March, April, 1929.

Oration by John T. Hogeboom at Centennial Celebration, Hudson, N. Y., July 4, 1876.

Papers of the Sloop *Experiment*. New York Historical Society.

REEDS, CHESTER A., *The Geology of New York City and Vicinity*. New York: American Museum of Natural History, 1930.

Report of Special Committee appointed by the Common Council of New York to make arrangements for the reception of Governor Louis Kossuth. New York: Published by Order of the Common Council, 1852.

Report of the Hudson Valley Survey Commission to the Legislature, March 1, 1939. Albany, N. Y.: J. B. Lyon Company, 1939.

SKINNER, ALANSON, *The Indians of Manhattan Island and Vicinity*. American Museum of Natural History.

SMITH, PHILIP H., *Legends of the Shawangunk*. 1887.

SPINGARN, J. E., *Henry Winthrop Sargent*. Reprinted from the 1937 Year Book of the Dutchess County Historical Society.

U. S. Coast and Geodetic Society. Special Publication. Washington, D. C., 1934.

VAN BERGEN, ROBERT HENRY, *Ye Olden Time*. Published at Coxsackie, 1935.

VAN DEUSEN, H. L., *Old Ulster Days*. (Newspaper essays.)

Newspapers and Periodicals

Albany Argus, 1845.

KELLNER, SYDNEY, "The Beginnings of Landscape Painting in America," in *Art in America*, an illustrated quarterly, Vol. 26, No. 4, October, 1938.

Kingston Daily Freeman, 1937.

Knickerbocker Press, Albany, N. Y.

Long Island Star, 1832.
Morning Courier and New York Enquirer, 1845.
New York *Herald*, 1845.
New York History. Published Quarterly by the New York State Historical Association.
New York *Morning Post*, 1783.
New York *Post*.
New York *Times*, 1852.
New York *World-Telegram*.
New York Zoological Society *Bulletin*, March, April, 1929.
Owl, A geneological quarterly magazine published in the interest of the Wing family of America.
Poughkeepsie *Eagle*, Souvenir Edition, 1889.
Poughkeepsie *Eagle News*, 1938.
Poughkeepsie *Journal*, 1806.
Poughkeepsie *Republican Telegraph*.
The Voice of the People. Delhi, N. Y.: 1844.
Thrift Messenger. Poughkeepsie, N. Y.: October, 1935.
Ulster County Press. Stone Ridge, N. Y.
Ye Olde Ulster, Kingston, N. Y.

Index